I0187502

Discipleship:
God's Plan for Parenting

Bringing Parents and Children Together
Through the Intimacy of Biblical Discipleship

Proverbs 24:3-4

———

"The most extraordinary thing in the world is an ordinary man and an ordinary

woman and their ordinary children." G.K. Chesterton

Discipleship:
God's Plan for Parenting

Bringing Parents and Children Together
Through the Intimacy of Biblical Discipleship

MARCELO A. TOLOPILO

Edited by Julie Giese

Chart & Compass Press
Temecula, California
Discipleship: God's Plan for Parenting

Discipleship: God's Plan for Parenting
Bringing Parents and Children Together Through the Intimacy
of Biblical Discipleship

Copyright © 2016 by Marcelo A. Tolopilo

Published by Chart & Compass Press
www.chartandcompasspress.com

Scripture quotations taken from the New American Standard Bible®, Copyright © 1960, 1962, 1963, 1968, 1971, 1972, 1973, 1975, 1977, 1995 by The Lockman Foundation. Used by permission (www.Lockman.org).

All rights reserved. No part of this publication may be reproduced, stored in a retrieval system, or transmitted in any form by any means, electronic, mechanical, photocopy, recording, or otherwise, without the prior permission of the publisher, except as provided by USA copyright law. For information on acquiring permission for reprints and excerpts, contact ask@ chartandcompasspress.com.

Cover design and typesetting by David J. Roberts

ISBN 978-0-9821032-1-0

Dedicated to the glory of my Redeemer, Jesus Christ,
the Son of God, the Son of Abraham, the Son of David,
The Messiah of Israel, and the Savior of the world.

With deepest thanks
to my beloved wife, my partner in life,
the mother of my children,
and my dearest friend on this earth.

Contents

APPENDICES

Why Should I Read Yet Another Book on the Family?

Some will ask, "Why another book on the family? Hasn't enough ink been spilled over the subject? How many more pens must run their lives dry before the final exclamation mark spears through this copious and tired theme? Enough already!" If these concerns have flitted through your questioning mind, let me assure you that I am mostly using a word processor, and only a few pens have been harmed in the writing of this book. Yes, plenteous offerings have been penned about the Christian family, and no doubt many more will be written in years to come; however, there are four reasons why I feel compelled to write this book, and why I think you ought to read it.

1. What does God say...

First, we need to see God's plan to shepherd the family through the lens of Scripture. Some authors, even Christian authors, have primarily approached this subject from a behavioral or psychological angle, but in my humble opinion more needs to be written about the matter from a biblical point of view.

Let's face it, God designed and created the family. He is the divine Architect of the home; therefore, His instructions regarding His beloved institution should energize our powers of discernment. My chief goal in writing this book is to ask the simple yet all-important question, "How would God have us raise (disciple) our children?" To do justice to this query, we must go to God's own testimony, the Scriptures.

2. "Say again?"

Secondly, I am compelled to address this critical issue because important truths bear repeating, and they bear repeating because all Christians suffer from a measure of B.A.D.D. (Biblical Attention Deficit Disorder—I just made that up, but hey, it works!). We easily get distracted from God's precepts or forget what God has said, and unless we are reminded of God's truth, we lose our way in a sea of opinions and worldly wisdom. The old hymn sums up our tendency and struggle with a simple phrase: you and I are "prone to wander."[1] We need to be reminded of what God has said so that we may walk by the light of His wisdom, not man's (Psalm 119:105).

Because of our spiritually wayward, listing tendencies, reminding Christians of what we already know has been a staple of faithful shepherds since the days of the early church. The apostle Peter, for example, wrote his general epistles to encourage the church at large toward holiness in the midst of a wicked antagonistic world. In doing so, he employed the important principle of biblical redundancy to get his message across. Seeing the end of his life approaching he wrote,

> *Therefore, I will always be ready to remind you of these things, even though you already know them, and have been established in the truth which is present with you. I consider it right, as long as I am in this earthly dwelling, to stir you up by way of reminder, knowing that the laying aside of my earthly dwelling is imminent, as also our Lord Jesus Christ has made clear to me. And I will also be diligent that at any time after my departure you will be able to call these things to mind... This is now, beloved, the second letter I am writing to you in which I am stirring up your sincere mind by way of reminder, that you should remember the words spoken beforehand by the holy prophets and the commandment of the Lord and Savior spoken by your apostles* (2 Peter 1:12–15; 3:1–2, emphasis added).

Truly, repetition—stirring the memory to recall truth—is a mainstay of biblical, pastoral instruction. As a pastor and Bible teacher, my exhortation is spent not on teaching God's people new things but in reminding believers of what God has already said, and much of the time, what they already know. In fact, if I ever teach something new, some new interpretation of Scripture that has somehow escaped the careful scrutiny of the great divines of the last two thousand years, do me a favor: put a sock in my mouth, secure it with duct tape, fit me with a nice snug straitjacket, and book me a room at Happy Acres where I may occupy myself with something more productive than speaking fantasies, something like stringing beads. I assure you, that would be more productive and far less harmful than teaching "new doctrine."

Pastors and teachers may find creative ways of communicating biblical propositions, but deep, expositional, biblical truth is what faithful men of God will teach. Why? Because we need to recall God's proven words so that we may remember His ways and thereby walk in them. Otherwise, my friends, we simply forget the way of the Lord and merrily go off the beaten path. And when we forget and stray from God's truth, we stumble into dangerous terrain and put ourselves and our families in harm's way.

I believe it is in our fallen human nature to forget or neglect truth, not because we're stupid, but because living by God's truth is harder than doing what we want or living by what feels right to us. In a sense, maturity in the Christian life (sanctification, becoming more like Jesus Christ) comes through the process by which we live less and less by our clouded intuition (what feels right to us, the thoughts and behaviors that come naturally from our flesh) and more and more by our biblically enlightened volition. For that process to be sustained, we need to be reminded of God's truth often. Again, I'm not saying we're a congregation of dull dolts, but repetition of the truth is necessary to conform and transform our often reluctant will.

Worth repeating

Repetition is not only the essence of faithful pastoral ministry, but it is also at the core of effective parenting. Good parenting involves a lot of tireless repetition. Take for instance the not-so-critical, yet socially valuable art of proper table manners. Parents spend 80% of their early years at the dinner table cutting everyone else's meat and reinforcing good table etiquette. That's why we don't put on as much weight when our children are young. Who has time to eat when you're constantly on Polite Patrol!

If I were to dine in your home, I would probably walk away impressed by how your older children conduct themselves at the table, remarking to my lovely wife, "My, those kids are so polite! It's always 'please' and 'thank you' with them. Did you notice they don't hold their utensils like cavemen, and they eat with their mouths closed too! Lovely family!" Hopefully you would say the same thing after eating with my kids—hopefully.

If your children are teens and they have good table manners, that's wonderful! However, the larger question is, "How often did you have to instruct your kids on proper table etiquette?" Once they progressed beyond the pureed-mystery-food-in-a-jar stage when the food gets more on the baby then in the baby, once your children were introduced to the civilized world of real food, how often did you have to teach your kids how to conduct themselves at the table?

How many times did you tell your son, "Now Billy-Bob eat with your mouth closed, son. I don't want to hear your squishy, smacky noises! You sound like a lion gnawing on a carcass. I feel like I'm watching an episode of *Animal Planet* when I watch you eat." How often did you remind your daughter, "Beulah, honey, sit up straight at the table. You don't want your profile to look like a banana. We've read *The Hunchback of Notre Dame*. You've seen the artist's rendering of Quasimodo. How do you think he got that awful hump? That's right, he had terrible table manners; he refused to listen to his parents and then one day, BAM! He looked like a question mark for the rest of his life! His life I tell you! Now sit up straight before you get locked in that position. What? It could happen!"

How many times did you admonish and encourage your children with those instructions—well, maybe not those instructions but a boatload of others like them... kind of like them? Once, twice, a dozen times? If your children are anything like mine, table etiquette was part of the daily menu. "What are we having for dinner, Mom?" "Good nutritious food and assorted corrections, now go wash your hands." At times I remember growing discouraged by the daily grind of the recurrent corrective routine at the table.

Raised by wolves

I recall one frustrating evening when the repetitive instruction was flowing from my mouth like promises from a politician's lips. Finally in frustration, I told my children, "You know what, guys? Someday I'm going to write a book, and I am going to entitle it, *My Children Were Raised By Wolves*! because no matter how many times we instruct you on proper table manners, you seem to do the very opposite. Hence, I have a theory. I think at nighttime, when your mother and I are asleep, wolves come into this house. Yes, that's right, not harmful but wild, ill-mannered wolves!

"I'm talking big wolves who can speak English and sound like they're from Brooklyn. They sneak into the house and whisk you away to their den, and there these rude ruffians teach you the ways of the uncivilized wolf. They growl their instructions at you, 'Eat with your mouth open. Don't use a fork! Push the food around on your plate with your paw. Yeah, that's it. You got it! Good! Now tussle with your siblings over that last piece of garlic bread. Go ahead, snarl. Pretend it's still alive. You guys learn pretty fast for humans! Now let's get you back to bed before your parents find out what you've been up to.' And you kids thought I would never find out, didn't you? Well, I know all about your nocturnal mutiny!"

The initial wide-eyed stares on my kids' faces gave way to a puzzled concern for their father and eventually to reluctant laughter as they got my point. Their father, in a rather delusional, frustrated sort of way was trying to remind them of how to properly conduct themselves at the dinner table. What's more, it's not that my children were being disobedient or disrespectful to their mother and me, it's just that they would temporarily forget what they knew to do and then resort to what came naturally.

And so, it fell to my wife and me to remind them of their manners or lack thereof, just as the duty fell to my parents and to their parents before them, and their parent's parents, reaching all the way back to that first Passover meal. "Kids, I know we have to leave Egypt in a hurry, but that's no excuse for poor table manners. Please, sit up straight and chew your matzo with your mouth closed—but eat quickly, we have to plunder the Egyptians and it's getting late."

You see, the responsibility fell to my wife and me to constantly help our children recall what they knew until it became ingrained in their behavior. For the most part, now that my four children are grown they have abandoned the ways of the wolf—and it only took about two-plus decades.

All of us, like our children, need frequent reminders of the truth, so that it may become ingrained in our thinking and expressed in our behavior. This is certainly true of parental discipleship, aka biblical parenting. In my travels throughout this country, it has been my observation that many have either forgotten or simply don't understand much of what God prescribes for the Christian family, and especially that God has called Christian parents to biblically shepherd their children. Sadly, as the church progressively abandons biblical preaching, I fear that many have never been taught God's pattern for the home.

And so, I am writing this book in large measure to remind and instruct—myself, my maturing children, and my fellow pilgrim parents in Christ—of the Lord's design for this supremely important institution that He has created, this training ground for disciples, this stage for the gospel, this pillar of society, this marvelous entity which we call the Christian family. Biblical repetition is a good remedy for Biblical Attention Deficit Disorder (B.A.D.D.), so I encourage you to read on.

3. My family wants me to write this book!

The third reason I am writing this book is because my dear wife and children demand that I do so; therefore, in order to keep peace in my home and keep my family happy, I have written this book. While the tone of this third reason is somewhat comedic, it is nonetheless a real force behind this humble effort. Often I have grown discouraged in its writing largely because of my personal shortcomings as a husband and as a father. At my lowest times I have put this work aside, yet my wife—and often my children—have lovingly rebuked me and exhorted me to push on. A number of times they threatened my wellbeing with sharp and pointy things if I did not press on. Well, sure that's an exaggeration, but you get my drift. Valorie and my kids have greatly desired to see this book written, and through their encouragement I have persevered. Of course, by reading this book you will also help keep my family happy, and that's good because they have earnestly prayed that you would be encouraged by it.

4. Parenting is discipleship!

Lastly, briefly, but most importantly, I am writing this book to remind my fellow Christians that parenting is discipleship. A Christian parent's primary duty before the Lord is to lead their children to God and teach them to walk in the content of biblical faith. Christian parents need to hear and embrace this message with renewed vigor. I am praying that countless numbers of believing parents will be encouraged to heed the call to parental discipleship and that the lives of myriads of young people and their future families will come to know the God of their fathers and become equipped to walk with Christ and impact the world for His deserved glory.

Mentoring our children spiritually

The biblical premise of this book is that parenting is discipleship. For some of you, this may force you to look at parenting differently! I believe it would be fair to say that many Christian parents draw too great a distinction between parenting and the discipleship process. The conventional thinking seems to be, "Parents raise kids, and the church makes disciples. Mom and dad bring up their little ones, but the church primarily trains them to be followers of Jesus. Discipleship falls under the umbrella of the Great Commission, and that is the domain of the church. Parenting and missions/evangelism are distinct and separate undertakings."

I would agree there are responsibilities unique to each of these two categories, but I would also suggest that at its core, parenting is discipleship. Furthermore, the great missionary endeavor to make disciples of the nations (the Great Commission, Matthew 28:19–20), for believing parents, begins at home and from there radiates outward to the world.

The priority and importance of discipling our children

The basic exhortation behind the Great Commission is essentially to lead people to saving faith in the Lord Jesus through the gospel and to teach them to observe all the things Jesus taught us, i.e., the sum of biblical doctrine.[2] That is discipleship. Certainly the Lord's charge to "*make disciples*" applies to those of our own household. Indeed, our children are no less needful of salvation and nurture in Christ than other human beings on the face of the earth, and from a logical perspective they must become the first and primary targets of the Great Commission for Christian parents and grandparents.

"You mean to tell me that missions, evangelism, the discipleship of other Christians, ministry within the body of Christ are replaced by my need to spiritually mentor my home?" Not at all, but the necessity to make disciples of our own family members—for those of us who have been given the gift of children—must stand at the top of our spiritual priority list. We must always strive to put and keep our own spiritual house in order, or, like Eli the priest who neglected to shepherd his sons, we may lose the spiritual battle for our children and in the process potentially forfeit the privilege of ministry to others as well (1 Samuel 3:12–13).

Sadly, not everyone in the church recognizes the priority that parents have to strengthen the spiritual vitality of their own homes first. Whether this is due to ignorance, negligence, indifference, or a different ideology, in the long run, failure to embrace this parental priority can weaken our service to the body of Christ and cripple our outreach to the world. Putting our home (not just our children but our spouse as well) at the top of our spiritual priorities is necessary for the sake of gospel ministry. Consider the following four points that underscore this necessity. The priority of spiritually mentoring our family is necessary from the standpoint of the following considerations...

1. Integrity—To go out into the world to make disciples but to overlook those closest to us with this task is a contradiction. Our loved ones are part of the scope of the Great Commission and the most obvious first recipients of our obedience to it. Minimizing our primary duty to spiritually edify our own spouse and make disciples of our own children really calls into question how much we value the gospel message and the teachings of Christ. If we truly love missions, how can we ignore the need to "go" to our own first? Such a misguided priority could result in the permanent unbelief of our loved ones and obscure the message we preach. Closely akin to this idea is the following point.

2. Believability—How can we expect the world to embrace a message that we don't preach to our own, or even worse, that doesn't significantly impact those nearest to us, those who are at the center of our sphere of influence? If our message of salvation and transformation does not impact our homes, how can we tell people that the gospel will transform their lives and expect them to believe it?

3. Loving Priority—The deepest affection God gives us as human beings is for our spouse and children. God gives us a unique relationship to our families. For example, God's design (for most Christian adults—barring death) is for us to marry one person for life, with whom we are one flesh. That relationship is so special that the Holy Spirit uses it to illustrate the unique and glorious relationship of God the Son to His people, the church (Ephesians 5:22–33). For each one of us, our spouse is singularly given to us, and we are especially devoted to their welfare above all other men and women.

Likewise children (whether born to a family or grafted in through adoption) are sovereignly and uniquely given to parents by God. I love all children. My wife and I are certifiably absurd baby geeks. When we see parents toting little ones in a grocery store, my wife and I have been known to crane our necks just to get a peek at their little dudes (or dudettes), to catch their eye and evoke a smile. We love kids! It makes my day when a little person smiles at me. Little people are absolute miracles of divine creativity. I could stare at a sleeping baby for an hour and get lost in admiration of God's creative genius—that's not an exaggeration! Every child is a treasure!

Yet, as much as we are able to appreciate the children we meet, Valorie and I do not have the capability emotionally and physically to care for all the beautiful children we encounter. Before the Lord, my wife and I bear a special responsibility and love for the children He has given to us. As mere mortals, we have a finite capacity to care, and therefore the Lord gives us an unmistakable and special bond and charge over the human beings He brings into the world through our specific nuclear family. The children in our home were given first to us to care for and to love as only parents can. As much as we love children, we are simply incapable of loving all children as we love our four, and that's the way God meant it to be. My wife and I must see to their spiritual health first, or we are working against the grain of the natural affections God has given us.

It is hypocritical and self-deceiving to nurture a love for "the lost out in the world" or to desire to mentor fellow Christians in biblical truth and not—with equal or deeper passion and compassion—pursue the spiritual welfare of those souls whom the Lord grants to us as our first and greatest spiritual priority in life.

4. Good vs. Bad Discipleship—Leading our children to faith in Christ and teaching them His ways is good discipleship. It nurtures our family spiritually, but it also models godly behavior for those in the church who are observing us— and believe me, people are watching us and learning from us! Neglecting to prioritize our family's spiritual development is, simply put, bad discipleship. It teaches those who are learning from us that it is acceptable to de-emphasize, trivialize, or fail at discipleship at home just as long as we "get the job done" out in the world. It tells those who are learning from our example that, "Priority #1 is to make disciples of others; family discipleship is not necessarily related to that endeavor and does not affect it." That's a bad message and terrible discipleship. Conversely, speaking from experience, few things have impacted people spiritually more than observing the Great Commission worked out in our home. It has multiplied personal ministry for us and by God's grace encouraged many families to aspire to glorify Christ through the platform of their homes.

The call for Christian parents to mentor their children spiritually is truly essential for gospel ministry and in many ways central to the health and holiness of the church. If the rank and file of believing parents faithfully sought to feed themselves spiritually through the prodigious resources at their disposal for spiritual growth and sought to pass on these truths sincerely, consistently, sacrificially, as a matter of first priority to their sons and daughters, the impact on the church over time would be visible.

I am convinced we would see the spiritual and emotional healing of countless families and therefore greater holiness in the church, leading to a revived gospel testimony in our communities. We would certainly reap a greater harvest of souls among our young people—instead of helplessly watching the massive defection of Christianized unbelievers in young adulthood. Certainly, we would live to witness a wave of new missionaries to the world. We would see spiritual awakening in proportion to our obedience to God's design, i.e., loving God, walking with our God in truth, and discipling our sons and daughters in that same and glorious way.

The Importance of the Family to God

&

The Centrality of His Word in Discipling Our Children

CHAPTER 1

Whose Job Is It Anyway?

Eternal treasures

Parents have been blessed by God with a marvelous, immeasurably valuable stewardship, their children. Scripture testifies of this precious treasure with the words, *"Behold, children are a gift of the LORD, the fruit of the womb is a reward. Like arrows in the hand of a warrior, so are the children of one's youth. How blessed is the man whose quiver is full of them; they will not be ashamed when they speak with their enemies in the gate"* (Psalm 127:3–5).

According to this passage of Scripture, children are a gift, a reward, a defense, and a blessing. In fact, these verses clearly tell us that having multiple children is a blessing. This straightforward biblical verity exposes a harmful attitude embedded in our culture's understanding of children. Without even discussing the blight and atrocity of abortion, children are often believed to be "cute but inconvenient" or worse, a liability, a hindrance to adult freedoms.

Scripture tells us the very opposite. What's more, children are not only a treasure beyond description in this life, they are potentially a trophy of God's grace and glory for eternity. That's ultimately how we need to view children. They are a gift, a reward, a defense, a blessing, and a stewardship from God entrusted to us so that we might lead them to God. That truly describes the goal of Christian parenting, doesn't it—to value our kids so much that our ultimate aim is to lead them to the Lord and in the Lord? With that principle clearly in mind, the great J.C. Ryle once wrote,

> *Precious, no doubt, are these little ones in your eyes (our children); but if you love them, think often of their souls. No interest should weigh*

with you so much as their eternal interests. No part of them should be so dear to you as that part which will never die. The world, with all its glory, shall pass away; the hills shall melt; the heavens shall be wrapped together as a scroll; the sun shall cease to shine. But the spirit which dwells in those little creatures, whom you love so well, shall outlive them all, and whether in happiness or misery (to speak as a man) will depend on you. This is the thought that should be uppermost on your mind in all you do for your children. In every step you take about them, in every plan, and scheme, and arrangement that concerns them, do not leave out that mighty question, "How will this affect their souls?" [1]

God has put the eternal treasure of our children in our hands to nurture in His ways so that one day they might embrace our God, follow Him, serve Him, and lead the next generation in the same life-giving path. That's our divine call as parents, and there are few endeavors that are as challenging, as important, as joyful or potentially sorrowful as this one (Psalm 127:3–5; 1 Samuel 2:12; 3:13b; 4:11). We would do well to recognize the value of this stewardship (our children) and the eternal importance of this mission (leading them to God). Indeed, this goal is the starting line of evangelism and discipleship. Our grand missionary enterprise (the Great Commission) flows from our homes out to our community and from there to the world.

"Whose job is it anyway?"

Please don't underestimate the urgency and seriousness of shepherding your children, and please, please understand that God entrusts this awesome charge primarily to you, the Christian parent. Ultimately, we carry the sobering and wonderful responsibility of mentoring our children spiritually.

Occasionally this great duty is forfeited to another because of death or abandonment, or because God saves some children from unbelieving homes. Consequently, other shepherds must step into the mentoring void—e.g., grandparents, pastors, fellow Christians, surrogate Christian families. However, we must realize that, barring a few exceptions, God has entrusted parents to raise their children *"in the discipline and instruction of the Lord"* (Ephesians 6:4).

Consider the testimony of the following Scriptures. They confirm that parents must take the lead in the discipleship of their children.

For I have chosen him [Abraham], *so that he may command his children and his household after him to keep the way of the Lᴏʀᴅ by doing righteousness and justice, so that the Lᴏʀᴅ may bring upon Abraham what He has spoken about him* (Genesis 18:19, emphasis added).

And when your children say to you, "What does this rite mean to you?" you [parent] *shall say, "It is a Passover sacrifice to the Lᴏʀᴅ"* (Exodus 12:26–27, emphasis added).

And it shall be when your son asks you, in time to come, saying, "What is this?" then you shall say to him, "With a powerful hand the Lᴏʀᴅ brought us out of Egypt" (Exodus 13:14, emphasis added). The historical context assumes father to son, but the application certainly involves both parents to their children.

Remember the day you stood before the Lᴏʀᴅ your God at Horeb, when the Lᴏʀᴅ said to me, "Assemble the people to Me, that I may let them hear My words so they may learn to fear Me all the days they live on the earth, and that they [parents] *may teach their children"* (Deuteronomy 4:10, emphasis added).

These words, which I am commanding you today, shall be on your heart. You shall teach them diligently to your sons and shall talk of them when you sit in your house and when you walk by the way and when you lie down and when you rise up (Deuteronomy 6:6–7, emphasis added).

When your son asks you in time to come, saying, "What do the testimonies and the statutes and the judgments mean which the Lᴏʀᴅ our God commanded you?" *then you shall say to your son,* "We were slaves to Pharaoh in Egypt" (Deuteronomy 6:20–21, emphasis added).

Let this be a sign among you, so that when your children ask later, saying, "What do these stones mean to you?" then you shall say to them, "Because the waters of the Jordan were cut off before the ark" (Joshua 4:6–7, emphasis added).

He said to the sons of Israel, "When your children ask their fathers in time to come, saying, 'What are these stones?' then you shall inform your children, saying, 'Israel crossed this Jordan on dry ground'" (Joshua 4:21–22, emphasis added).

For He established a testimony in Jacob and appointed a law in Israel, which He commanded our fathers that they should teach them to their children, that the generation to come might know, even the children yet to be born, that they may arise and tell them to their children (Psalm 78:5–6, emphasis added).

Hear, my son, your father's instruction and do not forsake your mother's teaching (Proverbs 1:8, emphasis added).

Hear, O sons, the instruction of a father, and give attention that you may gain understanding (Proverbs 4:1, emphasis added).

Hear, my son, and accept my sayings and the years of your life will be many (Proverbs 4:10, emphasis added).

Train up a child in the way he should go, even when he is old he will not depart from it (Proverbs 22:6, emphasis added).

Listen, my son, and be wise, and direct your heart in the way (Proverbs 23:19, emphasis added).

I would lead you and bring you into the house of my mother, who used to instruct me (Song of Solomon 8:2, emphasis added). Here a bridegroom is speaking to his bride as he brings her home.

Fathers, do not provoke your children to anger, but bring them up in the discipline and instruction of the Lord (Ephesians 6:4, emphasis added).

Just as you know how we were exhorting and encouraging and imploring each one of you as a father would his own children (1 Thessalonians 2:11, emphasis added). Here Paul is using the analogy of a father and the known duties of a godly dad.

For I am mindful of the sincere faith within you, which first dwelt in your grandmother Lois and your mother Eunice, and I am sure that it is in you as well... and that from childhood you have known the sacred writings which are able to give you the wisdom that leads to salvation through faith which is in Christ Jesus (2 Timothy 1:5; 2 Timothy 3:15, emphasis added).

Timothy, Paul's young protege, was impacted spiritually primarily by his grandmother and mother. Timothy's *"sincere faith"* was seeded and nurtured in him through the word of God, which he learned since childhood from his maternal mentors.

I believe the point of all these verses is inescapable. God has given us (Christian parents and grandparents) His ways in His word so that we might embrace them personally and teach them to our children. It is our responsibility to disciple our sons and daughters. I don't care how loudly others voices beg to differ, the Scriptures speak perspicuously to this issue, and we must obey the clear instruction of God's word.

Don't buy the lie

Sadly, our service-minded, consultant-driven Christian culture has convinced many, if not most, that moms and dads are unskillful and inept at discipling their own kids and especially their preteens and teenagers. The drivel is familiar to us all, "Parents can't mentor their own kids! They're too old, out of touch, irrelevant, retro, lacking style, devoid of savvy, bereft of trendy-up-to-the-minute vocabulary, not to mention they don't have a repertoire of bodily fluid jokes. Bottom line, parents are simply incapable of relating to, let alone discipling their children." If you believe that, or you have been made to feel that way, you have been fed a lie.

No, my friends, neither the state nor the church is primarily responsible for developing the moral character of our children or leading them to God. I suppose it is safe to say that ninety-nine point nine percent of people who read this book would heartily agree the state cannot interfere with the upbringing of our children. Government must allow parents the widest berth and freedoms (barring criminal activity) to raise their children as seems best to them. None of us want local, state, or federal governments, or international bodies telling us how we should bring up our kids.

When it comes to our children, the farther the state stays away from us the better! Right? Of course, right. (There's a little Yiddish grammar for you. Dangle that adjective for all to read at the end of an incomplete sentence.) Remember the movie *Fiddler On The Roof?* At the beginning of the film, as the audience is introduced to the precarious tensions existing between the Jews of Anatevka and the gentile authorities, one man asks his rabbi, "Rabbi, is there a proper blessing for the Czar?" "A proper blessing for the Czar?" the rabbi thinks aloud, then states with a knowing twinkle in his eye, "Yes, may the Lord bless and keep the Czar... far away from us!"[2] Most of us understand the absolute necessity for parental freedoms and minimal government intervention and that the job of rearing children belongs to parents, not governmental agencies. I can hear the chorus of "Amen!" echoing through the land on that one! I add my "Amen" to the chorus! And yet, when it comes to the church, it seems many present-day parents willingly and gladly acquiesce the spiritual training of their children to professional clergy.

"But really, what about the church?"

Someone may ask, "What about the church? Ultimately, isn't the church, through its youth ministry, responsible to train our children in the faith?" I would say the vast majority of Christians today accept that tenet to some degree. This is especially true when it comes to our preteens and teens. This common opinion, however, does not pan out biblically. The community of believers, the church, does play an indispensable supportive role in the discipleship of our children, but not the primary one. That function has been entrusted to parents.

The church's main function is to equip believers for service (Ephesians 4:11–12), and in my opinion, one of the greatest needs in the body of Christ today is the need to equip parents to serve their families through discipleship. As with any equipping ministry within the church, the building up of parents and families must come primarily through biblical instruction and encouragement, and by providing biblical accountability and support to moms and dads in every phase of parenting. The goal of such a ministry is to enable parents to carry out the job God has placed before them.

Your local church and its pastors are not there to take your place as the primary shepherds of your children. That task and privilege has fallen first and foremost to you, the father, the mother, believing parents, and by logical extension, grandparents. In spite of that, I'm afraid many parents in the church have relinquished much of that role to contemporary youth ministry. I can hear the "motor boaters" now, "But, but, but, but, but, but, but, wait a minute, Marcelo, we have a fine youth program and a marvelous youth pastor to disciple our kids." That may be true, but nowhere in Scripture does the Spirit instruct us to relinquish the discipleship of our children to a vocational pastor or youth professional.

I'm not really sure how this default system came to be; but sadly, it is virtually universal in the North American evangelical church and increasingly the norm throughout the world. The general consensus is that we, Christian parents, are there to nurture children spiritually in the younger years. We read them Bible stories before bed; we teach them to pray; we correct their sinful behavior with biblical instruction; we take them to church with us; we help them understand the Bible lessons they learn there, and assist them with their memory verses. That is pretty much expected fare from parents. But then when our children are on the cusp of one of the most important developmental periods of life, preteens and young adulthood, we are told that we must surrender them to the youth experts and the local youth group for further biblical education and spiritual development.

We would do well to think outside the "cultural box" and process this call to disciple our children biblically rather then simply acquiesce to the accepted present pattern without question. It must be noted that the New Testament was written in a time when there were no such entities as "youth groups" functioning as default systems to shepherd kids spiritually.

The key issue

Does this mean that youth groups are unbiblical or wrong? No! The Scriptures give us great latitude to shepherd the flock of God. The Bible doesn't say anything about "men's retreats," "men's and women's ministries," "all-church pancake breakfasts," or "mega church garage sales" to raise money for missions either; however, the absence of chapter and verse for such outworking of biblical ministry does not make such organization of ministry illegitimate. Whether or not a church has a youth group is not the issue. The key issue is who is being primarily empowered to nurture children spiritually? Biblically speaking, it must be the Christian parent, and I believe all youth programming must be subservient to that primary goal.

I recognize that this is a sensitive issue for many, and honestly, my intention is not to offend anyone. It is our duty, however, to think through our accepted norms in the church in a biblically informed manner, and that is what I am attempting to do (see verses listed on previous pages). Let me acknowledge the positive impact youth ministry has had on countless Christians. I do not want to diminish that for one moment. I realize lives have been changed for eternity and for the glory of God through the sincere and tireless efforts of faithful youth pastors and spiritually dynamic youth ministries. We all know that the mission fields of the world and the pastorates of our land are filled with the fruit of youth ministry. Again, I am not anti–youth ministry. I myself have been a youth pastor to middle school, high school, and college students. Truth be told, I have a genuine affection and compassion for youth pastors, because when we hire them we often put them in an impossible situation.

Many churches bring a youth minister on staff and, without a whole lot of shepherding oversight, demand that his abilities and ministry stop just shy of raising the dead—maybe that too! His daunting job description usually includes—but is not limited to—saving the lost, bringing the earnest to maturity, and taming the rebellious. All too often the focus, or the unspoken expectation, when churches hire a youth pastor is for that third purpose, "taming the rebellious." We hire a young man to "straighten out" the troubled wayward teens—especially Deacon Alphaeus's ruffians who are too young for him to kick out of the house.

In other words, we usually demand that he render our young people (the unsaved, fledgling, and rebellious) spiritually mature and ready to serve God in all walks of life. We require all of this in one, or two, or possibly three hours per week while working with the young people mostly in a group setting. The church, in essence, expects the youth pastor to do what the Scripture requires parents to do, but in a fraction of the time. Moreover, when he fails to straighten out Deacon Alphaeus's kids, we fire him and go searching for the next youthful victim. Never mind that parents have had their children for 12 to 18 years, and have them under their watch for the better part of the remaining 165 hours in a week; if the youth pastor can't "straighten out" our youth in a couple of hours each week over the course of a year or two, there's something wrong with the guy!

My friends, it is not the singular task of youth pastors to disciple our children. The very time and logistical constraints of their availability remind us that their role is supportive in nature at best. And again, I'm not denying that fruit has been borne of such labor, nor, as I said, would I ever want to denigrate such wonderful results. However, ultimately we (the church) should not judge a ministry or method solely on its apparent success or popularity. On the contrary, we must measure all ministry against the plumb line of the revelation of God's infallible word.

Whether or not God has used youth ministry to shape your life or the lives of others for the better is not the central issue. The question is not, "Can God use youth ministry to disciple young people to spiritual maturity?" The simple answer to that question is "Yes He can." God can use, and often does use, many secondary or tertiary alternatives to accomplish His desired will (Read the book of Esther!). That said, the best and most productive way to accomplish God's good purposes is by carefully following the primary prescription God provides in His word. In the case of training our children spiritually, God's prescription calls for parents to lead the way.

Shifting our focus

Perhaps the time has come for the church to rethink its philosophy of youth ministry and shift its focus toward equipping moms and dads to become better parents and spiritual mentors to their children, as well as emphasizing parental leadership in ministry activities. We need to reinforce to our young people that parents are the leaders of their families. I believe we need to abandon the ubiquitous perspective that views young people as the spiritual domain of the youth program, and in many cases, to the exclusion of parents. All too often parents are eager to relinquish the spiritual development of their preteens and teens to young men whose primary qualification to shepherd our kids is "youthfulness." How many fifty-year-old youth pastors have you met? My apologies to the few of you who might read this book.

Most often lack of experience disqualifies a person from a job. That's why we don't allow people under 35 to become president. But frequently "youth" is a primary consideration when hiring a man to shepherd one of our most precious stewardships from God—our children. Often it seems we hire the least experienced to shepherd some of the most vulnerable among us, and then we encourage parents to surrender their impressionable young people without hesitation to the youth professionals and to stay out of the way as much as possible. Why? Because the young and inexperienced shepherds—who in most cases have either very young children or no children—are more capable of discipling young adults (in two to three hours per week) than parents who have nurtured them for all of their lives and who live with them for most of the time? How does that work? That seems like fishy math to me.

Let me reiterate once more, I am not against youth pastors, neither am I anti–youth group and youth programs. I believe there is a legitimate place in church ministry to shepherd young people and bring them together for study, prayer, fellowship, evangelism and play—especially with the leadership and participation of parents and, in particular, dads. However, I believe that churches need to rethink the structure and function of youth ministry because so much of contemporary youth programs are led by the least experienced and have been shaped by the secular educational system (strict segregation according to age, separation from parents, other adults, and community life) and heavily influenced by the ever changing, frivolous, and often dangerous world of pop culture more than by Scripture.

Let's face it, our children are our flesh and blood, and if adopted, we have chosen and pursued them to be our very own family. The Lord has placed our children in our care for the better part of their first two decades of life, and we share our lives together hour upon hour, day upon day. That's why Deuteronomy 6:1–9, God's call to parents to teach their children the ways of the Lord, was not addressed to a special class of Jewish youth priests, and Ephesians 6:1–4, Paul's exhortation to spiritually mentor our children, is not aimed at the professional clergy. Both of these passages, as well as the wisdom literature dealing with the spiritual mentoring of young people, is addressed to parents! Why? Because this is God's design, and there is no one better qualified in God's economy to accomplish this great task.

Furthermore, if parents take to heart their calling and embrace this divine mandate, there will be no one more rightly motivated to see the process through. I will tell you plainly, other fine Christian men and women love and appreciate my children (including a history of godly youth pastors), but no one cares for them and the welfare of their eternal souls like their mother and me. God has hardwired parents to fulfill this eternally important duty. This is how it has always been. Remember Genesis 18:19? *"For I have chosen him* [Abraham], *so that he may command his children and his household after him to keep the way of the LORD by doing righteousness and justice"* (emphasis added). God has given the authority, right, and privilege of spiritually rearing children principally to one entity, believing parents.

Role recognition

Does this mean that we should give a dismissal slip and severance package to all youth pastors? Not at all! I always welcome the influence of godly men and women (regardless of their age) on my children. I can never expose my children enough to godly people. What this means is that youth workers and parents must recognize their roles. The role of fathers and mothers is to train their children in the truth of Scripture—that is God's heart for His people revealed in the Old and New Testaments—and youth pastors can play a helpful part in augmenting and affirming what the parents are doing and teaching in the home.

There are growing numbers of Christian families who adopt worldly patterns of parenting partly because they have never been effectually shepherded with God's truth. Shepherds in the church—including youth pastors—would do well to shift a good portion of their ministry effort to train and walk with parents to fulfill their God-ordained function in the home. I realize that sounds ironic, but the lion's share of youth ministry, in my opinion, should be aimed at the parents, to equip them to train their young for life and service.

I do not believe that many churches will rethink their philosophy of youth ministry because of this book—though I pray some will be encouraged to rethink how and in whom they should invest their resources. My greater hope is that many Christian parents will rethink their spiritual responsibility to their children and conclude that they must take a lead role, an active part in the discipleship of their children of all ages. We will explore what this looks like in succeeding chapters.

Parenting, an awesome task with abundant provision

Dear parents, God has charged us with the awesome and rewarding task of training our children spiritually so that we may prepare them for life and Christian service, and to spiritually impact their future families. I realize discipling our own children, becoming a youth pastor, a shepherd to our kids may sound intimidating to some of us. We may feel inadequate for the task. If so, join the club. The task is great and we're all sinners with character flaws and weaknesses that threaten to undermine our duty to shepherd our homes. This is true, but remember we have a great Savior who walks with us and the Spirit of the Lord who will enable and strengthen us for the task God has called us to fulfill.

The Bible holds many examples of people who were overwhelmed by the charge God called them to execute. The great servant of the Lord, Moses, is a prime example of a man convinced of his own inability to fulfill the mission God placed before him to deliver the sons of Israel from their bitter bondage in Egypt. God's call to Moses was direct and unmistakable. Appearing to Moses in the burning bush, the Lord said, *"Now, behold, the cry of the sons of Israel has come to Me; furthermore, I have seen the oppression with which the Egyptians are oppressing them. Therefore, come now, and I will send you to Pharaoh, so that you may bring My people, the sons of Israel, out of Egypt"* (Exodus 3:9–10).

There was no ambiguity in God's mandate to this Levite, yet in the face of the clear call of God, Moses could think of several reasons why he was unfit for the job. The challenge set before him was enormous, and Moses felt altogether too small for the gargantuan undertaking. He said, *"Who am I, that I should go* to Pharaoh, and that I should bring the sons of Israel out of Egypt?" (Exodus 3:11). His reply to the divine summons was, "I'm a nobody. Who am I that You should entrust me with this important work? You've got the wrong guy." God's simple reply to His servant is enlightening. In essence, God informed Moses that it didn't matter what his strengths, weaknesses, and failures were. The mission did not hinge on Moses, but on the God who calls, sends, and enables. The upshot of the Lord's response can be found in the first part of Exodus 3:12. *"Certainly I will be with you,"* i.e., "I will be with you, behind you, before you. I will be your strength, Moses!"

God never gives us responsibilities that we cannot fulfill by His abundant grace (Matthew 19:26; Mark 9:23; Philippians 4:13; 2 Corinthians 12:9). This includes the labor-intensive, joyful, and rewarding journey of raising children in the Lord.

If we feel inadequate for the job of mentoring our own kids, I have good news. God has called us to this task, and He is with us to strengthen and enable us for this great mission. Let's make God's promise to Paul, and Paul's boast in the Lord, our very own rallying cry to disciple our sons and daughters. *"And He has said to me, 'My grace is sufficient for you, for power is perfected in weakness.' Most gladly, therefore, I will rather boast about my weaknesses, so that the power of Christ may dwell in me"* (2 Corinthians 12:9). You might want to print this up and place it somewhere where you can see it every day. I encourage you to fulfill your God-ordained role as mentor to your children in the power and grace that God supplies! He has called us to this, He will supply the grace and strength we need to meet this challenge.

God's providential grace working through our weaknesses

I wish I could tell you that I decided to mentor my kids because I possessed a clear and profound biblical vision for this task early in my greenhorn years as a father. If I did, I would be lying through my teeth. Alas, like most other important decisions in my life (marrying my beloved wife, choosing a ministry, parenting resolutions), God's gracious providence led me to a place where I was confronted by my own inadequacies and shortcomings, then He unveiled His surpassing wisdom and enabled me to take a step in the right direction by His abundant grace. Such was the case when I began to disciple my eldest son, Joshua.

Josh and I began meeting one-on-one in earnest when Joshua was twelve years old. He is now 29, and the depth of our father/son relationship in many ways began to develop at age 12 when he was becoming a young man. We always had a loving connection because he was my boy and I was his daddy. We played and laughed together; we prayed and talked about God together in his early years; but when he was on the cusp of becoming a young man, the flower of a new relationship between us started to blossom. At this time we began to know and love one another in a wonderful and more profound way.

This growth in our personal relationship came about as a result of the decision to more actively disciple Josh at this critical juncture of his life. He and I began meeting regularly to search the Scriptures together. This was a habit he and I enjoyed for as long as God enabled us to meet, and it remains a treasured memory for the both of us, not to mention a touchstone for our relationship. In fact, now that Josh has finished his graduate studies and has come back to Southern California (at least for the near future), he and I meet over coffee for extended times of fellowship and biblical give and take.

When Josh and I began to meet together initially, I taught him basic principles of inductive Bible study (see Appendices A, B, & C) so that he could study the Bible accurately on his own, and this eventually launched us into several years of fellowship together around God's word. These were rich years where we grew together in our knowledge and love for Christ, as well as in our love and respect for one another.

I had a chance to reflect back on that pivotal decision to mentor my son after spending a day with him on his college campus. I had set the day aside to spend with my budding chemist (Josh was a chemistry major) on his turf, the beautiful campus of UC Irvine and its environs. We met for an early lunch, studied together at the science library for five hours, enjoyed dinner at our favorite Mexican restaurant, and capped off the evening with an extended walk through the sprawling complex of shops and eateries on Newport's Fashion Island near the UCI campus. We found ourselves intermittently strolling, sitting, sipping coffee, enjoying the cool October seaside weather, all the while talking, always talking about anything and everything.

One minute we would find ourselves musing about the superficial, e.g., the dismal season our beloved St. Louis Rams were having, who they should draft in the spring, our favorite coffees, movies that made us laugh. The next moment we would be eight feet deep in a Bible passage, discussing the finer points of sovereign election, or how to prepare one's heart for marriage and raising children. We enjoyed one another's company when quietly studying and spent the balance of the day in meaningful dialogue.

After our prolonged fellowship that day and evening, I drove my son back to his dorm, gave him a tight hug and watched him walk up the stairs to "his" apartment. A mixture of gratitude and contentment struck me. Watching Josh climb the stairs to his door, I realized he was now a young man walking his own path in life, a path God was blazing for him. He was independent of his mother and me, flourishing in the place where God led him. As a parent, I was suddenly and immensely gratified that my son was making a successful transition to adulthood. When I pulled away from the parking lot to make my way home, I was especially grateful for the close relationship I shared with my eldest.

As I said, the quality of relationship we share as father and son, and man-to-man, began to flourish when I started taking a purposeful, proactive role in mentoring Josh in God's word. The decision to start meeting with my son came about in a divinely serendipitous manner. It was actually a difficult time in our lives. My wife and I had come to the unfortunate but inevitable decision that we had to leave our local church.

The philosophy of ministry had evolved to the place where there was no longer much need for a Bible teacher in the assembly. The ministry focus shifted from training God's people to do the work of ministry and take the gospel to the highways and byways of life, to gathering the unbelieving in the auditorium every Sunday and carefully crafting our church environment to accommodate their antichurch sensitivities. Home Bible studies morphed into "share your personal story" sessions based on questions from biblically thin Sunday sermons. Independent expositional Bible studies were frowned upon and publicly discouraged as well. Every aspect of ministry, Sunday morning worship, preaching, small groups, any and all activities, had to reflect an accommodation to the perceived needs of the unsaved. We knew this would ultimately lead to an erosion of the spiritual vitality of the church, the weakening of God's people, conflict, the softening of the gospel, and diminished evangelism. What's more, the leadership was sold out to this new philosophy of ministry. The course was set and no dissenting voices were tolerated. Clearly, we perceived that I would not be able to exercise my gift as I should in such a setting because I was, and am, a Bible teacher. We had to leave.

It was difficult leaving dear friends, and my wife and I grieved over having to pull our eldest son, Joshua, out of his beloved youth group. What made it tougher to leave was the fact that the youth group was arguably the healthiest ministry in the church—biblically speaking. The youth pastor was a wonderful and godly young man. He strove to teach the kids the Scripture and to nurture them in the things of God. Several years later he left the church for the same reasons we felt compelled to leave, but at the time of our departure he was leading a dynamic and healthy youth program. This young man also took an active interest in our son and genuinely cared for him, much to the delight of both his mother and me.

When we made the decision to leave the church, I knew I had to tell Joshua of our decision and plans personally. I didn't want him learning of our intentions through the grapevine and risk wounding his heart. I was his dad, he trusted me, and I had to tell him. I decided to inform him of our decision over breakfast, and so one morning we went out to one of our favorite restaurants in town. After chitchatting about life for a while, I cleared my throat and began to unfold our decision to our son and to explain our reasoning to him. I also apprised Josh of the difficult reality: that we would leave as a family, and we would find a new church to join as a family. In other words, we were not going to view the church as a ministry Pez dispenser, a service provider, and piecemeal a "church experience" by parceling ourselves out to multiple churches depending on our particular desires and their specific programs.

I've seen many people lump together a chaotic church experience in this manner: "We'll go to the Presbyterian church for worship and attend the Community church's men's & women's ministry events. We'll join the Bible church's home Bible study, send the kids to The Church of What's Happening Now for their youth group, and last but not least, drop off the younger kids at the Baptist church for Awana so my wife and I can slip over to Starbucks on Tuesday evenings." We live in a world where choice is king and we sometimes wrongly perceive the church as a buffet of services. I didn't want my son growing up with such a cavalier and utilitarian understanding of the body of Christ. I knew Joshua would want to continue to attend the youth group at our former church, but I was convinced we needed to commit ourselves to a local body of believers so that we might worship and serve the Lord as a family.

I'll never forget telling my son of our decision and watching his eyes well up with tears. I felt as though my heart was breaking with his. When I finished explaining myself, he wiped the tears from his eyes and told me with a quivering voice, "I understand your decision Daddy, and I completely trust you and Mom." I felt like saying, "You do?", but all I could do was express my love to my son and assure him that God would take care of all of us.

For the next thirty minutes or so, we talked about Joshua's youth group experience over the past year, about how neat his youth pastor was and what Josh had learned from the study of God's word through this pastor's teaching. He informed me how he had planned to become more involved in the youth discipleship program, and as we talked, I had an epiphany. I suddenly experienced an uncomfortable realization. I became acutely aware that I was allowing another man, a good and godly man but another man nonetheless, to disciple my son. All I could think about was, "Whose primary responsibility is it to nurture Joshua in the things of God? Who needs to teach him the Scripture? Who needs to hold him accountable and ask him how his thought life is going, whether his love for Christ is waxing or waning? Who was showing him and encouraging him to love God?" In short, I was faced with the question, "Who should be discipling my son in the Lord?" The inescapable answer ringing in my head was "Me. 'Knock knock, hello?'" I remember thinking, "Joshua's spiritual growth and welfare is essentially my responsibility, and God will hold me accountable for my son's spiritual health." That was the answer that settled in my mind.

I felt so convicted about my lack of biblical vision for my own son. It wasn't that I had made a deliberate choice to shirk my parental spiritual duty. I had simply and unwittingly surrendered my responsibilities to the status quo. I was just going along with the program without ever biblically scrutinizing or questioning the accepted norm, or evaluating my obligation as a Christian father. I was shocked at my own ignorance and troubled that I had not been a scripturally vigilant dad. At the same time, I was grateful that the Lord had revealed my negligence, and doubly grateful that I had woken up in time to invest more deeply, spiritually in my boy who had begun his journey toward manhood. I woke up just in time for Joshua's bar mitzvah, so to speak, and so from that day we began to discuss and comment on the Law of God together. What a joy that was and still continues to be!

He and I started to meet together that week and did so pretty much for the balance of his teen years. In the process, we learned how to study the Bible, and we discovered much about God, His Son, His Spirit, the church, God's plan for the ages, Christian responsibility, personal purity, and much, much more. We also nurtured a deep and abiding love for one another and shared a level of intimacy that I could only wish for all dads. Meeting as father and son, we not only learned great truths, but we became greater friends, and in the journey my son became a man! A godly man no less, who will live for Christ wherever the Lord leads him and who will one day bring up his son in the fear and admonition of the God of his fathers.

When I drove home from that lovely Friday evening spent with Joshua at UCI, I had an intriguing thought. I considered the possibility that I could have continued down the path I had been on with my son during his preteen years. Nine years had passed since we had begun meeting together. What if we had allowed the status quo to continue for all that time? Josh could have continued to become more and more involved with one youth ministry or another under the tutelage of some capable youth pastor, and chances are, he would have turned out to be a good Christian man. Josh had a loving home; his mother and I were not disengaged parents; he was on the right path. He likely would have been okay.

However, had he been discipled—say by his beloved youth pastor— I would have forfeited much of the closeness I now enjoy with my son because we never would have had such rich times together—as we did when we studied the Bible and shared the closeness it afforded us through his teenage years. His primary spiritual mentor would have been someone other than me, his dad. Ironically, even the youth pastor that was so much a part of Joshua's life when he was twelve would now be completely out of his life, and yet I would still be Joshua's father, but the precious years to nurture my son would have been a lost opportunity. I was so thankful that God allowed me to redeem those years with my boy. Our relationship will always be richer because of it; Joshua's life will always be fuller because of it, my life will always be fuller because of it and so will the lives of future generations.

CHAPTER 2

The Value of the Family to God

The importance of the family... from God's perspective

One of the greatest joys I experience as a father is hearing my children clearly articulate and embrace a value they have heard and seen modeled in our home. I find that gratifying as a parent because I want my children to comprehend my instruction and to live by biblical convictions. In a nutshell, having our children understand us and seeing them walk in our counsel is a reward of biblically shepherding our children.

As the apostle John wrote to his spiritual children, *"I have no greater joy than this, to hear of my children walking in the truth"* (3 John 4), so I rejoice to see my children hear and obey. No doubt you feel the same way, and if this is true of us as earthly parents, how much more must God, our perfect heavenly Father, delight when we treasure His words, take to heart His values, and align our lives by His principles. This is why the Lord has given us His counsel in the Scriptures, so that we might know Him, live by His precepts, and honor Him with our lives. Certainly this is true in every area of life, but it is poignantly applicable to the focus of this book, which is the spiritual mentoring of our families.

God longs for us to wrap our arms around His plan for the family and own it, to walk in it. And my friends, in order for God's familial precepts to take root in our hearts, we must first understand how important the family is to Him. Owning God's priority for the Christian home begins with an understanding of the high esteem the family enjoys in God's economy. It is from such understanding that we will be able to hold a conviction that echoes God's own heart for the home, and with that conviction we will find ourselves equipped to lead our families in a way that truly mirrors His design and therefore experiences His blessings.

How significant is the family to God Almighty? For the Christian, there is no more consequential question regarding the family than the one that sits atop this paragraph. Answer this question and the opinions of men either line up or simply dissolve in the light of God's revelation.

So what is the testimony of God regarding the importance of the family? Simply put, the Bible reveals that God holds the institution of the family in the highest esteem. This is clearly seen in two ways. First, we see the divine importance of the family reflected in the way God values marriage, the hub around which the family thrives. Secondly, God's value of the family is exemplified in the role it plays in the outworking of redemption.

The worth of the family preserved within the sanctity of marriage

In the following few pages I want to highlight God's high esteem for marriage. First we will see God's immense value for marriage and the family from a negative perspective—God's aversion to the destruction of this precious institution. Secondly, we will see how priceless the family is to God from a positive angle— His description of the church as the holy bride of His Son.

I realize the negative argument will be difficult for some of you to read because your lives have been deeply scarred by moral failure and/or divorce—either because of your own moral failure or through victimization. Please understand, God's grace covers all our sins, and He through His infinite power and love can rebuild and restore broken, devastated lives as demonstrated for example in the life of King David (see Chapter 12). Without question, where would we all be if not for the abounding grace of God? If you have placed your failures and sins at the foot of the cross and turned to the Lord with a humble heart, then the Lord has taken away your sin and He is in the process of creating a miracle of grace out of your life. Recognizing that, once again, my point in this section is not to unnecessarily burden anyone, but simply to highlight how precious marriage and the family is to God. That argument is made powerfully by considering how much God hates the violation of the family He designed and instituted.

Few institutions enjoy the divine sanction and blessing as much as the marriage relationship, and it is this unique relationship that forms the root of the family. The husband and wife union is inviolable and precious in God's sight because He has ordained it. Indeed, it is the first human institution God established. In Genesis 2:24, shortly after creating Eve, Adam's suitable companion and partner for life, the Lord sanctioned marriage with these words, *"For this reason a man shall leave his father and his mother, and be joined to his wife; and they shall become one flesh."* Eve embodied everything Adam needed, and Adam completed Eve. Together they formed a whole, a union for life. This marital design remains intact to this day.

It is through this union that God also formed the wellspring of the family (Genesis 1:28). In other words, God ordained marriage and through it the home. Marriage is precious to God and by extension so is the family. This is precisely why the Lord fills the pages of the Bible with admonitions against violating the purity of this exalted and holy union. The Lord Jesus, echoing the sanctity of marriage recorded in the creation account, added this sober warning to any who would violate the marriage bond, *"So they are no longer two, but one flesh. What therefore God has joined together, let no man separate"* (Matthew 19:6). This teaches us that what makes the marriage union indissoluble is God. If then a person violates a marriage relationship, they are desecrating what God Himself has ordained. Such a person finds himself or herself warring with God, not man.

With the inviolability of marriage clearly in mind, the author of Hebrews reminds us and warn us, *"Marriage is to be held in honor among all, and the marriage bed is to be undefiled; for fornicators and adulterers God will judge"* (Hebrews 13:4). When instructing the Thessalonians on sexual purity, Paul includes this similar sobering caveat to those who would destroy a marriage because of sexual gratification, *"the Lord is the avenger in all these things"* (1 Thessalonians 4:6). God promises to put those who violate the holy union that He Himself established on His opposition list.

Let me tell you, that should scare to death anyone flirting with the thought of adultery, because to follow through with such intentions is to put oneself in opposition to God, having ravaged and obliterated a union God has made for His own pleasure and His own glory, and which He holds dear! To destroy a marriage, and by extension to ravage a family, stirs God up in righteous indignation. Why? Because He holds marriage and family as precious and inviolable.

The dangers of divorce

Nowhere is this more clear than in the Lord's absolute contempt for divorce, which He expresses in the last book of our Old Testament canon, Malachi. Toward the close of the Old Testament period, the people of Israel had grown spiritually lazy and unfaithful to the Lord. They maintained a religious facade, but their hearts were far away from the God they pretended to worship. Relationship had deteriorated to religion. They wound up their ceremonial observance and allowed the clockwork of religiosity to run its course. For most, there was no zeal for the truth, no love of obedience, no passion for the Lord in their dead rituals.

Predictably, their lack of spiritual vitality expressed itself in a life of pervasive unfaithfulness, including the area of marriage, and a lack of discernment about their own terrible condition. As always, spiritual tepidness manifests itself in manifold evil not the least of which is a kind of moral blindness. When a person's heart is cold toward God, sin flourishes as does his dullness to comprehend personal culpability and sin's deadliness. Remarkably, it is not uncommon in such spiritual stupor to blame God for the misery we have brought upon ourselves through our own disobedience.

This is exactly where Israel found itself when the Lord dispatched the prophet Malachi to sternly rebuke His wayward people. Their hearts were far away from God, their ritualism served no purpose, their self-righteousness was astonishing, and one of the sins that encapsulated their blind, unfaithful, self-indulgent lifestyle was the betrayal with which men treated their wives. The marriage vows made before God in their youth meant nothing when lust demanded gratification. Consequently, as the years wore on, faithful life companions were set aside like old worn-out clothes in order to satisfy the diminishing, prurient desires of faithless men. The treachery of divorce ensued. God's disgust with this situation and divorce in particular is evident in the book of Malachi. Listen to the stinging rebuke God delivers to His people through the pen of His servant:

> This is another thing you do: you cover the altar of the LORD with tears, with weeping and with groaning, because He no longer regards the offering or accepts it with favor from your hand. Yet you say, 'For what reason?' Because the LORD has been a witness between you and the wife of your youth, against whom you have dealt treacherously, though she is your companion and your wife by covenant. But not one has done so

who has a remnant of the Spirit. And what did that one do while he was seeking a godly offspring? Take heed then to your spirit, and let no one deal treacherously against the wife of your youth. "For I hate divorce," says the LORD, the God of Israel, "and him who covers his garment with wrong," says the LORD of hosts. "So take heed to your spirit, that you do not deal treacherously" (Malachi 2:13–16).

Breaking the marriage covenant for any reason other than infidelity is treachery in the eyes of God (Matthew 5:31–32; 19:9). It is to clothe ourselves in the filth of our treason (*"him who covers his garment with wrong"*) before the righteous Judge who becomes a witness against us. That is strong and damning language! Why does God feel so strongly about infidelity and divorce? Because He created the holy institution of marriage, a union He designed to blossom into godly families (*"offspring,"* Malachi 2:15).

We see God's esteem for marriage in His disdain for divorce. That's making an argument from a negative point of view; however, the Bible makes the same case for marriage from the positive angle as well. In fact, the New Testament raises this divinely sanctioned union to dizzying heights of honor in Ephesians 5:21–33. Here the apostle Paul under the inspiration of the Holy Spirit likens marriage to the exalted and pure relationship that exists between Jesus Christ and His holy bride, the church. Consider the words of Paul as he teaches us about marriage, and more importantly, as he helps us understand the heavenly realities of our relationship to our Lord, Christ.

And be subject to one another in the fear of Christ. Wives, be subject to your own husbands, as to the Lord. For the husband is the head of the wife, as Christ also is the head of the church, He Himself being the Savior of the body. But as the church is subject to Christ, so also the wives ought to be to their husbands in everything. Husbands, love your wives, just as Christ also loved the church and gave Himself up for her, so that He might sanctify her, having cleansed her by the washing of water with the word, that He might present to Himself the church in all her glory, having no spot or wrinkle or any such thing; but that she would be holy and blameless. So husbands ought also to love their own wives as their own bodies. He who loves his own wife loves himself; for no one ever hated his own flesh, but nourishes and cherishes it, just as

Christ also does the church, because we are members of His body. FOR THIS REASON A MAN SHALL LEAVE HIS FATHER AND MOTHER AND SHALL BE JOINED TO HIS WIFE, AND THE TWO SHALL BECOME ONE FLESH. This mystery is great; but I am speaking with reference to Christ and the church. Nevertheless, each individual among you also is to love his own wife even as himself, and the wife must see to it that she respects her husband.

The point is clear, to compare the marital union of a man and a woman to the relationship between Jesus Christ and His church is to elevate the marriage relationship to a stunning place of honor in God's economy. God thinks so highly of marriage and values this relationship so much that He compares it to the eternally holy relationship between His Son and His people. That, my friends, is esteem indeed! And let's not forget the point of this section, which is this: as the Lord esteems marriage, in the same way by logical extension, He equally esteems the fruit of marriage, the family. He created marriage in order to create the family; one is the extension of the other, and the value of the first (marriage) is the value of the second (family).

Understanding the value of the family through redemptive history

How important is the family to God? We see its significance in the Lord's value of the marriage relationship. Secondly, we see the importance of the family in the critical role it played in God's redemptive plan for mankind. God is passionate about redemption, and He used the family as the holy conduit through which He would redeem a people for Himself.

I believe there is no better way to measure the value of the family to God than to consider the family's role in the most important program God has unleashed on this world—the salvation of men! There is nothing more significant and marvelous than God's glory, and the salvation of undeserving men will be history's greatest contribution to this magnificent end. The family, then, is infinitely precious to God because He designed it to play an integral part in the unfolding of redemption which will ring through eternity to His glory.

The Lord designed the family by His perfect and benevolent wisdom for the good of man but also, as we said, to play a central role in God's redemptive program. This has been true from the fall of man to the present day. To see this we need to think back to the fall of our first parents. Immediately following the devastating fall of Adam and Eve, which plunged our entire race into sin and death, God Himself promised to rescue man from the consequences of his rebellion. God would accomplish His heart's desire through a Redeemer (Genesis 3:1–7,15; Romans 5:12–15).

Through the ages as Scripture progressively unveiled the identity of God's promised Savior, God's word clearly revealed that this Redeemer would be the eternal, divine Son of God (e.g., Micah 5:2; Isaiah 9:6; Luke 1:31–35). In other words, the Redeemer would be God Himself, and He would rescue us from our fatal fall. And yet from the very beginning, the story took a fascinating twist. From the very first promise of redemption, God made it clear that the Savior of men would issue forth from the seed of woman (Genesis 3:15). In other words, the divine Redeemer would also be a man!

God would not simply come to earth straight out of heaven in His resplendent glory; instead, God would do the unthinkable! God Himself, in the person of His Son (the second person of the Trinity), would enter human history through the descendants of Adam.

Abraham's family

Clearly, from the beginning God bound Himself to accomplish His redemptive plan through the means of the family. He would come to earth but instead of simply materializing Himself among the family of man, He would enter our world in space and time through a conventional human clan and be a man. What a remarkable miracle that promised to be! And so in the succeeding centuries after Adam's fall, God chose and identified a specific family, the family of Abraham, through whom He would send His Son to bless mankind with salvation (Genesis 18:18). It is at this early juncture of redemptive history that God not only revealed the familial lineage through which He would send His Son, but the uniqueness of this privileged family. They would possess a distinguishing trait that would set them apart from all the tribes of the earth. You see, the family of God's eventual Redeemer would know God, trust God, and live life by God's standards and not the world's. Abraham was unique among men because he had an intimate relationship with the God of heaven and earth. James reminds us of the closeness of this relationship between Abraham and His Creator when he tells us that Abraham *"was called the friend of God"* (James 2:23).

Imagine that! In a day when nearly all men were polytheistic pagans—with few exceptions, e.g., Melchizedek and those under his influence—Abraham knew and loved the One and only God. Abraham's neighbors lived in constant fear of the entities they worshiped. They knew nothing of a caring relationship with their gods; their deities were erratic, capricious, and unapproachable. Generally, pagans preferred to keep their deities at a distance—kind of like some of your out-of-state relatives. And so they labored to keep their unpredictable, pernicious gods placated, at bay, or at arm's length. And yet, Abraham drew near to God, was beloved of God, and indeed was the friend of God. Abraham possessed a knowledge of the Lord and a trusting relationship with Him that transformed his life and reflected God's character to the world around him. It was precisely this knowledge, relationship, and righteous life, this work of grace in Abraham that set him apart from all the clans of men. Furthermore, it was this triumvirate of virtue (knowledge, relationship, and a righteous life) that he was to pass on to his sons in order to ensure God's plan through him.

God himself confessed of Abraham, *"For I have chosen him, so that he may command his children and his household after him to keep the way of the LORD by doing righteousness and justice, so that the LORD may bring upon Abraham what He has spoken about him"* (Genesis 18:19). This verse outlines in a very straightforward way the outworking of God's promise to bring about the salvation of man through Abraham's righteous family. That being so, let's briefly look at this text line by line.

Verse 18 begins with, *"For I have chosen him."* Simply put, God's sovereign plan of redemption was ordained through Abraham's family, the Jews. The Lord Jesus underscored this truth to a woman who did not want to believe in God's sovereign choice of the Jews as His conduit for salvation. In John 4:22, Jesus told the woman at the well, *"You* [Samaritans] *worship what you do not know; we* [the Jews] *worship what we know, for salvation is from the Jews."* The chosen familial conduit through which God would redeem men was the seed of Abraham, the Jews.

God's choice of Abraham in Genesis 18:19 is clear and so was Abraham's responsibility before the Lord. *"For I have chosen him, so that he may command his children and his household after him to keep the way of the LORD."* The term *"command"* can also be rendered "instruct" or "charge" and is used to speak of a father's instruction to his son. In essence, God called Abraham to teach his children and all those under his care what it meant to walk with God just as he himself had walked.

As a father and leader, he was charged with explaining to his sons and daughters, his extended family, his servants *"the way of the LORD"* i.e., who God was, why He was worthy of their trust, and what God required from them. His duty was to communicate the joy of knowing the one true God. It was his responsibility to nurture in his offspring the same kind of relationship he enjoyed with God. Ultimately, *"the way of the LORD"* was expanded and elucidated to Abraham's descendants through God's word, the Law, and the sum of God's revealed truth in the Old Testament. At this point in God's unfolding plan of salvation, Abraham was to pass on his firsthand knowledge of God to his household and they, in turn, to their children.

Then the text reminds us of the purpose for which Abraham's family was to know and pass on God's ways. They were to embrace and teach *"the way of the LORD"* in order to live godly lives, or as the text tells us, for the purpose of *"doing righteousness and justice."* In other words, the evidence of God's truth received and passed on was obedience, that is, a life lived in practical righteousness and justice.

Finally, it was through this faithful reception of, transmission of, and obedience to the truth that the Lord promised *"to bring upon Abraham"* what He had *"spoken about him,"* which was salvation to the sons of men. In other words, Abraham's family (and its integrity) was an essential part of God's plan for His Son and for His people.

God's trustworthy promise

And so, God bound Himself to bless Abraham (Abram initially) and work through his godly and prodigious lineage. This was quite a pledge since he and his wife Sarah had no children and especially since Sarah was beyond her childbearing season of life. Even so, God guaranteed Abraham he would have a son, and more than that the Lord promised his descendants would be as the stars of the heavens (Genesis 15:5). In Southern California, where we have lived for most of our lives, that would constitute a rather modest promise. I can see Abraham looking up toward the heavens on a typical Southern California night and thinking, "Okay, I'm going to have about nine descendants, that's reasonable." However, looking up at the evening windswept desert sky of Abraham's preindustrial day, the illustration made its point. God's promise was truly astonishing. Abraham's descendants would be so prodigious that they would be beyond his ability to even number. This vow sealed by God's unilateral covenant was sure. God's words were true. God would be faithful to His promises. The Lord would bless Abraham and through him the world. Abraham's charge was to trust God, faithfully walk in His ways, and teach his household to do the same.

Because Abraham knew the One who declared His future blessing, he readily embraced the pledge even though God's promise seemed ridiculous on a human plane. The impossibility of the plan did not nag the believing mind of this remarkable patriarch. The Lord gave Abraham an unforgettable, if not an unbelievable illustration, and Abraham simply believed. Scripture states, *"And He [God] took him outside and said, 'Now look toward the heavens, and count the stars, if you are able to count them.' And He said to him, 'So shall your descendants be.' Then he believed in the LORD; and He reckoned it to him as righteousness"* (Genesis 15:5–6). Abraham understood and believed God could do the impossible, and through this faithful man and his family, God worked to bring salvation to the ends of the earth. The family was indispensable in the development of God's strategy to save mankind.

Yet someone will say, "Wait a minute. That sounds like a great plan, but the fact of the matter is Abraham's descendants proved repeatedly unfaithful to their calling. Israel regularly failed to trust God. They repeatedly transgressed the Law; they failed to diligently teach it to their children. They often failed to live up to the standard of Abraham." That is undeniably true. Any cursory student of the Bible could tell you that Israel's history is replete with their failure to follow God and to teach their children to walk with God.

No, Abraham's children were not always faithful to God; however, God was always faithful to Abraham's children. God knew the frailty of His people. The Jews were not a race of super humans. From birth, they were fallen men, prone to failure and unfaithfulness just like you and me. What kept them from being consumed by God's holy anger was the grace bestowed on them as the chosen and beloved of the Lord. David, the great king of Israel, confessing the waywardness of his people, exclaims in Psalm 103:7–14:

He made known His ways to Moses, His acts to the sons of Israel.
The LORD is compassionate and gracious, slow to anger and abounding

in lovingkindness. He will not always strive with us, nor will He keep His anger forever. He has not dealt with us according to our sins, nor rewarded us according to our iniquities. For as high as the heavens are above the earth, so great is His lovingkindness toward those who fear Him. As far as the east is from the west, so far has He removed our transgressions from us. Just as a father has compassion on his children, so the LORD has compassion on those who fear Him. For He Himself knows our frame; He is mindful that we are but dust.

Israel often failed and often experienced the chastening hand of God. In fact, many of Abraham's descendants died in unbelief, yet Israel was not wholly consumed because God in His grace made a unilateral covenant with Abraham to secure his blessing. In other words, God made a binding contract to bless Abraham based on God's faithfulness alone (Genesis 15:17–18; Romans 11:26–29). Because of this covenant, even in the darkest chapters of Israel's history, God in His faithfulness preserved a remnant among His ancient people and through them secured the hope of redemption for the nations (Ezra 9:8,13–15; Isaiah 10:20–22; 11:11; Jeremiah 23:3; 31:7; Micah 2:12; Romans 9:27; 11:5).

The tribe of Judah and the line of David

The prophet Micah expresses this truth beautifully in Micah 7:18 when he wrote, *"Who is a God like You, who pardons iniquity and passes over the rebellious act of the remnant of His possession? He does not retain His anger forever, because He delights in unchanging love."* Unlike His people, God through the ages proved faithful to His word, and from the clans of Israel the Lord identified successive families among the Jewish people through whom the Deliverer, the Messiah (literally, Anointed One) would come. After Abraham, God singled out his son Isaac as the son of promise (Genesis 21:12; Romans 9:7). Thereafter, the Lord called Isaac's son Jacob and his family to be the conduit for His glorious plans (Malachi 1:2–3; Romans 9:13). Jacob as you know had quite a large family, and from his twelve sons one was chosen to be the progenitor of the Messiah. He was identified at the end of Jacob's life. On his deathbed, the patriarch prophesied of days in the distant future and declared that the Messiah would issue forth from his son Judah. *"The scepter shall not depart from Judah, nor the ruler's staff from between his feet, until Shiloh* [another name for the Messiah] *comes, and to him shall be the obedience of the peoples"* (Genesis 49:10).

With this prophecy of Genesis 49:10, the field was narrowed to one family, one tribe among the sons of Jacob. And yet, more specificity was required still. You see, Judah grew to be the most populous tribe in Israel by the time of the conquest of Canaan and increased even more in number as the people settled in the land (Numbers 26:19–22). The field of families became even more focused several hundred years later when the Lord pinpointed the narrower branch of the Messiah's lineage. It was in the early years of Israel's monarchy when God identified the family of David of the tribe of Judah, and subsequent king of Israel, to be the familial stock through whom the Redeemer King would arise (1 Chronicles 17:10b–14). Even with the choice of David, the coming of the Messiah was more than a millennium away. Many families within David's lineage would run their determined cycles before the Messiah was born.

Finally and gloriously, the promise to King David was fulfilled one thousand years later through two of his direct descendants. Joseph (the Messiah's legal father), a humble carpenter from Nazareth, and Mary his betrothed who conceived a Son while a virgin by the Holy Spirit and gave birth to our beloved Messiah and Savior Jesus Christ who is blessed forever (Luke 1:26–56; 2:1–40)! These two descendants of David would form the familial root for the advent of the promised Redeemer.

God's humble servants

The wonderful story of the appointment of Joseph and Mary has been related to us many times. We hear it every Christmas, and yet we never tire of it because it is so remarkable. It is an astounding story not simply because of the thrilling supernatural events that attended the birth of Christ, (e.g., the angelic messengers, the divine conception of Jesus, the supernatural leading of the wise men to our Lord, signs in the heavens, heavenly dreams), but also because God chose these two obscure Israelites to be the guardians of His eternal Son.

Why were Joseph and Mary chosen? "Well, they were descendants of David." True enough, that was a nonnegotiable part of the promise, but let's face it, there were no doubt many other viable descendants of David in the territories of Israel. Joseph and Mary were among the humblest of the great king's prestigious line. Joseph was a modest craftsman whose noble background catered him little if any privilege in the Jewish culture of his day. Mary was but an unassuming, young peasant girl (14 to 16 years of age) in a patriarchal society. She was on the low end of the totem pole as far as prestige and influence.

Together they were poor and lowly people whose status is reflected by the humble offering they presented to the Lord for the dedication of their Son, the Lord Jesus, at the temple, *"a pair of turtledoves or two young pigeons"* (Luke 2:24). This was the prescribed offering for the poorest of the people of Israel (Leviticus 5:7; 12:8; 14:22). So, once again, why were they chosen from among all the descendants of David? Certainly they were not called out because of their impressive earthly resume.

They were selected because God in His sovereign grace chose servants who were faithful to the pattern He called Abraham to live by and pass on to his children. Remember Genesis 18:19, *"For I have chosen him, so that he may command his children and his household after him to keep the way of the LORD by doing righteousness and justice, so that the LORD may bring upon Abraham what He has spoken about him."* The biblical testimony discloses that Joseph and Mary—like their ancient father Abraham—knew and loved their God and walked righteously.

Matthew chapter 1 reminds us that Joseph, an ordinary man by the cultural standards of his day, was nonetheless a righteous man, a just man. He was faithful to walk in God's ways. That was the pattern of Joseph's life. We see a reflection of God's values in his compassionate attitude toward Mary when during their betrothal he discovered she was pregnant, and once enlightened by God as to the nature of her pregnancy, we see his practical righteousness in his willingness to obey God regardless of how this obedience made him look to the incredulous people around him. In a shame/honor based culture, Joseph was asked to take a wife who was not carrying his child, and—in obedience to God—he did!

> *And Joseph her husband* [they were betrothed, and though the marriage was not consummated, their engagement was legally binding], *being a righteous man and not wanting to disgrace her, planned to send her away secretly* [I.e., to dissolve the marriage contract discreetly so as not to bring further shame to Mary].

But when he had considered this, behold, an angel of the Lord appeared to him in a dream, saying, "Joseph, son of David, do not be afraid to take Mary as your wife; for the Child who has been conceived in her is of the Holy Spirit. And Joseph awoke from his sleep and did as the angel of the Lord commanded him, and took Mary as his wife" (Matthew 1:19–20, 24).

He received God's word humbly and ordered his life by its light—even when obedience left him open to criticism and surely resulted in ostracism by the world around him. We also learn that his betrothed, Mary, while socially insignificant, was favored by the Lord because of her trust and love for the God of Israel. (See Mary's response to the news of the angel Gabriel, Luke 1:26–38, as well as her hymn of praise, the Magnificat, in Luke 1:46–55). This couple faithfully walked in the steps of their father Abraham, and this was the family unit through whom the Lord would keep His promise to save the world. Joseph and Mary not only fulfilled the prophecy made to King David, but this humble couple mirrored the godly family legacy of their patriarch Abraham, and through them God brought salvation to Israel and the world in the Lord Jesus.

God preserved the line of the Messiah and brought about the blessing of the nations (salvation) by means of families, men and women who walked in obedience to God's revelation and faithfully passed on God's ways to their children and their children's children. God didn't choose perfect families but redeemed families that reflected His righteousness, starting with Abraham and down through the centuries to Joseph and Mary, to bring His Chosen One, the Messiah to this earth. Please don't miss the significance of this simple truth: God used the vehicle of the family to bring His Son into this world and through Him the salvation of men for His eternal glory! This is how important the family is to the Lord. The family was an essential instrument used by God to bring about redemption to the four corners of the earth.

How important is the family to God? From the beginning, God has had a passion for the integrity of the family. Through the divinely sanctioned and blessed institution of marriage, God brought forth the home and through it the Redeemer into the world. In that Savior, God secured His redemptive plan and established the church, for whom He desires the practical purity that is hers positionally in His Son and which is essential for the effective proclamation of the gospel of redemption. That, my friends, is advanced or thwarted to a great degree by the spiritual integrity of the family. If our families are failing, the gospel will ring hollow to many who are in desperate need of it. That's how important the family, your family, is to God!

If the spiritual vitality of the family is of such value to God, you can be sure the enemy will attempt to destroy your home. One of the chief ways he does that is by robbing your household of God's sanctifying truth. A weapon of choice that he wields with great effectiveness is biblical ignorance.

CHAPTER 3

The Threat of Biblical Illiteracy to the Christian Home

Illiteracy

While there are many weapons arrayed against the Christian family, one of the most dangerous is biblical ignorance. In spite of the unprecedented availability of biblical resources, vast numbers of Christians find themselves deprived of the spiritual food they need to grow. Biblical illiteracy is a growing problem in the church and directly threatens the vitality of the Christian home.

One of the most common tools in conflict (military or political) is the weapon of deprivation. The strategy of disabling your enemy by cutting off basic necessities is as old as war. Jerusalem fell, not simply because the Romans possessed superior offensive numbers, weapons, and military training. The Romans conquered Jerusalem in large measure because they succeeded in sealing off the city from the possibility of escape, then cut off the food and water supply and weakened the trapped population of Jewish pilgrims and residents, rendering them—in time—all but defenseless to the military might of Titus and his legions.

The enemy of the church, the devil, has long deployed the weapon of biblical deprivation against the people of God. He is a liar and continually seeks to twist and distort the truth through the offensive weapons of false teachers, doubt, etc., but he is primarily the enemy of truth and that's what he desperately wants to keep from God's people (John 8:44). His aims are just as well served by keeping believers from seeking or receiving the truth—biblical deprivation. Regrettably, he has plied this strategy against believers with great success in recent history.

There is an astonishing level of biblical illiteracy among professing Christians today. For reasons that lay beyond the scope of this book, for many Christians, the strength-giving stream of biblical truth has been diminished to a trickle. Whenever truth is blocked from flowing into and nourishing God's people, the impact is devastating, and few places has this been more visible than in the Christian home.

When the family is deprived of God's word, the outcome is tragically predictable. Parents who are weak in their knowledge of Scripture are not continually sanctified by God's word, i.e., they do not experience consistent transformation into the image of the Lord Jesus. This lack of personal growth diminishes the presence of biblically fed virtues in their marriages (selfless love, courageous leadership, humble submission, patience, kindness, joy, peace, faithfulness, goodness), and in the void created by a lack of growth, the toxic weaknesses of the flesh flourish (immorality, jealousy, strife, outbursts of anger, arguments, dissension).

You can also understand how the absence of biblical wisdom in Christian unions significantly limits parenting. Parents are seriously handicapped in their ability to teach propositional truth because of their personal lack of knowledge and evident hypocrisy. Unable to appropriately mirror Christ and the gospel, men and women cannot disciple their children. Without a knowledge of biblical precepts, they cannot impact their children with the power of incarnate truth (biblical virtue lived out in the context of life). The net result is weakened marriages and families susceptible to the ills of this world.

Make no mistake about it, biblical ignorance is a real problem for today's Christian family and a serious threat to the spiritual vibrancy of your home. Furthermore, the fight against biblical illiteracy is constant because we face the threat of it on multiple fronts. It is ubiquitous in our culture and has elbowed its way into the church.

The growing cultural gloom of biblical illiteracy

Lack of biblical knowledge hangs like a murky haze over our entire culture and casts its shadowy pall on far too much of the professing Christian community. For many, it is clouding their clear view of God and His tried and true paths found in Scripture. The causes of this state of ignorance and its influence on the church are manifold, and as I mentioned, far beyond the purview of this book, but generally speaking, I believe biblical illiteracy in North America has become dominant because of the mushrooming presence of aggressive secularism and the failure of Christians to recognize it and confront it.

Secular thinking in our culture is systemic. It has grown in its influence like the cold easterly shadow of a mountain eclipsing the countryside below. Today's America is most definitely not your grandfather's America. At the turn of World War II, who could have foreseen the coming assault of the sexual revolution in the sixties, the radical devaluation of life, the lawful infanticide of millions of unborn children since the seventies, or the unrestrained attacks on the institution of marriage and family over the last forty years. All the evils I mention above have come on the wake of antibiblical secularism, the momentum of which has not been stemmed but is actually growing.

Hostility to God's revelation continues to fuel radical elements in our country to eliminate any biblical reference points in the collective American mind. There exists a virtual panic among progressive humanists to expunge any reference to Judeo-Christian beliefs in the public sector. Whether through the revisionist secularization of our history, founding fathers and constitution, the fight to get the name of God out of our pledge and currency, the uproar over any public displays of the Ten Commandments, the de-Christianization of Christmas, the sway of secularism is stripping American culture of the vestiges of biblical reference points and continuing our slide into the neo–dark ages of postmodern, post-Christian thinking.

It appears that these influences are winning the day because we find ourselves living in a culture with only the dimmest recollection of the God of the Bible and His precepts for life. Culturally, we find ourselves in the thickening smog of biblical ignorance.

Do we have a biblical pulse?

A few years ago Jay Leno, then host of the Tonight Show, conducted an informal Bible quiz of his audience and asked them to name as many of Jesus' 12 apostles as they could remember. With all the Johns, Peters, Jameses, Andrews, Philips, Thomases, Alphaeuses—Hmm, okay, maybe not a whole lot of Alphaeuses out there, but we have most of the twelve covered in our dictionary of common names—you would think that a partial recollection of the twelve apostles in any random crowd would be a slam dunk. The staggering reality was that the television audience could not name a single one of the twelve apostles! In a revealing twist, the audience as a whole had no problems remembering all four Beatles.[1]

Anecdotally, Leno's survey demonstrates what research affirms, and that is that the vast majority of adult Americans are profoundly ignorant of basic Bible knowledge and especially of biblical, Judeo-Christian values that have shaped our nation.

We are becoming an increasingly secular nation

What is even more disturbing is the deepening biblical illiteracy among America's youth. Bible knowledge in America dips in direct proportion to age. The younger the population, the more profound the biblical illiteracy. I realize that may be hard to believe with all the plenteous and rich references to the Bible and Judeo-Christian values in popular music (laugh here!), but it's true. Research underscores the sad reality that the US is progressively becoming a secular nation.[2]

How far our contemporary culture has fallen when you consider that children in America were once taught to read with the Bible as a key reference point! The early settlers of New England, for example, helped their sons and daughters memorize the alphabet by means of a pictorial poem. Each letter was illustrated by a simple drawing depicting an event and then followed by a rhyme to capture the letter and its pronunciation in the mind of the child. Twenty-one of the twenty-four alphabetical characters had a biblical truth or event as a reference point.[3]

Once the alphabet was secured in the child's mind, the New England Primer (the first textbook ever printed on American soil) encouraged the memorization of a particular Bible verse to "instruct" the child "in his duty" and to encourage his "learning."[4] Biblical virtue was constantly reinforced throughout the pages of this early American primer. Among the poems included to help shape the character of children was the following:

Good children must,
Fear God all day, Love Christ alway,
Parents obey, In secret pray,
No false thing say, Mind little play,
By no sin stray, Make no delay,
In doing good. [5]

Similarly, in the "Alphabet of Lessons for Youth" (i.e., teens)—designed to stimulate their reading and intellectual growth—you find a list of aphorisms to help engage the memory. Every one of these adages is rooted in the Bible. Below are a select number of the lines used in the education of early Americans (the bold characters signify the particular letter illustrated by the line).

A wise son maketh a glad Father, but a foolish son is the heaviness of his mother. **B**etter is a little with the fear of the Lord, than great treasure & trouble therewith. **C**ome unto Christ all ye that labor and are heavy laden, and He will give you rest... **E**xcept a man be born again, he cannot see the kingdom of God... **I**t is good for me to draw near unto God... **K**eep thy heart with all diligence, for out of it are the issues of life... **M**any are the afflictions of the righteous, but the Lord delivereth them out of them all. **N**ow is the accepted time, now is the day of salvation... **R**emember thy Creator in the days of thy youth. **S**eest thou a man wise in his own conceit, there is more hope of a fool than of him. **T**rust in God at all times, ye people, pour out your hearts before Him.[6]

When viewed through our present secular educational paradigm, it seems staggering that The New England Primer was employed in American schools to teach our children how to read (gasp!), and to instruct them in the Bible (double gasp!!). What's more, this primer was so used in our country clear into the twentieth century (flatline _____). Not surprisingly, many of our country's greatest thinkers and planners were trained in literacy from this unabashed biblical textbook.[7]

There was a significant period of our history when Scripture was a chief source to inform the collective mind and soul of our people. Over the last one hundred years, the Bible has been progressively removed from our educational system and national conscience. The erosion of this scriptural soil has resulted in the appalling biblical wasteland that popular American culture has become. We have created a landscape of biblical ignorance out of which has grown a noxious weed of self-styled religion blooming many of the moral ills that threaten the future of our nation.

Unbiblical religion—what we have come to embrace

The progressive removal of biblical content from our social conscience has not simply created a void of religion, rather, it has replaced commonly held biblical beliefs with new unbiblical ones. There exist pervasive religious assumptions in our country that are the offspring of biblical illiteracy. This morphing body of beliefs is reflected especially in the "religion" of our young people.

Christian Smith, a sociologist at the University of Notre Dame, has researched religious beliefs in America, particularly among US teens. Out of these studies a creed has emerged. It is a loosely bundled system of beliefs (again, particularly in teens but not exclusive to them) which he has dubbed "Moralistic Therapeutic Deism"—just try to say that five times really fast! The central tenets of this self-styled religion include...

- A moralistic outlook on man, i.e., a belief that man is essentially good and "being good" gets you to heaven

- A pluralistic pragmatic perspective, i.e., whatever religion works for you is cool

- A utilitarian view of God, i.e., God is not sovereign but exists to secure our psychological happiness.

Christian Smith asserts that essentially the God of most young people exists chiefly to help us when we're in trouble and to make us feel better about our lives and ourselves. His summary of what most young people believe rings sadly true. He writes,

"In short, God is something like a combination Divine Butler and Cosmic Therapist: he is always on call, takes care of any problems that arise, professionally helps his people to feel better about themselves, and does not become too personally involved in the process."[8] My friends, that is the god—not just of most teens—but of a growing number of Americans who would consider themselves in the Christian camp.

"From what abyss does that religious mongrel arise?"

It is safe to say that the flourishing weed garden of religious beliefs in our land grows out of the milieu of our narcissistic culture, fed and supported by biblical illiteracy. We live in a social context wherein the individual is king; therefore, the gratification of the individual establishes the very purpose of life, and his/her feelings form the wellspring of truth framing all that is authentic or inauthentic. This is the new orthodoxy of our time: self-authenticating narcissism.

This self-obsessed, self-gratifying, self-deceiving worldview and its deity of necessity requires a societal seedbed devoid of biblical truth in order to germinate, sprout, and flourish. And never in the history of our country has our cultural landscape been so supportive of such self-serving religious beliefs like the ones we have just mentioned. Indeed, the only seedbed in which a false system like this can thrive is in the rocky soil of biblical ignorance, which as we have said is pervasive in our country.

The darkening shadow of biblical illiteracy on the church

This is the ideological atmosphere in which we live our lives and raise our families, and unfortunately Christians can't help but breathe in some of the polluted thinking surrounding us—it's everywhere. Bible-believing Christians regularly gasp to replenish their souls with the sweet breath of God's thoughts. We must constantly evaluate our thinking and behavior with God's truth in order to align our lives by God's precepts.

We are in a constant battle with secular, irreligious influences, and if we don't fight that fight consistently, the world's way of thinking can surreptitiously encroach its way into our minds and express itself in our lives.[9] Regrettably, Christians can lose sight of the ongoing battle and fail to shine the light of God's word on life's journey. As such, they find themselves in a haze of biblical illiteracy. Stupefied by the lack of scriptural vision, they are stumbling along treacherous roads not aware of the dangers they face.

It saddens me to say that biblical illiteracy is prevalent in the evangelical community. The present-day level of biblical ignorance among professing Christians is truly alarming and like no other I have witnessed in my lifetime. Perhaps sadder still is the reality that this lack of biblical knowledge among Christians is self-imposed.

From fog to famine

If I may change my metaphor, there is a growing famine of biblical understanding in the church, but it is not for want of good spiritual food. No generation of Christians has owned more Bibles, had so many study tools available to it, or possessed such a bounty of expositional preaching to feast upon. Technology has simply exploded the availability of sound biblical teaching for the body of Christ to consume.

For example, because of the Internet we have almost boundless resources available to us. If we desire it, we can be taught by some of the most prodigious, biblically faithful, and gifted preachers of our time. They are available to us with the tap of a touch screen. This is to say nothing of the availability of the breathtaking work of bygone servants like C. H. Spurgeon, Jonathan Edwards, et al., or the amazing Bible study tools we can unlock with the click of a mouse.[10] There is a lavish table of spiritual food available for Christians to feast upon.

There is simply no excuse for biblical illiteracy among present-day believers in developed countries, yet it is a present reality for many believers and sadly is a willful famine while sitting table side at the greatest biblical feast in the history of the church. Many have chosen not to eat and find themselves in spiritual ketosis, wasting away with little biblical appetite. Regrettably, the church has not escaped the ravages of our culture's pervasive biblical illiteracy.

Who's influencing whom?

Now granted, the lack of biblical knowledge I referred to earlier in this chapter reflects biblical illiteracy among Americans in general. So some of you are probably thinking, "This trend is alarming, but it doesn't pertain to true Christians. Arguably, our country has become more secular, but evangelical Christians surely have more knowledge of the Bible than your average cross-section of the American population... don't they?"

Unfortunately, that's not altogether true. Research seems to indicate that confessed evangelicals display virtually the same level of biblical ignorance as the rest of the American population.[11] I've preached all over this country, and time after time I have come up against an astonishing wall of biblical illiteracy among professing Christians.

"Mr. Emmaus?"

Our ministry was once called "Today's Emmaus Road" in reference to the post-resurrection events recorded in the twenty-fourth chapter of the Gospel of Luke. What a wonderful account that is! The events unfold on resurrection Sunday. The Messiah had conquered sin and death. The tomb was empty. The living Lord had kept His promise; His death was the road to atonement, but death could not rule over Him. He was alive and had appeared to a handful of His followers, sending reports of this astonishing miracle rippling through the circle of the Lord's disciples.

One would think the combination of the Lord's clear promises with respect to His death and resurrection and the veracity of the early accounts regarding His physical appearances would have filled all the disciples with great joy and eagerness to see Jesus once again (Matthew 16:21; 17:23; Luke 9:22; 24:6; Luke 24:1–12). He had made Himself manifest in the environs of Jerusalem. Undoubtedly, those who loved Him would soon flock to the beloved city to behold their risen Master. Yet on the third day after Christ's death, resurrection Sunday, we are introduced to two of the Lord's disciples laboring home from Jerusalem as if this were any ordinary post-Sabbath day. One was named Cleopas, the other remains anonymous; they were traveling home on the Emmaus road enveloped by unbelief and despairing of hope (Luke 24:17b–18).

Trekking the seven miles from Jerusalem to their home in the town of Emmaus, the two forlorn followers of Jesus poured out their hearts to one another, revisiting and reliving the mind-numbing events of the previous few days. Unaware of the thousand steps in their journey, the two immersed themselves in the somber recollections haunting their minds.

Engaged in their thoughts, the pair eventually crossed paths with a stranger who, welcome or not, interjected Himself into their conversation. Their eyes veiled from recognizing the wayfarer and caught in a divine teaching moment impossible to imagine, the two unsuspecting disciples found themselves interacting physically with none other than the resurrected Lord Jesus. That doesn't happen every day!

In Luke 24:13–17 we read,

And behold, two of them were going that very day to a village named Emmaus, which was about seven miles from Jerusalem. And they were talking with each other about all these things which had taken place. While they were talking and discussing, Jesus Himself approached and began traveling with them. But their eyes were prevented from recognizing Him. And He said to them, 'What are these words that you are exchanging with one another as you are walking?' And they stood still, looking sad.

Few things can overwhelm a person as intensely as the recurring grief of sudden loss. Like a wall of churning surf crashing upon the unsuspecting, the straightforward question raised by the stranger hit the disciples with the full force of their sorrow. With this simple and penetrating inquiry, Jesus also pinpointed the precise source of the disciples' suffering, an unbelieving heart. I would guess the issue of their own unbelief was not remotely part of the discussion on the Emmaus road before this point—even though that was exactly their problem. The litany of vexation, grief, error, and incredulity springing from their hearts and pouring from their lips in verses 18–24 tells the sad story.

One of them, named Cleopas, answered and said to Him, "Are You the only one visiting Jerusalem and unaware of the things which have happened here in these days?" And He said to them, "What things?" And they said to Him, "The things about Jesus the Nazarene, who was a prophet mighty in deed and word in the sight of God and all the people, and how the chief priests and our rulers delivered Him to the sentence of death, and crucified Him. But we were hoping that it was He who was going to redeem Israel. Indeed, besides all this, it is the third day since these things happened. But also some women among us amazed us. When they were at the tomb early in the morning, and did not find

His body, they came, saying that they had also seen a vision of angels who said that He was alive. Some of those who were with us went to the tomb and found it just exactly as the women also had said; but Him they did not see.

They were bewildered by the very events that should have filled them with joy and confidence in God's promises. God's prophets foretold the suffering and atoning death of Christ (e.g., Isaiah 52:13–15; 53). What's more, Jesus clearly predicted it, but their lack of understanding and trust in God's revelation created a serious disconnect between what they actually believed at the moment (the Messiah had failed in His mission), what they consequently felt (despair), and reality (Jesus had gained the victory over sin and death) (Matthew 16:21; 17:23; Luke 24:6).

With their errant confession now out in the open, the Lord Jesus fully exposed the cause of their condition (reluctance to believe God's promises) and expertly applied the solution to their troubles, truth. *"And He said to them, 'O foolish men and slow of heart to believe in all that the prophets have spoken! Was it not necessary for the Christ to suffer these things and to enter into His glory?' Then beginning with Moses and with all the prophets, He explained to them the things concerning Himself in all the Scriptures"* (Luke 24:25–27).

This glorious Bible study lasted for the balance of their journey to Emmaus, perhaps for several miles. In fact, it continued into the last meal of the day, which they invited the Lord to share with them. It was at that point the Lord revealed Himself to His friends. Invited into their home and sitting down for a meal with them, Jesus gave thanks for the bread, broke it, gave them their portion, and simultaneously opened their eyes to recognize Him before instantly disappearing from their sight. *"When He had reclined at the table with them, He took the bread and blessed it, and breaking it, He began giving it to them. Then their eyes were opened and they recognized Him; and He vanished from their sight"* (Luke 24:30–31).

"Did not our hearts burn within us?"

Can you imagine the moment when these two disciples looked into the eyes of the Lord Jesus and recognized Him for who He was? Did He smile at them as He vanished? Did He wish them peace? Did He exhort them to take courage? We're not told and perhaps the reason for the lack of specifics is simply to draw our attention to one important reality: the wonderful heart-transforming power of the Scripture in the life of a believer.

Left holding their bread, the two disciples turned to one another and exclaimed in obvious wonder and joy, *"Were not our hearts burning within us while He was speaking to us on the road, while He was explaining the Scriptures to us?"* (Luke 24:32). What a tremendous testimony to the metamorphic impact God's word can have in our lives. The light of Scripture dispelled the shadows of unbelief and ignited the fire and bright light of hope in their hearts. Their minds and emotions were captured and changed not by the miraculous disappearance of the Lord, but by the penetrating power of His word.

As I considered what to call our Bible teaching ministry, I remembered this account and thought, "That's it! Perfect! That's what I want God to do through this ministry. I want the Lord to transform the minds and hearts of people through the power of His word." Consequently, after a little domain research, I settled on the name of "Today's Emmaus Road." I assumed people would hear that name and identify our ministry with what I thought was a familiar story in the New Testament. That didn't happen.

Eventually, I changed our name from Today's Emmaus Road to Walking In The Promises because most people were so unfamiliar with Luke 24 that they were completely befuddled by our ministry label. Some thought we were a Catholic ministry or a Methodist nonprofit organization that went by similar names. I actually had two folks—at separate events—ask me if Emmaus was my surname. Perhaps these folks were in the restroom or out getting a latte when I was introduced, but I felt a little awkward telling them I was not Mr. Emmaus. I was excited for the opportunity to inform folks about Luke 24, but I was shocked to discover the lack of familiarity many Christians have with this significant and instructive passage. Many of us are parched for spiritual knowledge even as we dwell at the great wellspring of Scripture.

Steven Prothero, professor of religion at Boston University (a non evangelical) chides evangelicals with our obvious hypocrisy. He says, "Despite their conviction that the Bible is the Word of God, evangelicals show scant interest in learning what the scripture has to say or wrestling with what it might mean." He concludes, "Even in the Bible Belt, the Good Book is fast becoming, as another evangelical puts it, 'The Greatest Story Never Read.'"[12]

There may be a proliferation of Bibles and "Christian" literature in the contemporary church, but as a people, we're not getting the meaning of the Book! We're not growing in our understanding of what God has said in Scripture. We give thanks to the "good Lord" for the "good Book," but we're turning to *The Shack* for our understanding of who God is.

We are increasingly becoming a people who venerate the Book, yet who willfully ignore it. Most Christians are willing to loudly affirm the inspiration of the Bible, but many don't bother to take the time or make the effort to study it, which in turn renders us incapable of applying it to our lives and families. This troubling inconsistency has an absolutely staggering consequence for our families. My brothers and sisters, we are losing our children to our own hypocrisy.

The staggering cost of biblical ignorance... the souls of our children

One of the tragedies of our broadening biblical ignorance in the church is that numerous Christians are failing to lead their children in the truth and ultimately to salvation. How can we teach future generations our faith (i.e., "the faith"— the biblical content of what we believe) and the way of salvation when we understand so little? Our lack of knowledge, in effect, has forced us to water down and redefine who and what a "Christian" is.

We have broadened the boundaries of Christendom to incorporate those outside the camp of salvation, many of whom are our own sons and daughters, but in doing so we do not gain one soul and in the process imperil many who are dear to us. We fail to see that we cannot keep those whom Christ has not purchased. Is it any wonder that "Christian" young people are abandoning their evangelical roots in early adulthood to the great dismay of many surprised parents?

According to studies conducted by several prominent evangelical organizations (the Southern Baptist Convention, the Barna Group, etc.) an alarming number of young adults raised in professing evangelical homes are leaving the church in their college years.[13] The numbers fluctuate dramatically from 50-plus percent to nearly 90-plus percent. The exact numbers are impossible to gauge, but these surveys taken as a whole, point to one shocking reality: we're not reaching our kids with the status quo, i.e., a tepid commitment to biblical truth in our homes and ministry to our young people.

Recently, I heard a conservative Christian college make a pitch to parents for their institution based on this disturbing trend. The basic spiel was this: "Isn't it terrible what's happening to kids from Christian homes? They're leaving the faith! Send them to our school." The implied message: parents can prevent their kids from apostatizing if they send them to the right college. I've got news for everyone, if we're losing our children to the world in college, guess what, we never had them in adolescence.

Unwittingly, some Christians are playing a shell game with the souls of their young people. Parents want to believe their children are truly saved because to contemplate the opposite reality is so distressing it is almost unthinkable. There may be little or no evidence of spiritual life in them (e.g., love for Jesus Christ, love for His people, respect for parents, an appetite for holiness, fellowship, worship, a distaste for the world, a hunger for God's word, a longing to walk intimately, humbly with God), but the conflicted heart of such parents—and often a weak view of the Bible—lead them to conclude that their son or daughter is simply "not walking with the Lord." In other words, they're saved but they've taken a hiatus from their relationship with God. That is one of the deadliest assumptions we can make and an assumption that is on the rise proportionate to biblical illiteracy in the church.

The only hope for the eternal happiness of our children is in Jesus Christ. We must lead them to the Savior and the road to Him is paved by God's word. We cannot afford to accept biblical illiteracy. The cost is simply too high. We must make it our ambition to know the Bible so that we may lead our loved ones to God and in God.

From ancient times God has targeted the family and laid out His blueprint for its welfare in His divine self-disclosure, the Bible. That has not changed. Like families of old, your family is exceedingly important to God, and He desires for your household to be spiritually prosperous. That is precisely why He has entrusted the treasure of Scripture to you. In this all-sufficient resource, God has given us the means to fully know Him and to understand His design for our lives and for our homes.

The resurgence of the local church pulpit

What's more, the pulpit is where the local church can and must meet this crisis. God's people need to hear from the shepherds God has appointed in each local church. As wonderful as preaching and teaching ministries are—believe me I know, we serve with one, Walking In The Promises—God has designed us, His people, to primarily respond to the truth in community, the local church. That's why so much of the New Testament consists of letters written to local churches or pastors of churches. To a great degree, the local church is truly where appetite for biblical truth should begin and grow.

Pastors must devote themselves more than ever to feeding their sheep, not only to strengthen them but, just as important, to stimulate in them a hunger for truth so that they may feast on other great pastures God has opened. We need biblically driven pulpits to awaken God's people to their great need for spiritual nourishment and God's amazing provision for their satisfaction and growth. To local pastors I say, we must bale the hay, strengthen the flock, and release them to the plentiful meadows of God's rich provision.

CHAPTER 4

The Indispensability of the Bible to Your Family's Health

The call to discipleship from Deuteronomy 6:1–9

Few texts of Scripture are as critical to the edification of the family as Deuteronomy 6:1–9. This text forms the clearest and most forceful call to parents to disciple their children in the truth of Scripture. It is the key passage for parental discipleship in the entire Bible and forms the backbone of what the wisdom literature and the New Testament have to say on the subject. In this text we will see that God exhorts parents to build up their children on the unshifting rock of His word. In order to comprehend how essential this text is, however, we have to understand a little bit of the background leading up to it. With that goal in mind, I want to spend the next few paragraphs unfolding the historical context in which this seminal passage is couched.

The painful purging of God's people

The book of Deuteronomy picks up the history of the nation of Israel just before the conquest of the land of Canaan. The instructive narrative engages us after Israel's 40 years of wandering in the desert. This was a young and chastened nation. The faithless generation of the exodus who refused to trust God for their inheritance (the land promised to Abraham, Isaac, and Jacob) had all died in the wilderness. That included everyone 20 years and older—what a staggering catastrophe of unbelief (Numbers 14:29)!

Think about that for just a moment, that's some two million people who perished in the wasteland of Sinai because they refused to trust God. What a tremendous price to pay for the failure to believe, yet the loss of this generation illustrates how important faith is to God. That's a lot of men and women who had to pass from the scene in order for Israel to recognize her need to trust the Lord and thus enable the people to move forward with their future.

A steep cost indeed, but the purification of the nation was not complete with the passing of the generation of the exodus. As staggering as that judgment was, Israel was in need of further cleansing. As the people made their way to the promised land, the spiritual pruning continued as an additional 24,000 Israelites died in the plague of Baal-peor. There, God severely judged His people for joining themselves to the false god Baal through the debauched worship rites of the Moabites (Numbers 25:1–9). The seriousness of Israel's sin at Baal-peor is also described in Deuteronomy 4:3, Psalm 106:28, and Hosea 9:10. Once more, the fire of God's righteous indignation roared through the camp of Israel, consuming the rebels who, left unchecked, would certainly corrupt the people on the very threshold of their promised land.

After God's judgment, as Israel approached her future home, the young nation found itself purged of many evil influences. The generation who doubted their unfailing God was gone. The licentious rebels willing to compromise the moral, religious purity of their kinsmen were removed from the fledgling tribal commonwealth. The people were therefore chastened, humbled, teachable, and ready to receive instruction from the Lord for the well-being of their nation.

Waiting for God's instruction

In fact at this point (the time of the writing of the book of Deuteronomy), the Israelites were perched on the plains of Moab, east of the Jordan River awaiting the "go ahead" to conquer their inheritance. The one thing they lacked was God's plan for the conquest. All the promises to the patriarchs, all the anticipation of previous generations, all their hopes as a people were on the cusp of being fulfilled. Israel was at one of the key crossroads of her early history. It is at this point in time that God delivered a series of instructions and addresses through Moses to His people which we have come to know as the book of Deuteronomy.

A faithful man's swan song

Adding a tone of gravity to the message was the fact that Moses communicated this collection of writings under God's direction in the last month of his life. This endcap of the Torah is the "swan song" of this faithful man's legacy. What's more, all of Israel was preparing itself for the departure of Moses. Everyone realized Moses' days on this earth were about to come to an end and that the words of Deuteronomy were his last words.

Moses and the people knew he would not enter the promised land (Numbers 20:12). They all understood God would gather Moses to his fathers east of the Jordan River. Very often great men are not fully appreciated until they have passed from the scene or until they are evidently near their mortal end. So it was in the case of Moses. Often vilified and unappreciated by the rank and file of Israel, he did not receive the deference he deserved for his faithful service until the close of his earthly life (Exodus 2:14; 5:21; 6:9; 14:11; 15:24; 16:2–3; 17:2–4; Numbers 14:4; 16:12–14). As the sun set on four decades of wilderness wandering, the clans of Israel willingly looked to their leader for wisdom as they grasped the reality that God's man would not cross the Jordan with them into Canaan. Logically, the Israelites were (for a change) deferential and respectful of their humble leader and eager to hear God's instruction through His messenger.

That's the book of Deuteronomy, and by the way, chapter 6:1–9, which we will consider, is the fulcrum on which the entire book rests. It is the central message in this important collection of discourses. Not surprisingly, verses 4–9 became Israel's central statement of faith, the Shema of Israel.[1] Deuteronomy 6:1–9, our focus, is the heart of the keynote address of the entire book and—according to the Lord Jesus—it is the balance point, the touchstone of the entire Old Testament (Matthew 22:37–40).

A unique convergence of factors

And so, we find an interesting confluence of factors here: the people at this historical juncture were purged, humbled, and teachable. Compounding the poignancy of the moment were the final words of their beloved leader. What's more, Israel as a nation was ready and eager to embrace her destiny—the conquest of the land of Canaan. Not least among these factors, Israel's prosperity within that land depended on their understanding of and their obedience to the instruction they were about to receive. God brought together these unique circumstances in order to instruct His people—He secured their undivided attention.

There's one more crucial point we need to wrap our minds around in order to appreciate this passage, because without this piece of the puzzle we lose some of the impact of the text. We need to understand the specific target audience God had in mind as He addressed the nation of Israel at this decisive, historic crossroad.

Who would you choose?

Let's take a step back for just a moment and ask ourselves a question. Say you and I had to pick the target audience for this seminal address at this critical time. Who would we choose to hear this essential instruction? If we had to single out the most important community in the nation to entrust with critical information before our day of manifest destiny, who would we target? You might reason, "Well, let's define the campaign first. The conquest of the land of Canaan was first a military campaign followed by a national/political outworking, the settling of the land. Therefore, it was a military, colonizing endeavor." And I would say, "You are right!" So whom would we choose to address?

I suppose, if we were going to gather a group of VIPs together and charge them with "make or break" information—considering the nature of what we were about to attempt—it would make sense to gather the military brass, wouldn't it? Get the generals and their men together to listen to God's instruction through Moses and strategize a plan of attack. Nobody can construct a better, more clever plan for war than the Israeli military. I'm being a little ethnocentric, but I think I'm right. It would make total sense from a practical standpoint to gather the military elite for this essential address.

You might also want to bring in the intelligence community. Remember the initial 12 spies who were sent out to get a lay of the land? Call in the Mossad. Put Joshua and Caleb in charge of intelligence. That would be a key group to talk to, wouldn't you think? You would certainly need to address the infrastructure gurus, the army corps of engineers, the planners, the managers who could figure out how to make things run smoothly as the conquest took shape and the people settled in the land. Just as important as any other group would be the judges of Israel, the succession of men who had helped Moses rule the people in the wilderness for so many years. They would boast some of the wisest, most respected men among the people and would likely constitute the future political pillar of the young nation.

Whom does God choose to address?

Those are a few suggestions. We could come up with others (economists, the wealthy, the powerful, the "connected"). But the critical question we need to ask is not, "Who do we think is essential to the triumph of God's people," but ultimately who was this pivotal group in God's mind? Whom did the all-wise God determine to be the most crucial demographic to address at this all-important point in time? Who was so essential to the birth and future of a people? Whom did God seek to instruct in order to ensure the welfare of the nation? The startling answer is the family!

I find that extremely telling. You have the most formative address of this essential book at this determinant crux in Israel's existence, and the key group to instruct—in God's eyes—is the family. We would pant after the military leaders, the politicians, the power brokers, the people with know-how and resources. God says, "If Israel is to conquer the land I have promised their fathers and thrive in it, I must instruct the parents (the heads of households), because the spiritual health of the family is vital to the survival and success of My people."

And so God assembled the tribes of Israel and spoke to them through the heads of households. In particular, contextually, God addressed the fathers, but implicitly the Lord addressed both parents as well as grandparents because in His design they all bore the responsibility for raising the generation to come. In this marvelous text, Moses called Israel to holiness by sanctifying their families to the Lord.

Here's the point we need to understand—allow me to be redundant—according to God, it is the spiritual stability, strength, and health of the family unit that is critical for the success and blessing of His collective people (Genesis 18:19). That was certainly true of Old Testament Israel, but in precept it is true of God's people through the ages, including you and me today. The spiritual integrity of the home is central to the proclamation of God's redemptive message and to God's blessing on His people.

Don't get me wrong, we don't worship the family; the gospel is not the family, but the proclamation of the life-changing gospel will ring hollow to the world around us if our families are falling apart. This is why Paul instructs us to take care of our homes in Titus 2:5 *"so that the word of God will not be dishonored."* God desires for our families to prosper spiritually so that our homes may become a stage for the glory of God's life-transforming message.

A stage for the gospel built on the word

In Deuteronomy 6:1–9, God in essence tells His ancient people, "The success of your conquest of Canaan and your prosperity within the land hinges on the spiritual vitality of your families." This gives us a glimpse into how valuable the family is to God and the outworking of His program, doesn't it? Having said that, just as important as the "whom did God address" question is the "what did He say" question. What did God give His people that was so crucial to their spiritual success and well-being? What was the critical provision God gave the Israelites and, by principle, endows to us so that we might nurture our families spiritually?

The answer is once again surprising—especially to those of us looking for a magic bullet. God's chief provision to build up the home is not the typical advice we would expect, e.g., "Call in the professional clergy!" or "Work on your communication skills," or find a better private school, or find a superior, more innovative reward/consequence system, or even the fail-safe axiom, "Eat more vegetables and try drinking more water," not at all. God's provision for the family is far richer and infinitely more comprehensive than any wisdom man has to offer. God's chief provision for the well-being of our families is the all-sufficient supply of His eternal word. We will see this precept stated and repeated multiple times in Deuteronomy 6:1–9.

The component most critical to the spiritual health of the home is the very thing the enemy of God (of our soul, of our family) attempts to deprive us of, God's life-sustaining truth. So as we approach these key verses outlining parental discipleship, we have the future of the nation of Israel hanging in the balance, and with the health of the believing household in mind, the Lord tells His people of His most important and most abundant provision for their spiritual welfare, the revelation of His mind and heart in His perfect Law.

Now this is the commandment, the statutes and the judgments which the LORD your God has commanded me to teach you, that you might do them in the land where you are going over to possess it, so that you and your son and your grandson might fear the LORD your God, to keep all His statutes and His commandments which I command you, all the days of your life, and that your days may be prolonged. O Israel, you should listen and be careful to do it, that it may be well with you and that you may multiply greatly, just as the LORD, the God of your fathers, has promised you, in a land flowing with milk and honey. Hear, O Israel! The LORD is our God, the LORD is one! You shall love the LORD your God with all your heart and with all your soul and with all your might. These words, which I am commanding you today, shall be on your heart. You shall teach them diligently to your sons and shall talk of them when you sit in your house and when you walk by the way and when you lie down and when you rise up. You shall bind them as a sign on your hand and they shall be as frontals on your forehead. You shall write them on the doorposts of your house and on your gates (Deuteronomy 6:1–9).

Driving the point home!

The single greatest provision God gave Israel to spiritually fortify the family was His revelation. This has not changed for us today. God's word is still the wellspring of truth that leads our homes into health and stability. Unfortunately, there are many voices that would seek to diminish this truth in our eyes.

With the smugness of the foolish they would claim, "Yes, the Scripture is helpful, to a point; however, the Bible is an ancient document out of touch with many of the complexities of modern living. We have new professional experts who can guide us through the varied and sophisticated challenges facing the family today. Honestly, we need less of the Bible and more skilled advice from experts." Still others would assert, "Of course we need the Bible. Great, but isn't that obvious? We need something more. After all we get the Bible preached to us every Sunday. Give me something more practical, something immediate, a seminar like, 'How to get my unruly, sullen teenager to respect me in a week or less.'"

God absolutely obliterates that perspective in Scripture (e.g. our present text, Deuteronomy 6:1–9 as well as Psalm 78:1–8, and many others). The Lord declares in principle, "My word is enough and it must have its central place in the home in the spiritual training of your children!" God's Spirit unequivocally hammers this point home in our text of choice, Deuteronomy 6:1–9. The preeminence of the Bible in the lives of God's people is not unique to Chapter 6. For example, this concept permeates the preceding five chapters of Deuteronomy and saturates the balance of the book, but specifically in 6:1–9, it forms the framework for everything God says to the believing home (heads of households). We need to understand the sufficiency of the Bible, and therefore the central place it must play in the home; we need to listen attentively to the instruction of this text of Scripture.

Let's dig in

The supremacy of God's word for the family echoes loudly and distinctly in the first nine verses of Deuteronomy 6. Note how the centrality and sufficiency of the word of God for the home is emphasized in these verses.

- In verse 1, Moses reminds the people of his principal charge from the Lord, to teach them God's Law. *"Now this is the commandment, the statutes and the judgments which the LORD your God has commanded me to teach you."* In a nutshell, this was Moses' divine mission: to fill the Lord's people with a true knowledge of God's word. Why? So that God's truth might dominate every facet of their existence and especially, contextually, their homes.

- In verse 2, Moses exhorts the people of Israel to focus on following God's precepts, *"to keep all His statutes and His commandments which I command you, all the days of your life."*

- In verse 3, Moses reminds Israel that listening to God's word with an inclination toward obedience would lead to their prosperity as a people. *"O Israel, you should listen and be careful to do it, that it may be well with you and that you may multiply greatly."*

- Based on the centrality of God's word (vv. 1–3), verses 4 and 5 tell of the ultimate purpose of God's Law, which is to reveal who God truly is so that they might love Him with all their being. *"Hear, O Israel! The LORD is our God, the LORD is one! You shall love the*

LORD your God with all your heart and with all your soul and with all your might"

- In verse 6, God's servant beckons his people to make the Law the sentinel of the inward person: *"These words* [the words of the Law], *which I am commanding you today, shall be on your heart."*

- This is followed in verses 7, 8, and 9 by strong commands to take God's words and *"teach them"* to their children, to *"bind them"* on their hands so as to guide their actions, and to *"write them"* on their gates so that God's precepts might rule in their homes.

Do you get the idea that this principle (the sufficiency and centrality of the Scripture in our lives and homes) is important to God? Do you understand that He has given us His word so that it may be well with us and with our families?

"Yes, but," the question may have arisen in your mind, "you say, and Deuteronomy 6 affirms, that the Bible needs to have a central place in my life and home, but is this book really all I need to guide my family spiritually, relationally? How exactly is the Scripture 'enough' for the spiritual health and development of my family?" The answer to that question is found in verse 1, specifically in the multiple titles Moses gives to God's revelation.

A multifaceted gem

Notice the names Moses strings together to refer to Scripture, *"Now this is the commandment,* [these are the nonnegotiable directives God places in our lives to protect and bless us],[2] *the statutes* [refer to precepts from the King for living],[3] *and the judgments* [rulings from the bar of the Great Judge that guide our steps and help us understand life],[4] *which the LORD your God has commanded me to teach you"* (emphasis added).

The terms *"commandment—statutes—judgments"* are all synonyms for the Bible, emphasizing slightly different facets of God's revelation and collectively drawing our attention to one key idea, the sufficiency of the Bible to direct our lives. To put it another way, the Bible is comprehensive in its coverage of life issues. It addresses all our spiritual needs. This is why Moses incorporates multiple titles to describe the Scriptures. He holds it up as a priceless, multifaceted gem that shines its brilliant light on all areas of life.

The multiple use of titles for Scripture is a common occurrence throughout the Old Testament (Leviticus 26:15; Deuteronomy 6:1; 11:1; 1 Kings 2:3; Nehemiah 9:13, and many others), but the quintessential example is Psalm 19:7–9. Consider the colors reflected by the prism of this lovely text.

> The law of the LORD is perfect, restoring the soul; the testimony of the LORD is sure, making wise the simple. The precepts of the LORD are right, rejoicing the heart; the commandment of the LORD is pure, enlightening the eyes. The fear of the LORD is clean, enduring forever; the judgments of the LORD are true; they are righteous altogether.

There in the span of three verses we find six titles for the word of God (law, testimony, precepts, commandment, fear, judgments), and even more, we also discover six characteristics that speak to the nature of Scripture (perfect, sure, right, pure, clean, true), and lastly six effects that Scripture brings about in the believer (restoring the soul, making wise the simple, rejoicing the heart, enlightening the eyes, enduring forever, righteous altogether). As in Deuteronomy 6:1–3, the point of these texts is to underscore the unrivaled riches of the word of God for the children of God.

What a marvelous treasure the Bible is! We don't have to grope about in the dark hoping that by some means we manage to live lives that are somehow pleasing to the Lord. He has entrusted to us His true and clear judgments, and by them He has laid out a sure path of unmistakable righteous living for us to follow.

So, if like me you need a comprehensive, trustworthy source of truth that is enduring and offers renewal, wisdom, joy, insight, life-transforming directives, and leads to righteousness, then I have good news. We possess the source, and it is God's chief provision for our personal welfare and that of our families! The waters of divine wisdom are flowing in a crystal torrent directly from the wellspring of God. That's what we have in the Bible. Drink it in and truly live!

The connection between the Bible and the family

Still someone might wonder, "I'm still unclear about how all of the Bible is beneficial for my family?" Here's the point: Deuteronomy 6:1–9 reminds us that the sum total of Scripture is for our edification and transformation (that is, growing into the image of God and His Son), and as we become more like Jesus, by that same process we become stronger, healthier, God-honoring, Christ-exalting families.

As the Spirit of God works His transformation in us through the word, He brings spiritual vitality to our souls and gives us wisdom for living. He fills our lives with joy through His promises and by the same gives us insight into the challenges we face on life's journey. By His truth, God's Spirit cultivates lasting change in our thinking and behavior and so produces the fruit of righteousness in us. That entire process, my friends, makes us better husbands, wives, fathers, mothers, sons and daughters, siblings, grandparents, aunts, and uncles.

That marvelous, supernatural transformation comes to us by way of the whole counsel of God, the Bible. That's why when I speak at family camps or to dads at men's retreats, I am free to teach from the life of David or the life of Christ, from the Old Testament or the New Testament—because all Scripture is profitable and sanctifies (2 Timothy 3:16–17). And whatever sanctifies (transforms) us—whatever makes us more like Jesus—renders us better able to love, to relate, to lead our homes. We need all of the Bible and its life-changing power in our lives and in our homes so that He may shape us as individuals and as families into His glorious image.

God's word is His chief provision for the spiritual vitality of our families. Specifically, as the text will instruct us, the Bible is His all-abundant provision so that we may walk in obedience and by so doing experience His gracious blessings. His word also reveals the sure path to loving God, and His promises hold the treasure of truth to disciple our children in His ways.

The Fourfold Benefit of Shepherding our Families with the Scriptures

CHAPTER 5

God's Word, the Road to Obedience & the Way of Blessing

Reaping the benefits of the truth—obedience

Those who enter into a personal relationship with God through the Lord Jesus become part of the glorious body of Christ, the church. As members of His body, we inherit the staggering spiritual wealth bequeathed to the family of God (Ephesians 1:3–23). As the old Amex slogan goes, "membership has its privileges." This is most definitely the case for those who belong to Christ.

No small portion of that treasure is the bounty of God's word—God's supreme provision for the family—that opens up to us a cornucopia of benefits. A discussion of the blessings that come to us via the word would take volumes, but the Spirit of the Lord has turned our focus to four particular benefits laid out for us and our families in Deuteronomy 6:1–9.

In the preceding pages we proposed that Scripture is God's primary provision for the welfare of our homes. How exactly are our families enriched by the Bible? God, speaking through Moses, outlines four specific ways our homes are supremely provided for by Scripture. In this important familial text, we will see that Scripture is God's abundant provision for our *obedience*, our *blessing*, for *knowing and loving Him*, as well as our *resource to spiritually train and impact our children*. If we embrace God's generous offering, our families will lack nothing for spiritual growth; in fact, they will overflow with God's riches to bless those whom we encounter.

The Bible is God's provision for our obedience

Do you want to live a life of obedience? Do you long to know the mind of God so that you may conform your life, your family to reflect His will? That should truly be the longing of every child of God. If your heart cries out to follow God's ways, then God has given you the means to glut your desire for obedience. The Bible is the source where God reveals His ways and His will so that we might merge our lives and our homes with His design and desires. Scripture is God's provision for a life of obedience.

In Deuteronomy chapter 6, Moses exhorts his people in this very thing, i.e., to receive God's instruction and to follow it. Beginning in verse 1 he teaches, "*Now this is the commandment, the statutes and the judgments which the LORD your God has commanded me to teach you.*" Why did Moses faithfully teach Israel God's Law? Was it because he didn't have anything else to do? He didn't have enough sheep and goats to tend, so he was killing time by teaching? No, Moses taught with a razor-sharp purpose in mind, and he tells us what that goal was, "*that you might do them in the land where you are going over to possess it*" (emphasis added).

God's servant didn't casually, off the cuff, tell the Israelites to obey. Moses repeated himself to drive the point home. Consider the purpose clause at the beginning of verse 2. Moses taught the people God's Law "*so that you and your son and your grandson might fear the LORD your God*" (emphasis added). What does it mean to fear the Lord? The balance of the verse tells us. It means, "*to keep all His statutes and His commandments which I command you, all the days of your life*" (emphasis added). Often in the Old Testament the word "*fear*" is used as a synonym for obedience (Job 1:1).

Yet again in verse 3 Moses exhorts, "*O Israel, you should listen* [to God's word] *and be careful to do it,*" that is, to obey God's directives unfolded in His revelation. God gave Israel His Law as a provision for obedience, and He entrusts us with His word for the same purpose. You may be thinking, "Yes, of course God has provided His word that we might obey it. I have to buy a book for you to tell me this? Isn't it obvious?"

I remember asking myself this very question one day as I was thinking through these verses. I thought about this hard until my noodle ached. Yet, the text repeats this conviction over and over again, and it seems so basic and apparent. I thought aloud, "Do I really need to tell people something that is so patently obvious?" It was at that very moment that another thought foisted itself on my mind with startling clarity. No sooner had I blurted out my question when I remembered the folly that fills my own heart. I was painfully reminded of the waywardness embedded in my flesh and how often I need to hear this truth.

Scripture is God's provision for my obedience. My friends, I need to keep this principle before me at all times. I need to keep this objective right in plain view because my heart is prone to wander and the distractions of this life are so numerous. My flesh fights against my desire to conform to God's truth; the busyness of life waves its arms and calls out to me, "Look over here!" Then, there are the baubles and shiny trinkets of this age that would lure me away from God's clear path. What's more, the world is constantly offering me substitutes for God's counsel. There are a myriad of worldly voices calling me to follow their counsel at the exclusion of God's! I wrestle daily to keep my heart from listing.

Unless you live on a desert island—and I know I don't—then this is your daily struggle as well as mine. As such, the truth Moses repeats in these verses must stand before us continually, and this is why it is stated so plainly and forcefully. We are all prone to wander, and the world is ever ready to offer us its erring counsel to our often distracted and listing hearts.

Allow me to make an iron-clad guarantee. At the time you read this book, there will be no shortage of unbelieving people offering you errant advice about your marriage, your parenting, and family matters. In time, the relentless droning of these faulty philosophies can affect our thinking and lead us astray. We need to know God's ways so that we might reject the counsel of this world and align our thinking, our marriages, our parenting, our lives with God's prescription.

The world is forever trying to marginalize the word of God in our lives with its mix of half-truths and, at times, outright lies. Let's face it, knowing the truth (God's provision) and clinging to it (obedience) is a constant battle we have to wage. If we let down our vigilance we could find ourselves whistling the world's tune.

"Get out of my head, jingle!"

Have you ever been exposed to a really obnoxious tune for a prolonged period of time, and you find yourself playing it in your head time and again, humming it aloud and tapping your toes to it—even though you can't stand it?[1] While that happens to me randomly more than I care to experience, I choose to make it happen once a year with such force that I nearly lose my mind in the process.

Most of my kids love roller coasters. I do too, my wife not so much, but I and three of my four kids can't get enough of them. Over the last couple of decades, I've taken my roller-coaster-loving kids to Six Flags Magic Mountain in Valencia, California, just to see how close we can come to tossing our cookies. Magic Mountain is simply an excuse to ride really fast, twisty rides that take you to the brink of blackout. That's why people go there. If you want a magical experience, go to Disneyland. If you want to jostle your vestibular system, go to Magic Mountain.

Through the years, the park has developed one mind-tingling (or numbing) ride after another, but our favorite all-time coaster is one called Riddler's Revenge. It's fast, smooth, corkscrewy—and judging by the looks on the faces of people who get off of it—life threatening. It's lots of fun. We love it. But the terrible thing about Riddler's is that in order to ride the beast you have to stand in line, sometimes for quite a while, and therein lies the rub.

You see the tormentors who designed Riddler's sadistically determined that high prices, long lines, and sticky handrails would not inflict sufficient grief on park guests. To this cocktail of misery, at least on Riddler's Revenge, they added a really tedious disco tune for their captive audience to "enjoy." It is a tune that cannot be moderated or silenced except by park closure or death. If you're going to ride, you cannot hide from the jingle of madness.

Obviously, we could choose to forgo the ride, but because we love the coaster and elect to ride it multiple times, in the front car and row no less, guess what? By default, we choose to listen to that repetitive, chafing ditty over and over again to the point that when we leave the ride, indeed even when we leave the park, we just keep hearing that maddening tune looping in our mind's ear. It's as close as I've ever come to waterboarding. It's a pretty rough experience. It would be easier to sit through a day-long insurance seminar without a bathroom break.

Even once we've arrived home and we are safely tucked away in our beds, I'll wake up in the middle of the night with the jingle still coursing through my brain. It just becomes an ingrained part of my subconscious until exposure to other music eventually flushes it out. It may even take two or three days on massive doses of Bach and Mendelssohn just to drive the mantra from my mind.

In a similar way, the droning, repetitive, flawed blather of our contemporary culture can ingrain itself in our minds, and we can find ourselves tapping our toes and aligning our lives and families to the rhythm of the world without even realizing it. We would do well to remember the words of Paul to his beloved Colossians, *"See to it that no one takes you captive through philosophy and empty deception, according to the tradition of men, according to the elementary principles of the world, rather than according to Christ"* (Colossians 2:8).

We need to be rooted, established in God's truth so that we may recognize the misleading counsel of men and order our lives, our homes by God's standard (Colossians 2:7). The world is constantly attempting to foist its broken designs on believers, particularly as it concerns us in our present study, our families. Let's take a few moments and in a simple, straightforward way compare the world's way with the word's (God's) way for our homes. By so doing we will understand more clearly that Scripture is God's provision for our obedience. Let's first look at the world's counsel regarding the foundational relationship in the family, the marriage union.

Counsel of the World | Worlds Apart | Counsel of the Lord

The world's way vs. the Word's way—the marriage relationship

We constantly hear the droning of our culture in regard to our marriages, don't we? Just turn on your television, pick up a newspaper, go to a movie, open your eyes and take your first conscious breath in the morning, and you will be bombarded with the world's misguided counsel on marriage.

The world's way: "Marriage is a 50/50 proposition"

For example, the world tells us that marriage is a 50/50 proposition. Sounds reasonable, doesn't it? In other words, you need to expect your partner to pull his/her 50% of the load in the relationship, and when you verify their half of the deal, then you fulfill your end of the bargain. That's fair; it's the American way. It's the time-tested Reagan Doctrine, "Trust, but verify!" That's great foreign policy. That shrewd piece of geopolitical wisdom worked like a charm with the former Soviet Union, but let me tell you something, it does not work well in marriage!

The problem with this 50/50 proposition is that the other person is usually waiting for you to fulfill your 50% of the contract before they budge significantly on their commitment. Hence you have two clearly entrenched sides in a stalemate waiting for the other to move; in essence, you have a divided house. Furthermore, who's to say what 50% really looks like? That's certainly debatable. This 50/50 mentality leads to suspicion, breeds selfishness, and will most certainly result in disappointment and emotional separation. The wisdom of this age tells us marriage is a 50/50 deal; sounds reasonable until you try to live by it. What does God say? What must we keep before us and submit to? What is God's prescription and provision for believing couples?

The Word's way: "I'm all in"

God tells us we have a new commandment to rule our relationships—including marriage—and it's to "*love one another.*" By the way, in the next few pages we're going to consider several passages that pertain to all Christian relationships and that most certainly govern the marriage union. It kills me when people think that the "one another" passages in the New Testament apply to our interactions within the body of Christ, yet somehow not primarily to the marriage relationship. That's absolutely false. For those of us blessed by God to be married, the marriage union is "ground zero." The "one anothers" begin at home with our spouse and radiate outward to the members of our family and from there to the church. If we can't apply these tenets at home, what leap in logic makes us think that we can put them to work in less intimate relationships? That's the road to hypocrisy.

With that in mind, listen to these forceful and familiar words of the Lord Jesus from the Gospel of John. "*A new commandment I give to you, that you love one another, even as I have loved you, that you also love one another*" (John 13:34); "*This is My commandment, that you love one another, just as I have loved you*" (John 15:12); "*This I command you, that you love one another*" (John 15:17).

Note the command tone in these verses. This is not simply an important or even strong suggestion to employ in Christian relationships. What we have before us is a divine imperative! God in the flesh issues a "*commandment*"—a word that could just as easily be translated "order"—to His followers. We have a new divine directive that must rule our relationships, and it is love.

Far from being an aloof and harsh requirement, Christ's Law is based upon the love with which the Lord Jesus loved us, and what kind of "love" is that?

It is a self-sacrificing love. The Greek term employed in the three verses just mentioned—and many, many other passages in the New Testament—is the ubiquitous verb *agapao* which is defined ultimately by the remarkable example of Christ's supreme love for His redeemed on the cross. This concept applied to us, therefore, means we must love others with their best interest as our primary motivation or in a similar manner to the way Jesus welcomed the cross in order to rescue us from sin. Jesus didn't simply love us sentimentally or when it was convenient or easy but with the full force of His redeeming actions. Does such a self-sacrificing love describe the way in which you behave (not feel, but act) toward your spouse?

My dear friends, we must love our life partners genuinely, sincerely from the heart with their welfare driving our decisions. Do you wake up in the morning asking God and yourself, "How can I meet my spouse's needs? What specific thing can I do today to bless her/him; to encourage him/her in their walk with Christ, in their work, in their parenting, in their friendships?"

For some of us, loving our spouse like that may seem like a pretty radical approach. You may be thinking, "Whoa turbo! That's hard to do, to live like that consistently." Yes it is, but we have a command from the King, a labor of grace. He has revealed to us how we must live, and frankly for those of us who belong to the King this is not a strange doctrine or a foreign experience. This is the love with which Christ has loved us. We are commanded to imitate His magnificent love and not mimic the self-obsessed, 50/50 mongrelism the world calls love.

Let me ask you, did Jesus Christ love you 50% of the way? Does He say, "Meet me halfway and I'll love you with 50% of my affections?" No, Christ loved us perfectly with 100% of divine love (John 13:1), and He calls us to reciprocate that love to others. What better place to begin than with our life partners. That's God's provision for our obedience. He tells us, "Do this! Align your marriage by this standard of sacrificial love and you will be walking in my provision for your marriage." Men and women, this is the kind of love that must drive our marriage relationships.

The world's way: "Looking out for #1!"

Here's another bone the world throws our way regarding the marriage relationship, and believe it or not, it is a downgrade from the 50/50 deal. The world will lure us into thinking that in a marriage relationship you have to look out for "Number One," yourself first! That's the new orthodoxy. You must love yourself first and watch out for your own interests. That's how you approach your wife or your husband.

Really? How does that work practically? Let's take that attitude and apply it to a common marital issue: resolving conflict. How do couples resolve conflict and the wounds they feel when hurtful words and deeds have been exchanged? What does the counsel of "Watch out for number one!" look like when resolving offenses?

Well, this popular wisdom informs us that we don't get pushed around. You stand your ground. If you get pushed, push back—harder! You mete out forgiveness in milligrams, not kilograms, and before you dispense any pardon you make sure you get your pound of flesh first. Furthermore, if your partner—in a moment of groveling weakness—apologizes for treating you poorly, file that admittance of failure against you in your memory because it'll prove to be effective ammunition for future battles and, most importantly, for future victories, winning the argument, and getting your way. Empower yourself! That's the world's counsel, "Look out for yourself and get your way." You resolve offenses by protecting yourself, gaining the upper hand over your spouse, and winning the argument.

The Word's way: "Put your spouse first"

In contrast, God's Spirit informs believers, "*Be devoted to one another in brotherly love; give preference to one another in honor*" (Romans 12:10). Is that not the opposite of the world's guidance? Pushing this grace even further, Paul, in Ephesians 4:32, gives us this emancipating principle for living with those we love, "*Be kind to one another, tender-hearted, forgiving each other...*" How? Just as long as you win the argument, get your way, or at the very least pull even?

No, God's counsel to resolve our offenses is to forgive "*... just as God in Christ also has forgiven you.*" How has God in Christ forgiven you? The exhilarating answer to that is... completely, exhaustively; He has removed our sins from us "*as far as the east is from the west*" (Psalm 103:12). God has taken our "*certificate of debt* [sins]... *which was hostile to us; and He has taken it out of the way, having nailed it to the cross*" (Colossians 2:14). With that bold stroke of grace, the Lord has removed our sin an infinite distance from us. That's how God in Christ forgives us, and He leads you and me to resolve our offenses with the same generous pardon He has shown us in our Savior, the pardon we have received, know, and love.

The world's way: "Treat 'em like Tupperware"

Let's quickly consider yet another brick of doltish advice from the common wisdom of our day. This one gets chucked at husbands. Husbands, popular macho wisdom tells you, "Women are a mystery! Don't try to figure them out. Just continue to treat them as one of the guys. They're like Tupperware. They'll bounce back! Just go on with your own life and domineer whenever possible. Assert your 'maleness.'"

That may seem insensitive in today's politically correct charged atmosphere, yet such attitudes are widely held by men of the world. Male chauvinism is alive and well in the secret counsels of the fairways, gyms, and water coolers of the land. Worse still is the reality that these prejudices are carried over to actual marriage partnerships. Unfortunately, the default wisdom directing the attitude of many men is that "guys need to bully their way through a relationship." The consequences of this approach to a marriage are devastating. Failing to understand their wives, men often deeply wound their partners, resulting in a litany of problems such as lack of honest communication, loss of trust, isolation, and bitterness.

The Word's way: "Treat them like crystal"

God encourages men through the apostle Peter, "*husbands... live with your wives in an understanding way*" (1 Peter 3:7). The term "*understanding*" in verse 7 is the familiar Greek word *gnosis* and carries the idea of possessing information about something or someone. Quite literally, it means "to know about, to have knowledge of, to be acquainted with."[2] In other words, God calls Christian men to be diligent students of their wives.

Peter continues addressing husbands with this relational insight, "*as with someone weaker, since she is a woman.*" That has a direct reference to a woman's more fragile physical and emotional disposition. Peter admonishes men to remember and to be considerate of how God has wired their wives physically and emotionally. Essentially, husbands are beckoned to treat their partners like Waterford crystal—something beautiful, valuable, and delicate—and not like a piece of unbreakable and common Tupperware. Save your head-butting, smack-talking, ear-thumping ways for the guys at the gym, gentlemen.

In fact, Peter takes the care of wives a step further by calling men to recognize the high standing each believing wife has before God. He writes, "*show her honor as a fellow heir of the grace of life.*" Peter reminds us that our wives, gentlemen, are fellow, equal sharers of the grace of Christ, heirs of all that Christ has. As someone has said, the ground is level at the foot of the cross, and as such, wives deserve the honor and dignity God gives them as children of God.

I don't have time to develop how radical Peter's statement was at the time it was written. Suffice it to say that in the Greco-Roman world at this point in history women were considered property, second-class citizens, subject to the despotic whims of their husbands, reflecting the chauvinism of the day. Peter teaches husbands, "Treat your wife as a fellow child of God!" To drive the seriousness of this obligation home, Peter adds an astonishing caveat, "*so that your prayers will not be hindered*" (1 Peter 3:7).[3] Peter says, "Be careful how you handle God's precious possession, your wife. If you don't, your prayers will be significantly impeded."

There are so many Scriptures we could bring to bear at this point, such as Ephesians 5:25, where the apostle Paul beckons husbands to envelop their wives with the love and tenderness with which the Lord Jesus embraces His beloved church, but space and time prohibit us. What we need to understand is the outcome of the world's way and God's way is as different as night and day. The common advice of the world to men regarding how to live with their wives results in shattered relationships. God's provision for husbands in their marriage relationship leads to understanding, respect, and unhindered communication with God.

The world's way: "Undermine and assert"

Ladies, the counsel of this world teaches wives to buck their husbands and undermine their leadership role in the home. This is especially true if the husband in question has ever failed you or the family (that, by the way, would certainly include every man that has ever said "I do"). For example, if your husband is insensitive to you, then in retaliation you bring him down! You deride him, you cut him down to his face in front of the kids and publicly as often as the opportunity arises. Whenever possible, "share" with others about his shortcomings so that you may garner sympathy for yourself. And until he treats you right, buck his leadership. "Submission? What, are you serious? That's not what the ladies on *The View* tell me. Give me a break!"

The Word's way: "Respect and rest in God's provision"

How does the heart of God instruct married women? God reminds wives in Ephesians 5:33, "*the wife must see to it that she respects her husband.*" The word "*respects*" could be translated "to reverence,"[4] "to be in awe of."[5] In this context, you could paraphrase it to read "to treat with respectful deference."

Here's the upshot of what Paul teaches married women. Wives are to regard their husbands as they would the Lord Jesus Himself. Perhaps you think that is a typo that bypassed the editors of this book. I assure you it is not. The apostle Paul reminds women in a marriage relationship, "*Wives, be subject to your own husbands, as to the Lord. For the husband is the head of the wife,*" i.e., the husband is a woman's God-given authority and protection. Paul draws this parallel directly from Christ's relationship to the church and says, "*as Christ also is the head of the church, He Himself being the Savior of the body*" (Ephesians 5:22–23). Ladies, to oppose and denigrate your husband is like the church opposing and disregarding Christ in the same manner. Bucking and undermining your husband's authority further isolates you from your life partner (your God-given protection) and leaves you vulnerable to the world's deception and devastation.

The world's way vs. the Word's way—the parent/child relationship

The world's way: "Tolerable rebellion"

This world has plenty to say about the parent/child relationship, doesn't it? It weighs in with such gems as "Rebellion is tolerable. It is a confirmed phase of the preteen/teen years. In fact, it is a 'rite of passage' for young people. Expect it, accept it, let it slide." This type of thinking is absolutely rampant in secular culture; and sadly, it is systemic in the Christian community. Perhaps this myth has shaped your perspective. If it does, my friend, that attitude could lead you to lose your sons and daughters temporarily (to this world, its philosophies and vices) and possibly for eternity (to hell itself). The path to ruin in this life and the road to eternal perdition is littered with the bodies and souls of young people who were not held accountable by their parents for their rebellious attitudes and behaviors!

The world tells us prideful defiance is a normal, acceptable, even a helpful rite of passage. "Self-will enables kids to discover who they are and helps them become their own persons, independent, rugged individualists," so preach the pop pundits. What's more, pop culture sells rebellion as a cool and hip, edgy, James-Deanesque quality that is actually desirable, commendable, and attractive. The entertainment industry, my friends, peddles much of its wares from this familiar cart and rakes in billions in profits while dispensing ruin to countless souls.

The Word's way: The path of obedience

Yet, Scripture warns us that rebellion is never acceptable at any age. It is the reflection of God's mortal enemy—the devil—in our fallen souls. Rebellion is at the very heart of who the devil is; it is his actual nature, and this is why God likens rebellion to occultism and idol worship. Speaking through His servant Samuel, God declared, "*For rebellion is as the sin of divination* [also translated "witchcraft," i.e., the dark craft of occultism], *and insubordination is as iniquity and idolatry*" (1 Samuel 15:23). That's pretty straightforward, isn't it? God's word puts rebellion on the same level as witchcraft and pagan worship.

Let me ask you something, is the practice of occultism and paganism acceptable in the lives of our children? Would it be okay for your teenage daughter to sacrifice a chicken or rabbit to her favorite demon deity, you know, to conjure up a little black magic to influence her friends and relatives, or to mediate a better SAT score? Would it be acceptable for your thirteen-year-old son to set up an altar to the love goddess Venus on his bedroom dresser and to adorn his room with pornography? Never, ever!

And just as such practices would never be acceptable to you, neither is the attitude and practice of rebellion acceptable to God, regardless of what pop culture pontificates. Conformity, obedience to God's ways expressed through divinely established and loving authority (i.e., parents), is always right and esteemed by God. Again, God instructs us through His prophet Samuel with these words of life, "*Has the LORD as much delight in burnt offerings and sacrifices as in obeying the voice of the* L~ORD~? *Behold, to obey is better than sacrifice, and to heed than the fat of rams*" (1 Samuel 15:22).

The world's way: "Parents are irrelevant!"

Here is yet another parenting axiom the world barfs at our feet and fully expects us to accept without question. More often than not our culture portrays parents as bumbling imbeciles completely out of touch with their kids and extraneous to their lives except to dole out goods. Essentially, parents are like yesterday's newspaper. Last night's news is a bundle of words, occasionally useful (e.g., comes in handy to line the bottom of a hamster's cage) but largely irrelevant. Likewise, parents are full of rhetoric (more like white noise), serve a menial purpose (to provide), and are considered peripheral, not central, to a child's life.

This tired refrain of worldly thinking tells us that children don't want or need to be close to their parents. They are simply not interested in nurturing a relationship with their mom and dad. In one way or another, parents hear the following undertones constantly: "You (the parent) are clueless about how to deal with today's generation; you're obsolete; you're too old. Kids relate best to other kids and young people. Let's face it, parents are primarily 'goods and service' providers. Your best course of action is to provide and step aside because young people don't want to relate to their parents, and frankly parents are incapable of relating to their kids."

A few years ago, a commercial for adolescent drug and alcohol prevention made the following spiel to encourage parents to talk to their kids about drug abuse— especially if their kids were already dabbling in recreational drugs or drinking. The pitch stated in part, "As a parent, it's hard to believe that your children would ever believe or listen to a word you say." "Well," I thought, "that should encourage parental involvement. Very helpful!"

You mean to tell me your kid is teetering on the precipice of a chemical addiction, his/her life hangs in the balance, and you might want to sheepishly broach the subject of the dangers of drug abuse with them—remembering all the while that your words mean little and your authority is nonexistent? Is that supposed to empower parents and help kids? This is how feebly parents are frequently characterized by our culture: "You might want to think about talking to your kids from time to time—especially if they're in trouble—but remember your words mean little to them because you have marginal credibility and even less authority."

The message that pitches to parents is disturbingly clear. Parents are largely irrelevant to their children, and logically kids have no real interest in having a close relationship with them. Moms and dads might as well own up to that reality, accept it, and pawn their kids off to the experts.

The Word's way: "Parents and children—hardwired for relationship"

Allow me to state this as clearly as I can: the popular opinions expressed in the previous paragraphs are false! What is God's provision, His prescription for families? Let me simply remind you of the clear assumption in the primary passage we are considering in this book, Deuteronomy 6:1–9, again, the premiere instructional passage in the Bible for parental discipleship.

Deuteronomy 6:1–9 is built on the premise of relational intimacy between parents and their children. A simple cursory reading of the passage reveals this reality. The text demands an engaged, vital relationship between parents and their kids so that parents may lead their children to God and forge their character in the truth. Relational closeness is what God wants between parents and children because this is a primary context He uses to shape future generations of God-knowing, God-loving disciples.

This tight-knit affinity between parents and their kids is what God has designed for the family and how He has created us to function together. Deuteronomy 6:1–9 is bereft of impact without the presence of such a close familial connection. We would do well to remember that God has hardwired children and parents to live together, to lovingly relate to one another, to need one another. Far from being irrelevant, God affirms that no one can take the place of Mom and Dad in the lives of children. No other person or group of persons has more influence upon young people than parents, especially when it comes to their spiritual development.

Interestingly, not all secular voices affirm the popular conclusion concerning the irrelevancy of parents. A leading sociologist, researching spiritual development in American teens, bucks the trend. In his book *Soul Searching*, academic sociologist Christian Smith summarizes countless hours of research on the religious life of teens down to eleven key conclusions, one of which is the following. He writes, "Contrary to popular misguided cultural stereotypes and frequent parental misperceptions, we believe the evidence clearly shows that the single most important social influence in the religious and spiritual lives of adolescents is their parents."[6] You and I don't need to conduct thousands of research hours to conclude that moms and dads matter. We understand this on an intuitive, human, social level, but more importantly, we know this because God reveals in His word the critical life-directing role parents play in the lives of their children. If you have children, you are relevant to their welfare. God has created your sons and daughters to lovingly relate with you and to follow your lead.

My son, observe the commandment of your father and do not forsake the teaching of your mother; bind them continually on your heart; tie them around your neck. When you walk about, they will guide you; when you sleep, they will watch over you; and when you awake, they will talk to you (Proverbs 6:20–22).

The world's way: "The myth of powerless parents and autonomous children"

I suppose the old adage "repeat a lie enough times and people will believe it" is true when it comes to the myth of powerless parents and autonomous children. This spurious and prevalent falsehood is the first cousin of the "irrelevant parents" notion. It teaches parents to believe they have little authority over their children and indoctrinates children into thinking they are largely independent of their parents' leadership.

The discordant anthem of this particular message is rising to deafening levels in our day and age. There is a swelling chorus of voices in popular media, education, and political bodies to strip parents of their God-given rights and to emancipate children from the governance of their parents. Take for example the United Nations Convention on the Rights of the Child (CRC). It was introduced in the UN in November of 1989. Less than a year later, it was ruled binding law for ratifying countries. As of the writing of this book, 195 nations have ratified the treaty making it "the most widely-adopted human rights treaty of any kind."[7]

The only nations that have resisted ratifying the comprehensive treaty are the United States and Somalia—although Somalia will likely ratify the treaty soon. The Obama Administration revived efforts to ratify it and bring America under its binding laws.[8] Currently, the US is a "signatory" to the treaty but has not ratified it. The US agreed to act in good faith "not to defeat the objectives and purpose" of the treaty even though at this point it is not legally bound by its provisions and obligations.

That said, this sweeping and binding treaty threatens the very fabric of the family by stripping parents of their fundamental authority to raise their kids. At the same time, it would grant children broad and unprecedented "rights" to break free of their parents' influence. Under the CRC Treaty (which would override most existing American laws on children and families and—under international law—trumps our Constitution) kids would have the right to choose their own religion. Parents would be free to make suggestions, but they could not definitively lead in the arena of faith. The treaty also ensures children the legal right to appeal parental decisions they find objectionable. If children found certain rules or rulings disagreeable they would have guaranteed access to a governmental review. The ultimate authority in such appeals would rest with a government worker. What's more, one of the many rights granted to children under this treaty would be "a legally enforceable right to leisure," and the litany of this intrusive and ludicrous covenant goes on and on.[9]

I realize the CRC sounds ridiculous or scary. I assure you, it is both. I encourage you to carefully consider the reference for the CRC and its danger in the footnote section of this chapter. The information in it is well documented and written by an experienced, Christian, constitutional attorney (Michael Farris). Suffice it to say, at this juncture this treaty is an example of the forces at work to change the very structure of the family, especially in regard to the authority of parents and the biblical shepherding of children. Regardless of whether or not this treaty is ratified by the United States, the present cultural atmosphere opening the door to the CRC is the more immediate problem and poses a real threat to parents and children.

However the parent/child relationship is challenged in the short or long term, we need not wonder nor waver about what God would have us do. God's provision for this crucial familial relationship is clearly laid out for us in the revelation of His word.

The Word's way: Shepherding the household flock

Despite the inescapable presence of this message (Powerless Parents and Autonomous Children), the Bible clearly teaches that parents are morally bound to lead their children. Shepherding the household flock is a divine obligation God places on parents (Genesis 18:19; Deuteronomy 6:6–7; Ephesians 6:4). Children, for their part, are obliged and privileged to submit to their parents' leadership, and therein they will find protection and blessing (Exodus 20:12; Deuteronomy 5:16; Matthew 19:19; Ephesians 6:1–3).

At this point, I would like to briefly shift gears. I have spent—and will spend— most of this book addressing parents, and though I want parents to grapple with the biblical example we are about to consider, I would like to narrow my focus and in particular, though not exclusively, address my audience of young people for a handful of pages.

Until that day comes

While the hands-on-shepherding role of parents decreases with the passage of time (as children grow in maturity), parents never become obsolete. My dad was nearly 92 years old when he died and I still sought his counsel and regularly asked him to pray for the issues that arose in my life. I talk with my 29-year-old son often, but I relate to him as a fellow Christian man, and unless there is a sin issue, I speak to him as a come-alongside-mentor, as a friend. I can't remember the last time I had to remind him to eat his broccoli or zip up his pants. Well, I can't remember the last time I had to encourage him to eat his broccoli. Josh, like his dad, is a bit absentminded.

Young people, you will become increasingly independent of your parents. This process will eventually lead you to adult autonomy when God releases you to fully express the unique plan He has designed for your life. This is the marvelous process of becoming independent, and it is indeed an exciting journey for both parents and kids. It is one of the goals parents lovingly labor for and children joyfully anticipate.

However, until such a day (the day you leave your home when you marry or become economically independent), you are under the care and authority of your parents to some degree—more in the early years, less as you mature. That's the place God has provided for you to grow, and because that is God's design for your life, you can count on the world's opposition to it. As sure as that day approaches, the currents of popular culture will attempt to separate you from the safe harbor of your parents' authority. In western culture, this is especially true in the late preteen through teen years.

The world will try to convince you through its "wisdom" and hip "sophistication" that authority is way overrated. It will tell you that obedience is an archaic concept practiced by religious extremists and that your parents are out of touch with you and with youth. They don't fully understand you, and you can't expect them to lead wisely. The counsel of this age is trying to sell you the yap that, "Your parents have no right to foist their opinions on you, much less impose their decisions on your life, so question their authority at the very least and ignore their leadership if you must. Do what seems best to you even if it contradicts their counsel."

If some or all of those thoughts have ever crossed your mind, I would like you to consider one biblical example—there are several but let's simply look to one—that fleshes out the call of God for you in your youth. The reason this example stands out so beautifully is because it is the pattern left to us by the Lord Jesus Himself.

The template left by the Lord Jesus[10]

God Almighty appeared on the stage of human history as a baby and progressed developmentally like any other child. The Scripture tells us, *"And Jesus kept increasing in wisdom and stature, and in favor with God and men"* (Luke 2:52). This means that He matured in body and mind much like you and me. Yet because He was also God's Son (God in the flesh sent from heaven to save man from his sin), Jesus also increased in His understanding of why He was born, why He had been sent. In fact, as the young Lord Jesus approached adolescence, His redemptive mission became increasingly clear as the Father unveiled more of Himself and His plan to His Son.

Jesus, however, was somewhat alone in this knowledge. Not even those closest to Him could foresee or appreciate His life's purpose. His brothers and sisters were clueless as to His identity (God Incarnate) and life's work (the cross). His siblings remained unbelieving until after the Lord's resurrection (Mark 3:21; John 7:5; 1 Corinthians 15:7; Acts 1:14). Perhaps the Lord's parents had the clearest view of their son's future. After all, they had witnessed the many signs and words attending His birth, yet in spite of these wondrous things, they were not able to anticipate the radical turns in their son's road to the throne of David. Although Mary and Joseph understood something of the uniqueness of their son, they also could not fully enter into the vision for the mission Jesus was increasingly coming to know and own (Matthew 1:18–24; Luke 1:26–38; 46–55; 2:19, 51).

In fact, as the years passed and time diminished the clarity of those early days in Bethlehem and Nazareth, Joseph and Mary failed to adequately apprehend their son's growing, righteous appetites. Jesus as an adolescent could rightly say, "My parents don't understand who I truly am." That gap in knowledge and awareness between Him and His parents became distressingly clear one particular spring in the bud of our Lord's adolescence.

When Jesus was 12 years old, His parents took Him to Jerusalem. In the year of His thirteenth birthday and bar mitzvah, like most observant Jewish boys, Jesus was taken to Jerusalem to participate in the Passover feast. How that great experience must have thrilled His soul. His heart must have welled up with a mixture of excitement, reverence, and destiny. He was in the Holy City! He walked among the worshiping assembly of His brethren, the congregation of Israel... "*to go along with the throng and lead them in procession to the house of God, with the voice of joy and thanksgiving, a multitude keeping festival*" (Psalm 42:4b). He heard the priest sound the shofar in the temple courts, and most importantly, He worshiped in His Father's house. This is where He needed to be. He felt at home in the temple of God, where as an adult male member of Jewish society He could now discuss the Law He loved with the learned and the wise.

And the temple is exactly where we find the young Lord Jesus in Luke 2:46. It is interesting to note that we find the promised Messiah, the Agent of creation, the Son of God, the High King of heaven, respectfully dialoging with and asking questions of the teachers of Israel (Isaiah 9:6–7; Luke 1:31–33; Colossians 1:16; John 20:31; Revelation 19:16). Truly, he could have taught them!

We read that Jesus was "*sitting in the midst of the teachers, both listening to them and asking them questions,*" and even though "*all who heard Him were amazed at His understanding and His answers,*" His interaction was marked by humility and respect toward the adults under whose teaching He was sitting (Luke 2:46–47). Here, in the temple, we see the young Lord Jesus at home in

His Father's house, absorbed in God's Law. His heart must have cried out with the psalmist, *"Oh, how I love Your law"* (Psalm 119:97) and with David, *"Oh God, You are my God; I shall seek You earnestly; my soul thirsts for You, my flesh yearns for You... Thus I have seen You in the sanctuary, to see Your power and Your glory"* (Psalm 63:1a, 2).

And it is here at the temple where the story takes an unexpected turn. Shortly after the momentous Passover celebration, Mary and Joseph packed up their belongings and began their sixty-plus mile journey home to Nazareth assuming their son, Yeshua, was in the caravan of relatives. However, a day into their journey they discovered to their troubled surprise that young Yeshua was not anywhere in the convoy. Naturally, Joseph and Mary became exceedingly distressed. From a human standpoint, as a parent, I can completely understand their panic.

Desperate to find their son, they returned to Jerusalem, where they searched for Him for three days. They looked for Jesus high and low, their worries mounting with every passing hour. They looked everywhere in desperation, except in the most logical place of all: they didn't look within the temple complex. Luke 2:46 says, *"Then, after three days they found Him in the temple, sitting in the midst of the teachers, both listening to them and asking them questions."*

The simple question that gets to the heart of the matter is this: why did it take Joseph and Mary three days to find their son? The answer to this question is somewhat surprising and at the same time painfully obvious. The search for Jesus took three days because Joseph and Mary did not fully understand their son's heart, and they failed to accurately perceive God's plan for Him. What's more, their lack of understanding led to misplaced indignation. In Luke 2:48 we read, *"When they saw Him* [when they finally found Jesus in the temple], *they were astonished."*

The word *"astonished"* carries the idea of being so struck by amazement that one becomes overwhelmed by the sudden shock and emotion of the moment.[11] The Lord's parents were emotionally frantic at the inexplicable loss of their firstborn, and upon finding their son, all their mounting anxiety erupted in a flush of shocked surprise. Apparently, the dominating emotion when they found Jesus was not relief, but a sense of indignation because of their son's perceived misbehavior. Mary and Joseph blamed Jesus for their intense fear and distress.

This is reflected not only in the meaning of the term *"astonished"* but also in the scolding question Mary directed at Jesus, *"Son, why have You treated us this way? Behold, Your father and I have been anxiously looking for You."* Interestingly, the Greek participle translated *"anxiously"* meaning "to cause intense pain"[12] or "torment"[13] is in the middle voice, which makes it reflexive. What does that mean? In essence it renders that verse, "Why have you brought such great distress to us?"

Our Lord's answer to His parents revealed their inability to grasp the uniqueness of His person and mission and the logical place this comprehension would have directed their search. *"And He said to them, 'Why is it that you were looking for Me? Did you not know that I had to be in My Father's house?' But they did not understand the statement which He had made to them"* (Luke 2:49–50). Jesus' respectful reply was, "Mom and Dad, it should have been perfectly clear to you where I would be. I'm being faithful to My heavenly Father's call. I need to be near where His glory dwells." And their response to the Lord's answer was "What?" They didn't get it!

The Lord's earthly parents failed to carefully do the spiritual math regarding their beloved son. Contemplation of what Joseph and Mary factually knew about their Yeshua would have cleared things up for them. If they would have considered the wonderful truths revealed to them about Jesus 13 years earlier (the message of the great angel Gabriel, Joseph's vision regarding the nature of Mary's pregnancy, as well as the person she would bring forth, the report of the shepherds, the wise men, Simeon the righteous, Anna the prophetess), combined with what they perceived daily in their son's life—perfect obedience, an obvious passion for the God of Israel and His House, certainly a great love and grasp of God's Law—this information, properly triangulated, should have led them directly to the temple first (John 2:13–17; Mark 11:15–18; Luke 2:47).

The plain fact is the Lord's earthly parents were clearly out of step with their son's heart, which was perfectly in tune with the Father's priorities. If anyone had the right to lay aside the yoke of parental authority, it would have been the Lord Jesus. He was, after all, the Son of God. His earthly parents did not adequately understand heaven's prerogatives, which filled His heart. And yet our Lord at this particular stage of life and in the adolescent years that followed willingly submitted Himself to the authority of Mary and Joseph. Jesus, God in the flesh, obeyed His earthly parents whom He had created, for whom He would die an atoning death, and over whom He would rule as their resurrected, sovereign Master and Eternal King.

Given the human imperfections and limitations of His mother and father (they were frail sinners just like you and me) and the sinless deity of the Lord Jesus Christ, Luke 2:51 is truly remarkable and powerfully instructive. Following the incident at the temple, after His parents essentially excoriated Him for doing the right thing, for honoring God the Father, this is what Scripture records: *"And He went down with them and came to Nazareth, and He continued in subjection to them."*

The Lord Jesus submitted Himself to His parents not because they were better capable of directing His life than He was, but because this was God's pattern for the family. Furthermore, it was right for Joseph and Mary to lead their son, and it was obedience to God's word that compelled our Lord to follow their leadership for the first two-thirds of his life.

Not only does this example give us a pattern to follow, it clearly shows us the high regard the Father and the Son have for the familial structure God has ordained. Perhaps this is also why the first and second persons of the holy Trinity describe their perfect, eternal relationship to us with the terms "Father" and "Son."

Parents, don't buy the flimflam pandered by the world that lures you away from shepherding your kids. Young people, don't fall for the corrupting lie that you can buck your parents' authority without serious consequences for your life. Parents are not powerless providers nor are children an authority unto themselves. Parents have a divine mandate to lovingly shepherd their children, and children have the privilege to submit to their parents. This is God's provision for our obedience.

The world's way: "Life goes on! Ignore your aging parents"

There is one more contrast of the world vs. the Word that I would like to briefly bring to your attention so that we might see God's provision for our families. This comparison has to do with the relationship grown children have with their aging parents. The tune we hear the world whistle regarding this relationship is often discordant and shrill, especially when we compare it to the harmonious song sounding forth from God's revelation.

Contemporary wisdom often pushes adult children to live their own lives disconnected from their parents, especially as they become elderly and increasingly needy. In the minds of many, this is particularly justifiable in the case of parents who failed to shepherd their families well. Perhaps they failed to adequately provide for the needs of the household, or they were emotionally negligent or abusive. But the prevalent worldly attitude I have encountered toward aging parents (irrespective of their success or failure) is this: "Disregard your parents as they age. You have your own life to live." Sadly, this base inclination—expressed through many self-justifying excuses—is far too prevalent even in Christian circles. It seems that more and more adult children don't want to be bothered by the indignities and sacrifices associated with aging parents.

The Word's way: "Honor your father and mother"

God's perspective on aging parents could not be more different. The Lord tells children without reference to age (whether 10 years old or 60 years old), and without any qualifications on the part of the parents (notwithstanding if they were good or bad parents), "*Honor your father and your mother.*" This commandment was delivered by God through Moses, repeated by Jesus, and underscored by the apostle Paul to the church (Exodus 20:12; Matthew 15:4–6; Ephesians 6:2; it is likely Paul had this command in mind in 1 Timothy 5:3–4).

The Greek word "*honor*"—used in the New Testament references above and in the Septuagint translation of Exodus 20:12—is the term *timao*.[14] The verb means to place a value on something, to acknowledge the worth of something, hence "to revere, venerate,"[15] "to reverence."[16] God calls children to value their parents and therefore to treat them with deference and dignity. This is the privilege God places on children and grandchildren.

Without question, honoring our parents is not simply an intellectual exercise of esteeming them in our mind—though that's certainly part of it. It also involves varying degrees of sacrifice, and in obedience to Scripture we must step up and embrace this biblical command. Whatever the costs (great or small), children must honor their parents by seeking to meet their reasonable spiritual, emotional, and physical needs.

Honoring parents spiritually

We are compelled to approach our parents spiritually in much the same manner we relate to the unsaved or fellow believers with the added motivation of this divine imperative, *"honor your father and your mother."* If your parents are unbelieving, then ask God to increase your burden for their salvation. All too often adult Christian children don't like to entertain the possibility that their parents are not saved. I suppose this is chiefly because—as with unbelieving children—the logical consequences of such a thought are deeply painful: "My parents are lost, and they are marching toward the unimaginable horrors of a Christless eternity!" It's hard to go there. I understand, but the price of fooling ourselves or numbing ourselves to this reality is far too great for those we love.

Many true believers are content to regard their parents as Christians simply because they are decent people, hardworking folks, patriotic, or even churchgoers. But we need to think realistically with biblical clarity about their spiritual condition, and if they do not know Christ as Savior, then I encourage you to petition God to burden your heart with that reality regardless of how uncomfortable it may make you feel. Pray diligently for their salvation and seek every appropriate opportunity to lovingly talk to them about the nature of sin, its seriousness, the Savior, the gospel, heaven, and hell. If your parents are not believers, this spiritual approach honors them. It places an eternal value on them, regardless of how they respond to you and to the message of the gospel.

If on the other hand we enjoy the blessing of believing parents, then we need to covet their fellowship and seek their spiritual edification. Pray for them as you do for other fellow Christians, encourage them with the truth, look for opportunities to talk about the deep things of God, listen to the concerns and longings of their heart, request their accountability, and seek their counsel. To honor our believing parents spiritually is to relate to them as valued fellow Christians.

Honoring our parents by seeking their emotional well-being

What do I mean by this section title? I am simply addressing our responsibility (grown Christian children) to reach out to our parents in the sunset years of their lives. Generally speaking, it is easy to ignore aging parents in the whirlwind of daily life. The old saying "out of sight, out of mind" applies to the child/parent relationship more than most Christians would care to admit.

When I was a seminary student, I was employed by the community college system of California. My job was to visit assorted convalescent hospitals and retirement homes on a weekly basis. At each facility, I would conduct a forty-five-minute "Contemporary Issues" class covering a broad array of topics ranging from local to international politics, from human interest stories to the weather. It was really a program designed to engage folks on the fringes of our sophisticated culture—the elderly and the infirm.

It was a great job, and I enjoyed the relationships I developed with many of the residents. So many of them were eager each week to receive me, to listen to my ramblings, and to talk about their world. Soon after I began my weekly rounds to the numerous facilities on my list, I realized the reason these dear folks looked forward to my visits. It wasn't that I was an unusually gifted instructor or that my material was so gripping—it was essentially the morning paper mixed in with a little Readers Digest! They looked forward to my visits because I cared, and I talked to them. The preeminent issue in the lives of many of these dear people was loneliness.

I was surprised by the lack of contact these elderly folks had with their families, and I was saddened by the depth of loneliness they experienced. I can only imagine the corresponding depression and anxiety they shouldered as a result. Many of these precious folks were lucid, ambulatory, and engaging. Most had families, children, grandchildren, living within a reasonable driving distance, yet they remained largely alone and emotionally abandoned. I came to the personal conviction that more of the elderly needed to live with their families.

I held that job for the balance of my seminary training, and two years after I graduated, my wife and I took my parents into our home. They lived with my wife, my children, and me for 24 years. My mother Connie went home to be with Jesus ten years ago. She succumbed to the ravages of Alzheimer's at the age of 86, and we had the privilege of taking care of her at home for the entire duration of her illness. On June 24, 2005, her spirit ascended to her heavenly home from the loving environment of her earthly home. My dad went home to heaven in November 2013. When the kids were little, Mom & Dad enjoyed their grandchildren on their lap with a book. Those same grandchildren as young adults helped attend to their daily needs until their passing. Even though we experienced a number of challenges through the years, all our lives were enriched by the give and take of our mutual love.

Not all parents need to move in with their children—although I'm convinced more Christians need to consider this option—but as children, we must honor our parents by communicating with them regularly, involving them in our family activities, visiting them, engaging them, and recognizing them for the blessing they are to our families.

Honoring our parents with our hands, feet—and wallets!

For some, honoring parents will require physical, tangible support. Obviously, when parents become unexpectedly ill or simply grow elderly, some children will need to intervene with daily hands-on care, and for many this will demand a direct financial investment in their parents' welfare. It is noteworthy that two of the three references to honor parents in the New Testament revolve around a financial exhortation. First, consider the words of Jesus in Matthew 15:3–9:

> And He answered and said to them, "Why do you yourselves transgress the commandment of God for the sake of your tradition? For God said, 'Honor your father and mother,' and, 'He who speaks evil of father or mother is to be put to death.' But you [the religious leaders] say, 'Whoever says to his father or mother, "Whatever I have that would help you has been given to God," he is not to honor [financially support] his father or his mother.' And by this you invalidated the word of God for the sake of your tradition. You hypocrites, rightly did Isaiah prophesy of you: 'This people honors me with their lips, But their heart is far away from Me. But in vain do they worship Me, Teaching as doctrines the precepts of men.'"

In Christ's day, rabbinical tradition made it possible for grown children to circumvent the financial support of their parents by dedicating their wealth to God. By claiming this rabbinical exemption, their money was technically tied up in a higher purpose and "given to God as a gift." Since such vows to the Lord were considered inviolable, their wealth was, therefore, unavailable to help their parents. In effect, tradition trumped God's Law with a man-made clause. The injustice of ignoring the physical needs of elderly parents incensed Jesus! He excoriated the religious leaders for eclipsing God's clear word and through their tradition abetting deadbeat kids to abandon their frail parents. Obviously, the Lord Jesus felt strongly about the clarity of this commandment and the corresponding responsibility of grown children.

The Lord's astonishing sacrificial example

Christ explicitly taught us to honor our parents, and He also led the way with His astonishing sacrificial example. Hanging on the cross, His body and soul bearing the fierce judgment of God's holy hatred for sin, Jesus in His infinite compassion looked beyond His incomparable suffering to care for His aging mother. Taking note of Mary near the cross and recognizing she would need a loving environment after His ministry on earth was done, He entrusted her to the care of His beloved disciple, John.[17] As He atoned for Mary's sins (therefore meeting His mother's greatest spiritual need), He gave her a son to fill the void of His absence (thus helping to assuage the emotional pain caused by her loss). In this grand gesture, He also arranged for Mary's physical needs for the balance of her sojourn on earth. What a selfless example this is to us. The apostle John records this touching moment.

> Therefore the soldiers did these things. But standing by the cross of Jesus were His mother, and His mother's sister, Mary the wife of Clopas, and Mary Magdalene. When Jesus then saw His mother, and the disciple whom He loved standing nearby [John], He said to His mother, "Woman, behold, your son!" Then He said to the disciple, "Behold, your mother!" From that hour the disciple took her into his own household (John 19:25–27).

The words and the example of the Lord Jesus could not be more compelling. We can't atone for any of our parents' sins—only Jesus can work that great work— but we can follow in His footsteps and care for our fathers and mothers in their hour of need even when the difficulties of life envelop us and make it difficult to see beyond our needs to their distress. Enlightening is the response of John who obeyed His Savior's charge to personally care for Mary as his own mother. John didn't simply send Mary an occasional denarius and a clay greeting card, he cared for her by bringing Mary into his home to live with his family as his own mother.

The apostle Paul is also clear about the responsibility of grown children to their parents and even grandparents. Writing to Timothy—his son in the faith and pastor of the church at Ephesus—Paul carefully instructed this young shepherd about the role of widows in the church and the financial responsibility for their care. The first and straightforward financial axiom in Paul's discussion is this: children (and grandchildren) bear the financial responsibility for taking care of widows within the family (1 Timothy 5:3–8). Paul writes,

> *Honor* [financially support] *widows who are widows indeed; but if any widow has children or grandchildren, they must first learn to practice piety* [godliness] *in regard to their own family and to make some return to their parents; for this is acceptable in the sight of God* (1 Timothy 5:3–4).

The biblical message is clear, children are indebted to their parents, and if life circumstances demand it, they must see to their physical needs. For some of us, obedience will mean supporting needy parents financially, and in some cases it will involve taking parents into our own homes. This may be costly for us on several levels (money, time, freedom, privacy), but following God's precepts is always the best way, though not always the easiest. What's more, as we shall see in our next section, obedience does not come empty handed. It brings with it the smile of God to our lives.

Showing practical piety to our parents may be the most difficult option for some of us to assume, but it is the right and most blessed choice to make. I can say this confidently because Scripture plainly tells me so, and also because it is a decision my wife and I have had to make and live with. Twenty-five years ago, after a lot of prayer and dialogue between my wife, my parents, and me, we made the decision to bring my mom and dad to live with us. I would be less than honest if I didn't tell you that caring for my folks has been a challenge on multiple levels. That said, I would be remiss if I didn't also tell you that our decision more than two decades ago was right and that it has resulted in a boatload of joyful blessings simply too numerous to recount in this book.

The wisdom of our time will invariably challenge God's clear teaching on the family, and as we stated at the beginning of this chapter, we can easily find ourselves tapping our toes to the rhythm of our culture. We need to stop, listen, and identify the soundtrack playing inside our minds and hearts. Are we listening to the misguided droning of the world, or are we tuned in to God's message for our domestic relationships? Are we availing ourselves of God's provision for obedience?

"So, who are you going to serve?"

Obviously, there are many other divine truths about the family that stand against the failed counsel of the world. God's precepts are there for our good and for the taking. My dear friends, God has given us His word so that we might walk in His sure and proven paths. He has given us the Bible to steer us away from the precipitous ways of this world and the limited (at best) or dangerous (at worst) counsel of men. Aren't you glad God has not abandoned us to the folly of this age or left us to guess at what He wants, or to grope about in the dark for what is best for us and our households?

God has given us His word as our provision for obedience, yet this is a provision that can be neglected and rejected. We must decide what pattern for the family will shape our homes, the world's passing wisdom or God's proven eternal words (Matthew 24:35). If we determine to follow God's prescription for our families, make no mistake about it, that decision will be tested at critical crossroads continually. We will be mocked by the world; many will attempt to make us look foolish, unsophisticated, or stupid. We will be misunderstood—often by those closest to us—and we will be cajoled to forsake our biblical convictions; we will be tempted to abandon God's principles by the manifold seductions of our day, but like Joshua and his generation, we must resolve by God's superlative grace to stay God's course and follow Him alone.

> If it is disagreeable in your sight to serve the LORD, choose for yourselves today whom you will serve... but as for me and my house, we will serve the LORD. The people said to Joshua, "We will serve the LORD our God and we will obey His voice" (Joshua 24:15, 24).

God has provided an abundant resource for our obedience: Scripture; and yet, that's not God's only supply through His word, because obedience has a twin sister and she is called Blessing. The Bible—through obedience—is also God's provision for our blessing.

The Bible is God's provision for our blessing

Where truth and obedience meet, there you will find God's choicest blessings. Please understand, this is God's heart for you and your family. He longs to bless your home. He wants to pour out His manifold blessings on you, your spouse, your children, your grandchildren. His generous heart pulses to bring benediction to His people. Do you realize that? Is it a fixed truth in your mind that God loves to bless His beloved, or is your understanding of God's intentions blurred by the shadows of personal experience and the world's lies? Allow me to state this plainly: as sure as God wants you to obey, so He desires with equal passion to bless you and your family.

Speaking through His servant Moses, the Lord declares in Deuteronomy 6:3, "*O Israel, you should listen and be careful to do it.*" God pleads with His people to walk in His precepts. Why? Note God's clear purpose, "*that it may be well with you and that you may multiply greatly, just as the Lord, the God of your fathers, has promised you.*" God called Israel to obey so that He might fulfill all His plans to bless them. That was the Lord's heartfelt objective.

We see a similar impassioned expression of God's longing to bless His people in the previous chapter, Deuteronomy 5. There God erupts with, "*Oh that they had such a heart in them, that they would fear Me and keep all My commandments always*" (v. 29). God cries out, as it were, for the obedience of His people. The term "*Oh*" in Hebrew expresses a passionate longing.[18] It is used similarly in Psalm 55:6 where David, surrounded by the real and present danger of his enemies, cries out, "*Oh, that I had wings like a dove! I would fly away and be at rest.*" David groans the urgent and deep longing of his soul, which is a desire to escape from the terror of his enemies and experience the sweet peace of safety. This term ("*Oh*") expresses an impassioned cry.

Deuteronomy 5:29 reveals to us the fervent longing of God's heart. God cries out for a tenderhearted, obedient people. And why does the Lord so deeply desire the obedience of His congregation? It is because He yearns to bless them and the generations who follow them. Listen to God's visceral cry for Israel of old and for you and your family as well, "*Oh that they had such a heart in them, that they would fear Me and keep all My commandments always* [now notice the "why of it all], *that it may be well with them and with their sons forever*" (emphasis added). My fellow Christian parents, this is the heart of God toward you and your family.

God has given us His word as our provision first for obedience, and through obedience as His provision for His rich and manifold blessings. The Lord who created the institution of the family, who wisely established its function, who knows what the family needs, has revealed His design for our marriages and our parenting so that we might follow His pattern and in so doing experience His benevolent smile on our homes.

"But what about him... her... them?"

"What if I'm in a one-sided relationship?"—i.e., you truly desire God's blessing on your family, but you live with an unsaved spouse or unsaved, disobedient children who are older, perhaps even grown and gone. You may even live with parents who do not have a personal relationship with God through Jesus Christ. How can you bring about God's blessings on your home when you're the only one who cares to follow the Lord?

First of all, we can't bring about anything by our own power; only God can change lives, households. As with all things in life, we must entrust ourselves to God and focus on our own obedience. If we trust and obey, we can count on two things: God will never neglect our cry for help, and we can be certain the Lord will work out His good and perfect plan in our lives (Psalm 4:3; 34:17–18; 69:33; Romans 8:26–30).

Your chief concern regardless of the spiritual state of your home needs to be your personal trust in the Lord evidenced by a life of obedience. It's interesting to note that the biblical imperatives to parents, children, and spouses in the New Testament are given irrespective of the responsibility of other parties. God never says, "Parents, lead your children so long as they're docile and cooperative." "Children obey your parents only if they're Christians." "Husbands, love your wives if they're lovable." "Wives, respect your husbands if they've earned it."

God calls us to concern ourselves primarily with our own obedience and our personal trust in Him. Rest assured, He will bless those who are faithful to Him. What biblical role has God called you to fulfill? Set your heart to follow that path because that is where you'll find God's richest blessings. Remember, unless spouses or parents ask loved ones to contradict God's word, it is in the wife's and child's best interest to submit to their divinely appointed familial authority. It is the husband's privilege to selflessly love his wife regardless of his wife's spiritual condition, and it is the duty of parents to biblically shepherd their children. Make it your ambition to fulfill the role God has designed for you to play in your family, and trust the Lord to bless your life and home through His sovereign grace.

"Obedience + blessings = NO trials—right?"

God desires to visit our homes with peace, relational harmony, and palpable joy. My friend, isn't that what you long for in your home? If it is, then the good news is that the Lord has provided His path to lead you to the bounty of these blessings and many others. You see, when husbands lovingly lead, protect, and nurture their wives; when wives respect their husbands and follow their leadership; when children recognize the authority of their parents and submit to their guidance, the smile of God will rest upon our homes—even when life is trying!

Please understand, I'm not saying that if we simply endeavor to obey God's word we will not experience deep and difficult trials. I think this is our wishful fantasy at times, and there are even some who would erroneously claim freedom from suffering as a promise. However, neither wishful thinking nor false belief will exempt us from hardship. No one gets to fast-forward the difficulties in life.

Have you ever played Monopoly? One of the most coveted exemptions when the game turns hostile is the "Advance Directly to 'Go'" card. This little tool of fortune allows the player to skip all the toil and danger on the board and advance to "Go," where he or she collects a cool two hundred bucks because—because he drew the card. Hmmm, bypass all your troubles and get a reward for the smooth ride. That's a nice little bone to have thrown your way in Monopoly, but there is no such device in life. That is not God's design for us as individuals or as families. Jesus promised, "*In the world you have tribulation*" (John 16:33), and the apostle Peter reminds us in 1 Peter 2:21, "*For you have been called for this purpose* [suffering], *since Christ also suffered for you, leaving you an example for you to follow in His steps.*"

Plan on it, you and I will suffer in this life and we should not shrink back from God's severe mercy. Suffering is a useful tool in the Master's hand to purge and perfect us on our pilgrimage to heaven (Psalm 119:71; Acts

14:22; 2 Corinthians 4:16–18; 11:23–29; 12:9–10; James 1:2–4; 5:10–11; 1 Peter 5:10). Don't buy the false and debilitating notion that suffering is not from God (Psalm 119:75; John 18:11; Hebrews 12:9–11). The God who orchestrates everything for our good plans our suffering (Romans 8:28; Job 2:9–10). In fact, often the most marvelous blessings of obedience are found in the midst of suffering. As my all-time favorite pastor, C. H. Spurgeon, once said, "They who dive in the sea of affliction bring up rare pearls."[19]

One of the most grace-filled, joyful times in our family's history came during a great hour of testing. In February of 2005, my wife, Valorie, was diagnosed with breast cancer. Shortly after her diagnosis, she underwent a double mastectomy and began the harshest regimen of chemotherapy available in the medical arsenal against her type of cancer. In the subsequent weeks and months, she became deathly ill as result of her treatments. The noxious cocktail she received, combined with her slight frame and her particular reaction to the chemotherapy, put her on a bed of pain from which she struggled to rise. To this day, Valorie still deals with daily chronic pain from the poison that saved her life.

In the midst of her treatments, I often looked at my beloved wife collapsed on our living room couch, pale, listless, in obvious pain, wishing I could relieve her discomfort. The only thing I could do at times was sit by her side and pray, sometimes through irrepressible tears. (Happy footnote, Valorie has completed her tenth-year anniversary of being cancer-free, and her pain, though still present, has diminished greatly and is managed successfully.)

At the same time Valorie was in the throes of her cancer treatment, my mother—for whom we cared in our home—succumbed to the latter ravages of Alzheimer's and required 24/7 care. When Mom soiled herself, my children and I (often with Valorie's help) cleaned her and changed her clothes and linens. We nursed her bedsores; we tried with little success to assuage her confusion; we rushed to her side morning, noon, and night and comforted her when her fears overwhelmed her. We spoon-fed her until she could no longer eat; we held her hand and stroked her forehead when she lay in bed. We watched her brain slowly shut down until her body gave out and Jesus called her home. A corollary challenge we faced as my mother's mind and body faded was the care of my dad, who had his own medical issues and who had a difficult time processing the shocking degeneration of his life partner.

Compounding the medical challenges our family faced at that time was unforeseen difficulty in ministry. Unexpectedly, we found ourselves navigating through the most difficult ministry conflict of our lives. The church I pastored at the time had ballooned from a Bible study of three dozen or so to a fellowship of nearly four hundred people in less than three years. The people of the church loved us; they loved one another; and yet, concurrent with God's blessing, we hit an unexpected squall among the leadership that eventually led me to step down from the church's pulpit. In many ways, the heartache of that experience superseded the physical trials.

I will tell you, that was a difficult season of life for the Tolopilos. We wept often, sometimes deeply, soulfully. I remember Psalm 69 being my frequent daily bread in the shadow of that valley. But if that's all I told you about that period of difficulty, I would not be giving you the complete picture, because as we clung to God and His promises, God singularly blessed our family with a cornucopia of spiritual blessings. The members of the church I helped shepherd showered us with amazing deeds of love and affection.

In the midst of that hardship, we continually experienced the palpable presence and joy of Christ in our home. God gave us joy in Him and in each other. He amalgamated and coalesced our family in a deep bond of love that has only grown since then. Even more, though we did weep, I can tell you we laughed often, and sometimes we laughed so hard we cried. Knowing our God loved us and sovereignly held our lives in the hollow of His hand not only liberated us to see the humor in our condition, but it also gave us rest and peace as the storm of life raged around us. Our home, really the very crucible of our testing, was also God's oasis of comfort and joy.

God desires to build your home into a fortress of peace and joy. That's the norm God wants to establish in the church: strong, healthy, joyful families, citadels of light for the gospel in a dark and suffering world. Folks, God's ways are not broken, and He has given us the great treasure of His word so that we might walk in His ways and in turn experience His boundless blessings. The Bible is God's provision for our obedience, for our blessing, and also our road map for knowing and loving Him.

CHAPTER 6

God's Word, the Road Map to Knowing & Loving God

Scripture: The road map for knowing and loving God

As we have seen, God has abundantly supplied to our families the way of obedience and blessing in the treasure of His self-disclosure, the Bible. This great resource is also the Lord's provision for growing in our relationship with Him. The Bible reveals to us who God is so that we might know Him as He truly is and so that our affections might be kindled by the absolute beauty of His great person.

The number one goal of life

As we follow the flow of this life-altering text (Deuteronomy 6:1–9), we come to the most consequential principle not simply in the present passage or in the book of Deuteronomy, but the preeminent commandment in all of sacred writ, i.e., the Bible boils down to this one life goal. What we are about to consider in Deuteronomy 6:4–5 is the most important directive in the whole of God's revelation to His people. Here we have the highest, the most lovely and infinitely precious duty of all who are bound to God by relationship. This commandment stands as the monumental goal of every believer's life. What is that goal? It is our call to love the true and living God with our entire being.

> "Hear, O Israel! The LORD is our God, the LORD is one! You shall love the LORD your God with all your heart and with all your soul and with

all your might" (Deuteronomy 6:4–5). The Lord Jesus called this imperative "*the great and foremost commandment*" (Matthew 22:38).

The road map to get there

If this is the most essential pursuit in all of life, if it is the most important preoccupation of our existence, then we need to get about it; and therefore, the burning question becomes, how do we pursue such a grand goal? What is the road map that guides us to seek God and to love Him with our whole heart? Furthermore, how does this pursuit relate to shepherding our families? More of this in a moment, but first let's consider the primary question. What is the road map that leads us to know God as we ought and therefore to love Him for who He is?

In answer to this all-important question, the text of Deuteronomy 6 directs us to a familiar, tried, and tested set of navigational charts. We have seen that the Bible is God's provision for our obedience and blessing. Continuing in that same vein, we realize that God's word is also our provision, God's road map, if you will, for knowing Him in truth and loving Him to the utmost measure. No other source will do. Only God's perfect self-disclosure will lead us to who He truly is and ignite our affections for Him.

Any knowledge of God that contradicts or misrepresents Scripture is false and leads to idolatry. Think about what that means. To the degree that you and I don't properly understand what the Bible says about God, to that degree we can't love and adore Him for who He is. What's more, to the degree that we accept extra-biblical information about God, to that same degree our understanding of God is corrupted. This in turn robs us of the pleasure of loving Him and puts us at cross-purposes with God's greatest priority for our lives, to "*love the LORD your God with all your heart and with all your soul and with all your might.*"

Frankly, that's why I don't have a twig of patience for new and novel notions of God or "fresh words" of revelation concerning the person of God, cultural preconceptions of God, or intuitive presumptions of the person of God. We need tried-and-true paths directly from God that take us away (far away) from misguided, meandering, self-deceiving, and ruinous intuition (Jeremiah 17:9). We need the authentic, proven road map God has provided for us to follow so that we might know and love Him in the beauty of His self-disclosed glory. Just like the Israelites of old, we must guard against idolatrous ideas of God and seek Him, as Jesus instructed the woman at the well, *"in spirit and truth"* (John 4:23–24).

May the Lord equip us to that end. As we have just stated, the Scripture informs our minds about who God is and fuels our affections for Him. God's word is the divine road map that guides us to know God and to love Him, and that is the simple direction the text takes us. Let's track that trail and follow the flow of thought unveiled in Deuteronomy 6:4–5.

Verses 4 and 5 were so essential to the well-being of Israel that they (along with verses 6–9) became the principal confession of faith for the entire nation. These verses became a treasured liturgy recited twice a day by pious Jews who said of this duty, "Blessed are we, who every morning and evening say, 'Hear, O Israel, the Lord our God is one Lord.'"[1] This was Israel's prime directive stated in one simple yet ideologically packed statement and command. From the very first word of verse 4, *"Hear,"* we get a sense of the tremendous import these three sentences carry. The verb *"Hear"* (the Hebrew word *shema*) became the title for this central confession of faith, "The Shema of Israel."

"Stop, look and listen"

Standing like a theological beacon at the pinnacle of this lighthouse, the word shema doesn't simply mean "listen up." Rather, the term carries the idea of listening attentively, intelligently, with a view toward obedience.[2] When my children were little and I needed to communicate something important to them (usually regarding their well-being), I would sometimes have to stand them in front of me, calm them gently with my hand on their shoulder, and with the other hand cup their little chin, ask them to look me in the eye, let them know that what Daddy was about to say was really important, and then proceed to give them my instruction.

In Deuteronomy 6:4 and 5, God is holding the collective face of His people in His hands, and with their attention secured, the Lord calls Israel to listen to what He is about to say with discernment, with understanding, and with a willingness to obey. The Lord is commanding the Israelites to listen carefully and embrace truth that is critical to their survival as a people.

God's self-disclosure to His people

God revealed Himself to Israel in His Law. It is this self-disclosure God beckons them to obey in Deuteronomy 6:1–3 and to place on their heart in verse 6, and in this particular key statement of His Law found in Deuteronomy 6:4 the Lord unveils who He is, His relationship to His people, and the singular uniqueness of His person. By embracing this revelation, Israel would be set apart to fulfill the greatest commandment in the entire Bible, to walk intimately with the true and living God (v. 5).

The eternal, self-existent God

Listen to these illuminating and astonishing words God declares through His servant Moses in Deuteronomy 6:4. "*Hear, O Israel! the LORD is our God, the LORD is one!*" Right after compelling the Israelites to listen with a teachable heart, the Lord proclaims to His people who He is. He unfolds His character by declaring His name. Twice in the span of one short sentence the Lord emphatically proclaims His name to Israel, "*The LORD* [Yahweh] *is our God, the LORD* [Yahweh] *is one!*" This is the very name God revealed to Moses when He commissioned the humble shepherd to deliver His people from the oppression of the Egyptians (Exodus 3:13–15).

In declaring His name, God was not simply giving a designation of Himself to Moses and the Israelites, He was doing much more, for He was revealing His actual nature to them. God was declaring who He was. When we name our children we give them names that are sentimentally valuable to us. We often name our kids after beloved friends, relatives, or perhaps admired heroes. We may even give them names we hope will express their character, "Hope," "Charity," "Faith," "Honor."

It's a good thing we give human beings their names at the beginning of life's journey; otherwise, with hindsight and reputation our names might turn out slightly different. "I'll have to see some ID with your credit card, sir. Thank you Mr. Schlep-Lazy-Pants. Would you like some assistance out to your car? You would prefer a piggyback ride? Very well, I'll call one of our bigger couriers. You may slouch in this chair until he arrives," or "Welcome Miss I-Have-An-Anger-Problem. Will you be dining alone with your angry self tonight or will Mr. Passive-Procrastinator be joining you this evening? You say he doesn't know yet? Please try to keep your voice down. I'll order you a decaf." If people were named after their proven character, we would all experience some awkward introductions. Perhaps that's why we name our young sentimentally and early.

Names are hopeful devices for us mortals. For the Lord, His name is a statement of fact. It is a revelation of character, of being. With His name, God pulls back the curtain on His nature and reveals the glory of His great person to his beloved intimates, and in that name we find reason to worship Him, and we find benefit for our souls. In Deuteronomy 6:4, God proclaims His name twice, declaring to His people Israel that He is "*The Lord*," Yahweh.

A good translation of Yahweh is "the One who is," "the existing One," which points us to the mind-stretching reality that God is self-existent, completely self-sufficient, eternal, and absolutely unchanging. In other words, Yahweh—the Lord—has life within Himself. He is not dependent on any of His creatures. He has always existed and He will always be as He is. That being so, God is the source of all life and sustenance. All that creation needs and enjoys has its source in the self-existent One who gives generously to His creatures. To the men of Athens, Paul proclaimed God's self-existence with these words: "*The God who made the world and all things in it, since He is Lord of heaven and earth, does not dwell in temples made with hands; nor is He served by human hands, as though He needed anything, since He Himself gives to all people life and breath and all things*" (Acts 17:24–25).

In the name Yahweh, the Lord manifests that He completely transcends His creation, and yet, because He has created and sustains, we see that He reaches out in benevolent provision to His creatures. There is no one who has ever breathed a breath that he or she did not borrow from the existing One, the source of all life. Men are creatures who are dependent on God daily for life and sustenance. We need to eat and drink multiple times each day; we need to sleep for one-third of our lives in order to repair and restore our aging bodies. Men have a beginning and an end. They are born, grow, weaken, and die. We change from the moment we are conceived to the day our bodies are laid in the soil to return to the dust. We are reminded every day that we are mortal, dependent, finite, and fading.

Through His name, the Lord reminded Moses and the Israelites that He was transcendent, that is, beyond His creation and their experience. Unlike man, God is self-existent, eternal, unchanging. And yet in that same beautiful name,

Yahweh, the Lord manifested His immanence or His nearness to His people in that He was the inexhaustible supply for their every need and weakness. There was no deficit Israel could ever experience beyond God's ability to meet. Whatever the depth of want in His people—physical or spiritual—God's infinite resources, His indefatigable power would remain unchanged and dwarf any challenge, small or great. God's name, "Yahweh," preached these truths to Israel.

The God who is joined to His people

The revered name Yahweh speaks primarily of God's transcendent, incommunicable attributes.[3] It reminds us that God is massively great, so great that our finite minds struggle to comprehend the fringes of His awesome person, and that struggle brings with it tension. Pure greatness can be daunting for finite creatures such as ourselves.

To acknowledge that God is eternal and unchanging, to recognize that He is completely self-sufficient, independent of anyone and in need of nothing, is to be cognizant of God's aseity (God's absolute self sufficiency).[4] By itself, this realization seems more intimidating than comforting. Yet, the name of God is not proclaimed in a vacuum. God declares His name, Yahweh, in the context of a covenant relationship, "*Hear, O Israel! The LORD is our God* (emphasis added)." That possessive pronoun changes everything, doesn't it?

The great transcendent God had joined Himself to the people of Israel. This band of desert dwellers could claim the infinite God as their own! God and His people belonged to one another. Often in the Old Testament, Israel is called God's inheritance. "*For the LORD's portion is His people; Jacob is the allotment of His inheritance*" (Deuteronomy 32:9). The Lord possessed His people as a treasure. Likewise, Israel possessed the Lord as their portion. This is why David the king of Israel could write, "*The LORD is the portion of my inheritance and my cup,*" and Asaph echoed, "*My flesh and my heart may fail, but God is the strength of my heart and my portion forever*" (Psalm 16:5; 73:26).

Yahweh and Israel were in the mutual embrace of relationship: "*Blessed is the nation whose God is the LORD, the people whom He has chosen for His own inheritance*" (Psalm 33:12). Yahweh was not a far and distant Majesty. He was the God *of* Israel; and therefore, He and His manifold greatness was their inheritance as a people. "*Hear, O Israel! The LORD is our God.*"

The singular uniqueness of God's person

Lastly, in the text of Deuteronomy 6:4, God states the absolute uniqueness of His person to the Israelites. *"Hear, O Israel! The Lᴏʀᴅ is our God, the Lᴏʀᴅ is one!"* The Jews had fled from the polytheistic amalgam of Egypt. As a people they failed to stay true to Yahweh during their forty years in the Sinai desert. From the very onset of their exodus experience, the people displayed a deadly attraction to polytheism (belief in many gods) and syncretism (adapting false religions to the worship of the one true God, e.g., Exodus 32:1; Deuteronomy 9:16).

Polytheistic paganism proved a scourge to Israel not just at the beginning of their forty years of wandering but throughout their sojourn. In the book of Amos, God chided Israel for their flagrant spiritual harlotry while in the desert. *"Did you present Me with sacrifices and grain offerings in the wilderness for forty years, O house of Israel? You also carried along Sikkuth your king and Kiyyun, your images, the star of your gods which you made for yourselves"* (Amos 5:25–26). Israel as a people struggled to stay faithful to the one true God. Through their wilderness wandering, the Lord purged Israel of many of her compromising influences.

Now at last the people were on the steps of Canaan, eager to conquer the land promised to their fathers, but Canaan was a land filled with false worship. Canaan was a paganistic stew of false gods and deplorable religious practices, and given Israel's endemic allure to false gods, the conquest of Canaan was fraught with great spiritual danger. With that history and in this context, the Lord proclaims through Moses a truth that stood in stark contrast to the spiritual cancer of paganism. The Lord declared that He was the absolute and only God, King over all creation. He was the only One to whom the name Yahweh belonged. *"The Lᴏʀᴅ* [Yahweh] *is one!"* This simple clause obliterated the concept of polytheism and the notion of syncretism. The Lord reminded Israel that all other so-called deities were no gods at all. He alone was the eternal One, God in relationship with His people.

To know Him is to love Him

Deuteronomy 6:4 beckoned Israel to listen attentively and understand who the Lord was, Yahweh, that He was their God, and that He was the only true and living God, King of all the universe. And based on this right theology of God arising from God's Law, the covenant citizen was then commanded to occupy himself with the greatest pursuit of the redeemed: to love the God revealed in Scripture with his entire being. Chapter 6, verse 5 reads, "*You shall love the LORD your God with all your heart and with all your soul and with all your might.*" In this verse, God commands, yes, demands that His people love Him with their entire being. He was calling the Jew to engage his affections, his intellect, his physical strength and to consecrate his whole person to love God undividedly.

Perhaps it sounds rather odd to you that God would command the Israelites to love Him. How could anyone command another's affection? This is precisely why Israel was instructed to know God, to have a right theology of God, because to know the Lord in truth prepares and stimulates the heart to love Him. God revealed Himself through His Law to distinguish His true self from the pantheon of false gods among the people of Canaan, and He entrusted His self-disclosure to Israel so that they might know Him for who He truly is, and knowing Him, love Him with an undivided heart.

So how does this apply to us?

To this point we have briefly considered the first two verses of the Shema in its relation to the people of Israel (Deuteronomy 6:4–5). This is because it was written to instruct the Jewish nation at a critical crossroad in her early history. In order to comprehend a passage of Scripture clearly, we must understand it contextually. Having done that, how does this passage apply to Christians today and especially to our families?

Perhaps you're thinking, "Well, since this was written to the Jews way back at the beginning of their history as a nation, I'm probably off the hook. I can enjoy Deuteronomy 6 as part of Israel's historical narrative and let the story sleepily lay between the covers of my Bible, walk away and forget about it." If you are thinking that, stop it! Knock it off! It's not true! These truths reach down through the millennia and speak with relevance to you and me today. These precepts are at the heart of faithful living and therefore at the heart of discipleship in the home.

The cornerstone of biblical theology and faithful discipleship

My friends, knowing and loving God is truly the cornerstone of biblical theology and faithful discipleship. It is the greatest commandment in the entire Bible. It was given to us by God through His servant Moses and reiterated 1400 years later by none other than Jesus Himself (Deuteronomy 6:4–5; Mark 12:28–34). Christ's words are recorded in all three synoptic gospels (Matthew 22, Mark 12, Luke 10), and I would like to turn our attention briefly to the words of Mark. In chapter 12, the gospel of Mark informs us that the Lord Jesus was in Jerusalem. On this particular occasion, the Lord was arguing with the Sadducees and confounding His enemies by skillfully using the Scriptures to affirm the doctrine of the resurrection—which the Sadducees denied. Listening to the exchange between Jesus and the hostile Sadducees was a scribe who, after hearing the Lord's adroit response, came up to Jesus and asked a bold question.

Obviously, Jesus held an unparalleled understanding of the Scriptures, and the scribe, an expert in Old Testament Law himself, basically asked Jesus to prioritize the Bible down to one all-important commandment. Pretty audacious, isn't it? In essence he said, "Rabbi, reduce all of God's word down to one all-important thing. Give me a life priority list of one. What is the most important thing that I can ever do with my life?" or as it is stated in the gospel of Mark, "*What commandment is the foremost of all?*" (Mark 12:28). Jesus answered him with these familiar words, "*The foremost is, 'HEAR, O ISRAEL! THE LORD OUR GOD IS ONE LORD; AND YOU SHALL LOVE THE LORD YOUR GOD WITH ALL YOUR HEART, AND WITH ALL YOUR SOUL, AND WITH ALL YOUR MIND, AND WITH ALL YOUR STRENGTH*'" (Mark 12:28–30). Jesus told the scribe—whom the text tells us was asking this question earnestly—to occupy himself first and foremost with this singular priority. The Lord Jesus honored the question of this sincere scholar with the exhortation to engage himself, to abandon himself to this one great pursuit—to know and to love God!

My dear brothers and sisters, the necessity of this one pursuit has not changed for New Testament believers. In fact, because of the new covenant through the blood of the Lord Jesus—and the spiritual privileges that accrue to us as a result (e.g., the indwelling triune God, John 14:16–17, John 14:23)—we are far better equipped to fulfill this great commandment than Old Testament believers ever were.

Living out the Shema has to be the hallmark of a Christian. Jesus Himself made this magnificent pursuit possible through His life, death, resurrection, and ascension to heaven, from where He sent His Holy Spirit to fill His church and enable His people to live this truth. He also underscored its importance with His words in the gospels (Matthew 22:36–39; Mark 12:28–34; Luke 10:25–28), and even though Deuteronomy 6:4–5 is not directly quoted in the epistles, the exhortation to know and love God absolutely permeates the pages of the New Testament. This great commandment becomes pervasive in the New Testament.

Knowing God—not just a great book, but our ever present need!

Years ago J. I. Packer wrote one of the most needful books of the last hundred years. Its simple title was *Knowing God* and I still highly recommend it to Christians at every stage of maturity.[5] In two words, Packer summarized the ever present and profound need of all believers, to know the God of their salvation. Just as the Israelites needed a solid, growing comprehension of Yahweh, Christians must grow in their understanding of God and His Son.

Paul exhorted the Colossians to walk in a manner that was pleasing to the Lord by "*increasing in the knowledge of God*" (Colossians 1:10). Peter commanded his readers to crave God's truth—and therefore to thirst for a knowledge of God—with the same desperation and passion a newborn baby craves its mother's milk (1 Peter 2:2). What's more, it's interesting to note that Peter uses an imperative in his exhortation. He literally commands us to strongly desire God's word (see Chapter 10) and therefore to have a passion to know our God. In Peter's second epistle, the apostle prayed that grace and peace would abound in the lives of fellow believers through or "*in the knowledge of God and of Jesus our Lord*" (2 Peter 1:2). Three chapters later he commands (another imperative) these same Christians to "*grow in the grace and knowledge of our Lord and Savior Jesus Christ*" (2 Peter 3:18).

Believers today, like the Jews of the conquest, desperately need a growing, accurate understanding of God Almighty. Why are believers in all ages exhorted to grow in their understanding of God? In part, we need to know God because idolatry is always a threat. Not only do the temptations and baubles of this age continually threaten to dethrone God from His supreme place in our lives, but there are many counterfeit notions of God out there that would cheat us of a true knowledge of God. And frankly, a corrupted knowledge of God robs us of a greater capacity to adore Him, to love Him for who He truly is, and that deprives us of a deepening intimacy with God.

The old bait and switch

There is no greater spiritual theft Satan can devise than to keep the truth of who God is from the mind. One of the most effective ways the enemy pulls off this cosmic swindle is through the old bait and switch con. He offers people an inviting religious morsel that looks like the knowledge of God, but in reality he pawns off a poisonous imitation injurious to all who swallow it. With the advent of modern media, false ideas of God are rampant. Have any of them crept into your thinking? Consider the following.

The "Cosmic Santa" fraud

There are some who would tell us, for example, that God is duty bound—energized by our will, faith, and words—to bless us with vigorous health and unfettered wealth. This ideology views God as a Cosmic Santa willing and waiting to fulfill our every whim and fetch our every want. Poverty, suffering, sickness have one root cause in the minds of these folks, a lack of faith. God is not wholly sovereign over us—they would insist—but rather He is subject to us through our faith.

My friends, that is not the God of the Bible. Jesus Christ, God in the flesh said, "*In the world you have tribulation.*" Jesus reminds us that suffering is part of our life reality in this fallen world, yet Jesus also promised, "*but take courage; I have overcome the world*" (John 16:33). In other words, Christ encourages us to be comforted in our suffering because He has secured our ultimate victory through His death and resurrection, but don't lose that first point; He guarantees we will suffer in this life as He did. The apostle Peter reminds us that our Lord blazed the trail of hardship in this world so that He might shepherd us through it. "*For you have been called for this purpose* [to suffer righteously], *since Christ also suffered for you, leaving you an example for you to follow in His steps*" (1 Peter 2:21). The difficulties we encounter in life are part of God's divine plan, not an impediment to it.

The God of the Bible is absolutely sovereign (Psalm 103:19) and works marvelously through our affliction. This is precisely why the Psalmist writes, "*It is good for me that I was afflicted,*" i.e., "It's a good thing that I have suffered!" How could he possibly make such a statement? What shaped his perspective? It was the outcome of his affliction, "*that I may learn Your statutes*" (Psalm 119:71). The psalmist declares that his hardship drove him to God's word for comfort and wisdom, and there he found it, in abundant and gratifying measure. Four verses later, his soul sings, "*I know, O LORD, that Your judgments are righteous, and that in faithfulness You have afflicted me*" (v. 75) He could see God's faithful hand in the outcome of his suffering. God teaches and refines us through suffering. The life of Job illustrates this vividly.

At the beginning of the book of Job, God's servant is described in superlative terms. For example, in chapter 1, verse 1 he is characterized as "*blameless, upright, fearing God and turning away from evil.*" That's a pretty stellar reputation! What's more, in verse 3 he is chronicled as "*the greatest of all the men of the east.*" Among the powerful and the noble of the east, the nexus of civilization, no one was considered greater than Job. As if that were not enough, God's assessment of Job—truly the only assessment that really matters—is even more amazing. It is encapsulated in the divine confession of chapter 1, verse 8 and chapter 2, verse 3. There God proclaims, "*For there is no one like him on the earth.*" God declares that Job is the godliest man on the planet! Wow! Job knew God more intimately than any man on earth!

And yet, through his great affliction, Job grew to understand God as he had never known Him before.[6] Prior to God restoring his wealth and status, Job made a startling confession. In 42:5 he declares, "*I have heard of You* [God] *by the hearing of the ear; but now my eye sees You.*" Job was stating that through his deep suffering he (the greatest man in the East, the most righteous man on earth) had come to know God in a marvelous and superior way. He himself described the growth and intimacy of his knowledge of God as the difference between hearing—his former understanding of the great person of God—and seeing, the manner in which he had come to know God through his suffering. In this fallen world, hardships are inevitable, but for the child of God they are never random or wasted. God uses our suffering to realize His good and glorious design in our lives.

Happily, because of Christ's victory over sin and death, one day there will be no more suffering for His people. Our hardships, having accomplished God's purposes in our lives, will vaporize in the Lord's presence (Revelation 21:4). Seeing our glorious future, the apostle John wrote, *"the first things have passed away."* The brief time of suffering (human history since the fall) will give way to an eternity of unbridled joy in God. Our present suffering will result in glory unimaginable (2 Corinthians 4:16–17); however, until that day comes, God perfects us through the difficulties we experience in our terrestrial sojourn— poverty, illness, persecution, physical and emotional pain, loss, etc.

Hardship is an effective tool God uses to strip away our weaknesses and to strengthen us in this life, while producing unthinkable eternal glory for us in the splendor of heaven (2 Corinthians 4:17; 1 Peter 1:6–7). To claim that God is like a supernatural errand boy that we can manipulate by our faith to produce health and wealth in this age may sell a lot of books, but that's a false representation of who God is and how He works. If you worship that kind of god, you might as well bow down to a golden calf because that is not the God of the Bible.

"The Big Guy in the Sky" view of God

There are others who consider God to be something like a practical genie. He is not too demanding—He's bottled up in the Bible or in heaven someplace—but boy if you ever need help, He is there for you! Serving Him faithfully, sacrificially, seeking His honor and glory are not really the central issues, because life is really all about us, and God wants us to be happy. God desires that we come to church—except when it's inconvenient—but He expects us to come in our comfies, to relax, to enjoy a latte, a pastry, and listen to a facilitator who can cleverly weave some anecdotes and light Scriptures together to make us feel better about the week ahead. God is a low-maintenance God who primarily exists to make our lives happier, better. Somehow He owes us that.

He's like the "big guy in the sky," or like that perfect neighbor you've always wanted... warm, friendly, accommodating, tidy, helpful. His plans never encroach on yours. He's nice to visit once in a while; he'll help you move heavy furniture at a moment's notice; he watches your parakeet when you go on vacation; at Christmas you exchange cards and fruitcake, but he lives in his own place and lets you live your life in peace. He appreciates your need of him, but he respects your need to be your own person and your need for space.

If we peddle such a view of God, we may pack people into our auditoriums with that message, but we are not giving them the God of the Bible. The God of the Bible reigns supreme over all creation, and He demands and deserves our worship and wholehearted service. The Christian life is not about us; it's about following Jesus Christ, and that will require self-denial and hardship as we follow in His steps. Jesus said, "*If anyone wishes to come after Me, he must deny himself, and take up his cross daily and follow Me*" (Luke 9:23). You ask, "Is there any pleasure in committing ourselves to God?" Yes, there is exceeding joy in knowing Him, and He gives us deep and satisfying pleasure, the kind of pleasure that self-indulgence cannot mimic, but we find that joy and pleasure as we commit ourselves to Him and His well-deserved glory (Psalm 16:11; 73:25; John 15:11; 17:13; Romans 14:17; 1 Peter 1:8). Friends, being in the kingdom of God is not about us but about the glory of the King.

> *Oh, the depth of the riches both of the wisdom and knowledge of God! How unsearchable are His judgments and unfathomable His ways! For WHO HAS KNOWN THE MIND OF THE LORD, OR WHO BECAME HIS COUNSELOR? OR WHO HAS FIRST GIVEN TO HIM THAT IT MIGHT BE PAID BACK TO HIM AGAIN? For from Him and through Him and to Him are all things. To Him be the glory forever. Amen* (Romans 11:33–36).

The "Impotent Helper"

Then there is the "Impotent Helper" view of God that arises from the murky pools of the works righteousness swamp. These folks espouse the familiar dictum, "God helps those who help themselves." They would assert belief in a powerful God, with the caveat, "Oh yes, God is mighty, alright, but when it comes to salvation you have to contribute your part, share the load, pull your weight."

Not surprisingly, this weak view of God spills over into all of life. For example, when trials come there is an intellectual assent to the power of God, but there is a blind and willful commitment to one's own strength. The attitude is, "If we are going to get through real hardships we have to pull ourselves up by our bootstraps, lean into the wind and bear the burden." What ultimately arises from this errant perspective is utter despair. That's when the hardships of this world crash into our lives, devastate our flimsy self-confidence, wash us out into the merciless tides of uncertainty, and leave us adrift in the tumultuous sea of fear and hopelessness, grasping at shadows of God that are not true and therefore cannot deliver.

The Reformation rescued millions of people from this erroneous view of God and the gospel by asserting the biblical doctrine that salvation is completely apart from our works and by grace alone, through faith alone, in Christ alone (Romans 3:21–30; Ephesians 2:8–9; Colossians 1:13–14). Redemption from sin is man's most desperate need, and God is strong to save. Salvation is the most powerful miracle God works in the life of a person, and if the Lord can do the greatest work—making those who are spiritually dead eternally alive in Jesus, cleansing those who are vile sinners—then He is mighty to deliver believers from all their affliction—even when they are weakest and most vulnerable (Ephesians 2:1–10; Colossians 2:13–14; 1 Timothy 1:15–16).

Paul, a man who encountered many hardships in life and ministry, said it best in 2 Corinthians 12:7–10. Having earnestly asked God to take away his "*thorn in the flesh*," a persistent affliction that "*tormented*" the great apostle, he wrote,

> *Concerning this I implored the Lord three times that it might leave me. And He has said to me, "My grace is sufficient for you, for power is perfected in weakness." Most gladly, therefore, I will rather boast about my weaknesses, so that the power of Christ may dwell in me. Therefore I am well content with weaknesses, with insults, with distresses, with persecutions, with difficulties, for Christ's sake; for when I am weak, then I am strong* (2 Corinthians 12:8–10).

Just as God is powerful to save, so He is able to work powerfully in and through our hardships. The Lord is powerful to save and to sanctify. We need to surrender our burdens to Him.

I often minister to people who have a high view of salvation—the belief I have expressed in the previous paragraphs. They joyfully concur that God is powerful to save, yet many of these same dear people sometimes fail to allow that accurate view of God to affect their areas of struggle. In their day-to-day lives, they sometimes choose to adopt a view of God that is inconsistent with what the Bible reveals about Him. For example, in a valley of depression believers may feel God doesn't really care about their trouble. Others, overwhelmed by the enormity of their trial, view God as too small to deliver them. Some may even think they are alone in their plight, disqualified from receiving God's help because of personal failures.

Practically speaking, believers sometimes fail to trust God to take care of them in their weakness. Whatever the root cause of our distrust, we allow false concepts of God to shape our thinking and affect our living. The only remedy for the faltering believer is to immerse himself or herself in the clear streams of biblical truth, to drink in the pure, unadulterated veracity of the character of God and allow that truth to wash out error and nourish faith. Truly, we need to be "*increasing in the knowledge of God*" (Colossians 1:10). God's ancient call to Israel rings with relevancy for today's believers and Christian parents.

The outgrowth of knowing God: Loving God

The Shema challenged Israel to have a right theology, or understanding of God, and we have seen how that same call permeates the New Testament and applies to the contemporary believer. As we have pointed out, however, the Shema didn't stop with verse 4. Moses urged Israel to know the one true God, but on the basis of that knowledge they were equally exhorted to love God.

This holds true for you and me today as well. The New Testament with equal force engages us to love our God (Ephesians 6:24; James 1:12; 1 Peter 1:8; 1 John 5:2). It reminds us that Christ is grieved when our love for Him wanes (Revelation 2:4), and God's Spirit speaking through Paul anathematizes all who choose not to love God: "*If anyone does not love the Lord, he is to be accursed*" (1 Corinthians 16:22). Loving the Lord is serious business to God.

Based on a right theology of who He is, God beckons us to love Him with our affections, our intellect, our physical strength, indeed with our entire being. This is the basic call of God upon His people throughout the ages. More importantly for you and me, this is God's primary call on our lives. If you forget everything else I have written but you remember and occupy yourself with this one pursuit, you are on the road to a God exalting, satisfying life.

Without question this is the greatest pursuit of the Christian. It is the greatest biblical imperative we can dedicate ourselves to: to know and love God with our whole person! You ask, "What about feeding the hungry, curing disease, caring for orphans, proclaiming the gospel to all people?" Those are wonderful and noble pursuits, but the root of all acts of true love is our love for God. This is why

Christians throughout the centuries have started so many orphanages, schools, and hospitals. This is why men and women have left the comfort of home to die in strange lands for the opportunity to tell people of Jesus Christ and His saving gospel. It is the love of God that compels Christians to love so beautifully (Romans 5:5; 2 Corinthians 5:14).

The purest expressions of Christianity flow from a genuine love for God, including our love for the household of faith, our love for the lost, the exercise of spiritual gifts, and the noblest acts of evangelism. Knowing and loving God transforms believers from the inside out. So let me say it again, this is God's top priority for your life, pursue it with abandon!

"Great exhortation, but how does this relate to the family?"

Allow me to answer that question by stating a general precept first. Increasing in your knowledge of and love for God will make you a better Christian. How so? As you grow in your knowledge of and love for God, you will delight in the Lord more, and because you delight in Him, your heart's desire will be to please Him in every aspect of your life. This inclination will produce more obedience which will bring with it God's consistent, manifold blessings and compound your joy in the Lord. With regard to the family, this transformation as a Christian man or woman will have some of its most profound impact on those closest to us.

Allow me to share a very simple and straightforward idea that is virtually absent from the contemporary discussion about the family—so much of which seems to center around strategies to reshape behavior. This is so simple yet so important. Growing in sanctification (the process of transformation into the image of Christ, becoming more and more like the Lord Jesus, growing as a believer, becoming a more consistent Christian) makes you a better husband, wife, parent, son, daughter, sibling. In other words, whatever makes you more like Jesus Christ will surely impact all your relationships, especially with those who are nearest and dearest to you. Do you desire your family to heal, to grow in love and in Christian character, in harmony with God and with one another? Then increase in your knowledge and love for God because it will transform not only how you live, but it will impact those with whom you live.

I find it interesting and enlightening that this life priority list of one (Deuteronomy 6:4–5)—the essence of the Bible reduced to one commandment: to know and love God—is given to us couched in the preeminent biblical passage on training our children spiritually (Deuteronomy 6:1–9). Of all the places God could have inserted this essential commandment, why did He choose to put it here? Why did God have Moses give this injunction to the heads of households (parents)? Why do you think that is? I'll tell you why.

One important reason the foremost commandment is placed in this great familial passage is simply because there is nothing else that will transform parents more thoroughly, more radically, than an informed, growing love for God. And nothing will impact our children spiritually more than for them to witness in their parents a dynamic passion for the one true God. Do you want to make a profound impact on your children, your grandchildren, your whole family? Make it your ambition to know God more, to love God first, to love God most. Make that your prayer!

So often we reduce "good parenting" to strategies for changing our children, schemes to alter their behavior to fall in line with what we want (the same could be said for marital counseling). There may be parenting books and seminars (Christian and secular) that promise to help you change your children's behavior, but sometimes the motivation to "change" our children's behavior through strategies is mixed. Often we seek behavioral change in our kids to avoid being embarrassed or to try to look good. However, strategies that attempt to modify outward conduct in others without addressing our own heart and that of our children may bring a short-term change, but they will fail to transform anyone in the long run.

I am not suggesting that strategies, parenting techniques, and formulas have no value. There is a time and a place to employ these effectively. And yet, if our focus is simply to amend behavior through technique, that focus—by itself—is askew. In reality, it misses the mark. In fact, it can short-circuit and possibly circumvent God's plan. God doesn't simply want to tweak our children's behavior to prevent our embarrassment, or to make us look good, or to satisfy our sense of behavioral symmetry. His desire is to transform our children, but His priority is to transform us (parents) through a living and intimate relationship with Himself. He wants to profoundly change us first, from the inside out, in order to use us as catalysts for lasting transformation in our children. That's God's priority. God wants to reshape your heart and through you change those of your children as you shepherd them. God wants our children to intimately know Him and passionately love Him, but how can they find that road if we don't show them the way? Dad, Mom, who are they going to follow?

The road map for our #1 pursuit

I love my smartphone. I can be anywhere in the country, plug in a destination address, press "route," and my Little Buddy (that's what I call my iPhone. Yes, Mac people name their machines. We're sentimental that way.) will get me wherever I need to go and tell me where I can pick up good Chinese food in the process. Truth is, I enjoy maps of all kinds and the more details, the better I like them. Maps not only show us our destination—where we want to end up—but they unfold our journey; they tell us how to get to where we're going.

This is precisely what God has provided for the lifelong journey before us. He has penned His word to show us the way to Himself. We've considered how central God's word is to this text. The Scripture is God's chief provision for our obedience, for our blessing, and we are reminded it is also the divine road map for knowing and loving our God—what a gift! The Lord always supplies what we need to fulfill His calling, and in the case of this foremost commandment, He has furnished an abundant resource, a divine road map to guide us in our great pursuit.

Unlike ordinary guides and legends, however, this road map is more than mere information, data, or coordinates on a page. Rather, in His ample grace, God has given us living words, spiritually dynamic verities that reveal who He is and transform us from the inside out. In our pursuit of the Lord, God doesn't simply supply rote directions for His people to mechanically follow, instead He provides truths to internalize so that through them He might transform our thinking, our emotions, our wills, indeed our lives. My friends, the word of God is spiritually dynamic, imbued with God's power, and transforms people; it changes us as it reveals God to us.

A matter of the heart

Consider the sure path the Lord places before His people Israel, and in principle before you and me as well: "*These words, which I am commanding you today,*" Moses wrote, "*shall be on your heart.*" The road map to knowing and loving God consists of "*these words,*" God's words, the Scripture. The term "*these words*" is used in the broadest sense. In this context, it refers to the whole counsel of God's word revealed to Israel as mentioned in verses 1 through 3.

Remember, God is addressing the heads of households (grandfathers, fathers, and by logical extension the matriarchs as well, i.e., parents). Now notice the Lord's instruction to them. Does He command the Israelites to take the sum total of His Law and place it on the shelf with other great epic works of antiquity or to display the Law on the living room coffee table to impress visitors with its ponderous girth and to serve as the family talisman? No, that is not what the text teaches, is it? Where did God command Israel to house and manifest His truth? He wanted His Law to rest upon their hearts!

What does that mean? How is the word "heart" defined in the Bible? We need to be careful not to perceive this word solely through our contemporary cultural lens, because our present-day comprehension of this term is somewhat narrow. The biblical usage of the word "heart" is much richer in its scope. Today when we think of the term "heart," we almost exclusively associate it with the emotions, especially of love, the feelings of love. That's why when February fourteenth approaches, ubiquitous pink and red hearts pop up out of nowhere and adorn everything from flower shops to banks and confections to vacuums. Marketers do their level best to convince us that if we truly love someone we will buy their goods, and the icon they use to pump their products is the symbol of the well of affection, the heart.

Apparently it works. According to the National Retail Federation, Americans spent some $19 billion dollars on Valentine's Day last year.[7] That means the average lovebird coughed up just about $142 a piece. How do advertisers cajole so much cash out of our languishing wallets? By appealing to the intellect? No, they tie their appeal to Cupid's arrow and aim straight for our emotions, where they strike gold. In fact, the less you think, the more you feel, the more you'll spend. In early February, hearts abound in sentiment and registers ring in the cash. In western culture, the term "heart" has come to symbolize the hub of our emotions, affections, feelings, not our intellect or the seat of rational decision making.

In biblical nomenclature, however, the word "heart" has a much broader meaning than our contemporary term. The biblical term is used throughout the Scripture not only to describe the affections of love, but it is also employed to refer to the seat of the intellect and the will as well. The expression "heart" is used to speak individually of all three of these faculties, but often it refers to them as a bundle or as the inner person. In essence, the term "heart" in the Bible frequently identifies the entire immaterial person.

One commentator put it this way: "the word 'heart' in Scripture is considered the very core and center of life."[8] Another calls the heart "the inner, middle, or central part" of a person.[9] In other words, your heart is the real you. It is where you think; it is where you feel; it is where you will to do. Deuteronomy 6:6 uses the word heart in this fuller sense. So what is God telling His people through His servant Moses, and just as important, what is God telling us to do here?

My friends, God exhorts and commands His ancient people—in particular, parents—and by application He calls on His present-day people to take Scripture, which reveals who He is, and to rest it, settle it on our hearts. God is commanding us to allow the truth of who He is and what He says to saturate our entire being, to allow the glory of His character expressed through His word to shine its light into our thought processes, so that it may shape our passions and mold our decisions.

The plan remains the same

God's plan has not changed through the ages. In Colossians 3:16, we find a similar exhortation to the one we read in Deuteronomy 6:6. There, Paul commands his fellow Christians in Colosse to saturate their lives with Scripture. Paul's instruction is a New Testament parallel to the command given by God through Moses.

Paul writes, "Let the word of Christ richly dwell within you." Although our English translation makes Paul's instruction sound like a suggestion, in the Greek Paul is actually speaking in the imperative, that is, he is issuing a command. He directs the believers in Colosse to take "the word of Christ" which is a synonym for Scripture and to make it "richly dwell within" them.[10] That is a packed little phrase!

The word "richly" means copiously, lavishly, and can be rendered "abundantly,"[11] "in full measure."[12] Whenever I stop by my favorite coffee watering hole and order a cup of a favorite brew, the baristas generally ask me, "Would you like room?", i.e., "Do you want room for cream?" If I say "yes" they usually leave my cup a quarter empty, and so I reply, "Look, if I wanted more room I'd move to Alaska." (I say that only if I'm in New York City.) Just kidding, what I usually say is, "No room please. Fill it to the brim!" That's the idea behind the term "richly." God wants us to fill our lives to the brim with His word.

The command "*dwell*" is an interesting word. It is a compound word in the Greek made up of the prepositional prefix "in" and the verb "to dwell" (which is derived from the word for "house") and means "to live in, to dwell in, to reside in" and carries the idea of "remaining in."[13] Have you ever come home from a long trip? When you finally arrive to your residence in the company of your loved ones and the familiar surroundings, smells, sounds of the home you love, what's the terminology you often use to describe what you sense at such a moment? Typically we say or think words like "I feel so at home." You're no longer a stranger; you are welcome, and you fit in with the furniture and into your favorite chair. That's how naturally biblical truth needs to fit into our lives. Is the Bible part of your inward furniture? Is it at home in your mind, your conscience, your passions, your decision making, or does it feel like a strange presence in your soul like an unwanted guest, at odds with many of your values and your lifestyle?

God's Spirit is commanding us to allow His word, the word of Christ, Scripture, to come on in and be at home in us in a copious, lavish, super-abundant fashion so that it can have its divinely designed affect on our thinking, our feelings, our dealings, and in particular our relationship with God and others. We are commanded to put the word of God on our hearts because in it the knowledge of God is abundantly supplied to us, and God's Spirit will use that truth to change us into the very image of the One we long to know and love. And as that process progresses, we will be transformed into the kind of spouses and parents God wants us to be.

CHAPTER 7

God's Word, the Path to Familial Discipleship

The call to diligently mentor our children

In our important familial text, Deuteronomy 6:1–6, we have seen that Scripture is God's abundant provision for our obedience, our blessing, and God's road map for knowing and loving Him. As we continue to run on these same biblical rails, we will observe that Scripture is also our most important resource to disciple and impact our children for the Lord. God's word is indeed His provision for leading our children to salvation and maturing them in the faith.

It is absolutely necessary that Christian parents disciple their children, and that vital priority is especially delineated for us in Deuteronomy 6:7–9. This passage is essentially an amplification of the apostle Paul's summary exhortation in Ephesians 6:4, "*bring them up* [our children] *in the discipline and instruction of the Lord.*" This brief section of the Shema unfolds the crux of what it means to disciple our children. In these verses, we find "The Content of Discipleship," i.e., the subject matter employed in the shepherding of our children, "The Context of Discipleship," or the primary arena God has provided to mentor our kids spiritually, as well as "The Consistency of Discipleship" expressed in three principles for the effective spiritual training of our children.

The content of discipleship

Having worked our way through the text, little needs to be said about the content of discipleship except to underscore the obvious yet critical proposition that Scripture is the wellspring of truth to train our children. Deuteronomy 6:7 alerts us to this subject matter with the phrase, "*You shall teach them diligently.*" The antecedent of "*them*" is found in the opening words of verse 6, "*These words,*" which, of course, refer to Scripture (vv. 1–3). The content we must pass on to our children consists of the words, the truths God has entrusted to us in the Bible.

Interestingly, the entire phrase, "*You shall teach them diligently,*" comes from one forceful Hebrew verb that actually means "to whet," as with the blade of a knife.[1] Just as a skilled blacksmith takes a whetstone and sharpens a blade by honing it on one side and then the other and so renders a cutting-edge razor sharp and useful for service, so Christian parents—and contextually, by extension, grandparents (v. 2)—must take the word of God (God's sharpening agent) and carefully, diligently over time teach and apply it to their children's lives. By so doing, we will render our children useful to the Lord and able to successfully face life and its challenges.

Truly, one of the chief tasks of believing parents is to take God's revelation and explain it to their kids in every facet of life (from childhood to adulthood), using whatever means and circumstances (exhortation, correction, encouragement, ordinary events, once-in-a-lifetime experiences, one-on-one opportunities, family experiences, joyful times as well as sad, tragedy, triumph, failure, success, times of want, and times of plenty), and continually apply what God says to the world we and our children face. We must sharpen them, as it were, to live godward lives of enlightened obedience to the glory and honor of the Lord. Again, the content of this lifelong discipleship process is found in the words of life contained in the Bible.

Two critical questions

For Christian parents this begs two important questions. The first is, "Are we becoming a people of the word as Deuteronomy 6:1–6 implores us to be?" The only way we will be able to expertly apply God's truth to the lives of our children—an essential of parental discipleship—is to be saturated with and controlled by the truth (Deuteronomy 6:6). My dear fellow Christian parent, this must be an important goal in our lives. We must start where we are and with humble dependence on the Holy Spirit make it our ambition to grow in the knowledge of God which is revealed in Scripture. This is not only necessary for our own spiritual health, but it is essential in aiding our ability to shepherd our children into Christian maturity. Are we becoming men and women of the word?

Secondly, our brief discussion raises the question, "What are we pouring—or perhaps more accurately, allowing—into the minds and hearts of our children?" Are we being passive in our instruction and allowing the content, values, half-truths, and outright lies of this age to filter into the minds of our young? The idiom "nature abhors a vacuum" is true in our physical world, but it is also true in the realm of ideas. If we are not proactively pouring biblical truth into the lives of our sons and daughters, the world through its various philosophies and seductive means will certainly flood its beliefs and values into their souls. We can't afford to live quietly and simply hope our children catch our Christianity through the fog of our silence. We must actively seek to teach them God's ways.

Consider, for example, the words of Psalm 78, a marvelous exhortation to parents. In verses 1–7 God—through the author of this psalm—calls Israel to mentor succeeding generations of their children with purposeful determination so that they may trust in the Lord and walk with God. This goal is beautifully stated with the words,

> *That they should teach them* [God's words] *to their children, that the generation to come might know, even the children yet to be born, that they may arise and tell them to their children,* [and here's the purpose of their instruction] *that they should put their confidence in God* [i.e., come to fully trust in the Lord alone] *and not forget the works of God, but keep His commandments* [that is, that they might remember the faithful deeds of God and ultimately live lives of thoughtful obedience to the Lord] (Psalm 78:5b–7).

The psalmist beckons his people Israel to lead their children to saving faith and to a life characterized by trust and obedience. Such mentoring, as this psalm calls for, takes premeditation and a proactive willingness to speak truth into the lives of our children. That, my friends, takes effort and commitment because our human tendency is to say little when it comes to the great, deep, and vast subject matter of the Bible. The writer of this psalm recognizes this dangerous weakness.

He vows not to keep back God's instruction from future generations. In verse 4 he states, "*We will not conceal them from their children,*" that is, we will not conceal the instructive power of Israel's wayward history (a major theme of this lengthy psalm), and we will not shroud the great person of God and His wonderful deeds from future generations of Israelites (verses 4–7). Now obviously, no conscientious Jew—the first recipients of this psalm—and, in our case, no rational believer would ever hide or purposely obstruct biblical truths from their children! So what does the author mean by his vow when he says, "*we will not conceal them* [God's truths] *from their children?*"

I don't believe anyone reading this book would with malice aforethought obscure God's life-giving words from their children; and yet, the danger the psalmist is warning the Israelites and ourselves about is our own silence.[2] In other words, if we're not telling God's truth to our sons and daughters, we're concealing it from them, and if we fail to speak God's truth, that void could easily be filled by the worldly ideological deceptions competing for the souls of our children.

Our responsibility as Christian parents is to be purposeful in their discipleship and take the light God has given to us (the glory of His truth) and proactively pass on that torch to the next generation.

The context of discipleship

Deuteronomy 6:1–9 also makes it clear that the central context to pass on our faith is the home. God charges parents to bring His word to bear on the lives of their children in the ebb and flow of shared life. This classic command is not always understood. If you were to take a survey among Christian adults and ask, "What is the key institution to pass on God's truth to children and to future generations of Christian disciples?", many sincere Christians would tell you that responsibility falls to the church, to the professional pastors, to the shepherds of the flock, and to the programs they implement for the families of the church.

As mentioned in chapter 1, that thinking is widespread, and even though some would not completely affirm the proposition (that it's the church's sole responsibility to disciple our children), they nonetheless embrace this assumption practically. I have met numerous parents who agree with me that it is chiefly their task to disciple their kids, yet in actual practice they hand over the spiritual development of their children (salvation and discipleship) to the pastors and ministries of the church and trust that all will work out well.

What about exceptions to the rule?

The church with its various ministries—energized by God's Spirit through spiritually gifted believers—plays an important supportive role in the salvation and spiritual growth of our young people. That is an absolute; however, as I have mentioned (chapter 1), humanly speaking, the chief responsibility for the salvation and training of children belongs to parents.

That said, are there exceptions to the rule? The answer to that is "Absolutely!" Unfortunately, there will always be parents who leave their children on the doorstep of the church as it were and back away from their God-given call to shepherd their children. Furthermore, as the church reaches out to this broken world, God will save many who will need the members of the flock, the leaders of the church, to come around them and mentor them.

In fact, I would encourage those of you who have established Christian homes to embrace these brothers and sisters who need mentoring. If you know of young people or single parents who have come to salvation in Christ through the ministry of your church, adopt these brethren spiritually. Invite them into your homes. Show them what a godly family looks like—warts and all; disciple them with your lives and your words. Let your home serve as a real life display for biblical marriage, parenting, Christian living, grace, so that they may see what God expects of them as parents, or in the case of young people, what the Lord expects from them when He gives them families of their own. The church and, in particular, families must take a proactive shepherding role in the lives of single parents and young people who come from unbelieving and/or broken homes.

And just in case you missed it, let me state the obvious again. Your children will benefit greatly from the church's ministry to the body as well. For example, when I was a teaching pastor I always enjoyed having the children in the worship service. I think we grossly underestimate how much theological truth kids can process and apply. Conventional wisdom tells us we can't expect young people to sit through a fifty-minute or hour-long message. Yet we send them off to school to sit through multiple hour-long lectures in math, science, and English five days a week. Kids can wrestle with and understand profound concepts, including the truths of the Bible especially if they have embraced Christ as Savior.

I always enjoyed having younger kids in the worship service, and quite honestly, some of the kids got the point of my messages before the adults did. They often were the first to catch my humor. I had children draw pictures of my sermons for me. They would hear the words, the Scripture references, and give me their illustrations of my messages. Some of these artistic interpretations were quite interesting, more interesting than a few of my actual sermons. On a weekly basis, I would have kids ask me questions about something I said or tell me of their observations. Occasionally, they would correct me on a particular point. One ten-year-old girl informed me that I got the sequence of the plagues of Egypt wrong, and you know what, she was right! Our children will benefit from the pulpit ministry of the church, and they will be encouraged, admonished, instructed, and equipped through the multiplicity of gifts and ministries in our local fellowships.

Wrapping our minds around the key point

But here is the key point that you and I need to wrap our minds around at this juncture: the home is central to the salvation and effective discipleship of our children. As we have pointed out before, the Great Commission, God's missionary enterprise to the world, begins at home and radiates out to the world from there. This is the way God intended it to be, and if we minimize the role of the Christian home in the salvation and discipleship of our children, we stand to reap a bitter outcome.

As mentioned previously in chapter 3, an unbelievable number of young people raised in professing evangelical homes leave the church sometime in their college years. The attrition rate in these studies ranges from 50-plus percent all the way to 90-plus percent.[3]

Let's be conservative and assume the lower end of the spectrum more accurately reflects the defection of Christianized young people from their evangelical roots. You mean to tell me that five out of ten kids raised in professed evangelical homes abandon Christianity sometime in their college years? That is astounding! There are a couple of important thoughts that immediately strike me regarding these numbers. The first is that these souls who leave the church, who do not love the Lord Jesus Christ, were never truly saved, because one of the distinguishing hallmarks of a true Christian is perseverance (2 Timothy 2:12; Revelation 3:21; 12:11; 14:12).

The young people who are abandoning our churches may have been "Christianized," but they have not been led to saving faith in Christ, let alone to a life of faithfulness in Him. They are incapable of faithfulness to Christ because they do not know Him and their leaving is evidence that they never belonged to Him (1 John 2:19). The second thing this troubling trend tells me is that parents have not taken the responsibility for the salvation and discipleship of their sons and daughters seriously enough. Many professing Christian parents have defaulted to the church to spiritually mentor their young people, and God never intended the church to take the place of parents in the discipleship of children. God intended the home to be the ministry of greatest spiritual influence in the lives of our children. If we take the Christian home out of the discipleship equation, we will get the kind of frightening results we see today. Why? Because we are departing from God's blueprint for the discipleship of our kids.

Saving faith is most effectively nurtured, God's truth is most effectively passed on to our children, in the context of the home over time, where it is taught and consistently modeled by loving parents, and for that matter, godly grandparents. God's primary vehicle to impact your children is you—mom and dad, grandpa and grandma! The gospel and its attending truths are passed on best when they are couched in the warp and woof of daily life by the heads of households. There is simply no substitute for that!

This is how God instructed Israel to pass on His ways to their sons and daughters. It wasn't through a special secret formula, or through a seminar, or a magic pill, some kind of sanctified zap, or fun and savvy youth specialists, or yeshiva (Bible school). Nowhere in the Bible does God address the spiritual training, mentoring, discipleship of children apart from parents. Why? Because He works primarily through the home and mom and dad to impact children spiritually.

There's no place like home

The home is the principal place where children are led to God and transformed into committed disciples. This is really the thrust of Deuteronomy 6:7–9. Let's briefly look at the text—beginning with verse 6 once more for the sake of context. I will do a brief running commentary on these verses and then give you a summary.

As we approach this Scripture, keep in mind whom God is addressing through His servant Moses. The Lord is speaking to the fathers, grandfathers, the heads of households (parents and grandparents), in other words, those who bear the responsibility of raising the children in their midst. Facing the multigenerational audience of household shepherds, Moses states, *"These words, which I am commanding you today, shall be on your heart* [the seat of the intellect, emotions, and will, the inner person]. [Now notice Moses' exhortation.] *You shall teach them* [God's words] *diligently to your sons* ['sons' is a biblical expression frequently used to refer to all children male and female] *and shall talk of them* [the word that fills the heart will express itself in what is said] *when you sit in your house and when you walk by the way and when you lie down and when you rise up."*

This encompasses all of life, doesn't it? God says, "Because My word saturates your inner person, it will continually be on your lips, and so you will teach my precepts conscientiously to your children when you recline and relax in your home and when you go about your daily life and its duties." God commands His people to speak of His precepts in their simple, ordinary, daily, familial interactions. Then the Lord tells these household shepherds to talk of His truth to their sons when they call it a day and when they welcome the day. That is, in the conversations that fill the twilight hours and in the words that are first spoken when the dawn breaks. It is as if the Almighty counsels, "May My words be the last your children hear when off to sleep they drift so that My thoughts fill their dreams. And may My precepts be the first utterances you speak to them when they awake so that My statutes guide their footsteps through the day." In other words, all day long, all life long, God wants us to pour the treasure of truth that is on our heart into the open vessels of our children, our "disciples," literally our "learners."[4]

Moses continues in verse 8, "*You shall bind them* [God's precepts] *as a sign* [i.e., a vivid and constant reminder] *on your hand and they shall be as frontals on your forehead."* Deuteronomy 6:8 reminds God's people that the Scripture belongs in the mind as fodder for their thinking, but far from being simply an intellectual, theoretical abstract, God's truth rests on the mind in order to shape the character of one's life and drive the deeds and actions of daily experience.

This precept came to express itself in the Jewish custom of tefillin (phylacteries), or little wooden boxes with fragments of Scripture in them, bound to the forehead and to the left arm/hand by means of leather thongs. This was done by Jewish men to remind them that God's Law was to be perpetually on the mind, directing their thinking, and shaping and controlling their actions, i.e., the works of their hands. The "hand" in biblical nomenclature is often used as a reference for a person's life, his work, and his character (Psalm 90:17; 1 Timothy 2:8).

The phylacteries were symbolic of these truths to devout Jews. Unfortunately for many, the external tradition, the symbol, became the beginning, middle, and end of their obligation to Deuteronomy 6:8. The precept became religious ritual. God intended this to be an inward, life-shaping principle for household shepherds, expressed in a holy, exemplary life, lived out day-by-day at home before the eyes of their observing children.

The home as the mentoring context for our children is addressed with one final verse, Deuteronomy 6:9. "*You shall write them* [God's Laws] *on the doorposts of your house and on your gates.*" Not surprisingly this verse reminded the people of Israel, and by application all believing parents, of the dominant role God's word needs to have in the shaping of our home life. You have probably seen a mezuzah affixed to the doorposts of a Jewish home. It is also a small box, usually oblong and contains a copy of the Shema.

From the earliest days, Deuteronomy 6:9 and the outward tradition of the mezuzah instructed the believing family that God through His word rules in the home. God's truth stands as a sentinel over the believing household, guiding, nurturing, protecting those who live within. It is the Scripture that determines the life direction of a home. It is the Bible that acts as gatekeeper and determines what comes into the home and what stays out. The word of God feeds the soul and encourages the grace and character that drive daily interactions.

We have a mezuzah on the doorpost of our home.[5] It's not there as a charm, nor is it there as cult repellent, and neither is it there purely for tradition's sake because of my heritage. It is there because I need to remember, and my household needs to remember, my children need to remember that God and His revelation have authority over our home. Ultimately, even my authority as a husband and father and my wife's authority as a mother, our authority to lead our home comes from God's word rightly understood and applied, and so the Lord reigns through His word in our household.

God's word is the standard that governs our relationships and determines what is appropriate for our family—not contemporary culture, not what the neighbor's standards are, not what other people think or feel. Rather, God through His word rules our home. That's the point of Deuteronomy 6:9.

So what's the implication for our homes?

What is the essence of Deuteronomy 6:6–9? What is it teaching us today? It is teaching us that the main training institution to shape the mind, the values, the character, the moral fiber, and the faith of our children is the home, and the chief tool to accomplish that is God's standard, the Scripture! One precept we must grasp clearly in this text is the centrality of the home to accomplish our discipleship training. The apostle Paul embraces this in Ephesians 6:1–4,

Children, obey your parents in the Lord, for this is right. Honor your father and mother (which is the first commandment with a promise), so that it may be well with you, and that you may live long on the earth. Fathers, do not provoke your children to anger, but bring them up in the discipline and instruction of the Lord.

Paul tells young people they must esteem their parents and submit to their instruction so that they might experience God's blessing. Fathers must lead their sons and daughters with a biblically enlightened wisdom that corrects and enables children to live a life pleasing to the Lord. Most would agree that is a fair summary of Ephesians 6:1–4, but what we must also understand is the simple, undeniable, and nonnegotiable reality inherent in what Paul teaches, which is the same underlying reality found in Deuteronomy 6:6–9. It is that the discipleship relationship spoken of in both passages is between children and parents, parents and children, i.e., the home.

God tells us through His servants, Moses and Paul (from the Torah to the epistles, from the days of Old Testament Israel to the present-day church), that the home is the primary discipleship training ground for children. The family is the context in which the vast majority of all this relating, blessing, leading, correcting, instructing—in essence—discipleship is designed to take place. The primary context God has provided to disciple our children in the things of the Lord is the arena of the family unit, the Christian home. That, my friends, is a fundamental axiom many have lost sight of in the contemporary church.

Does the centrality of the home in discipleship mean I have to homeschool?

Am I suggesting every Christian ought to pull their children out of public or private school and homeschool them? That is not what this Scripture is teaching, and I don't want to put words in God's mouth. Common sense would suggest, and Old Testament history bears out, that the children of this young nation (Israel of the conquest) received formal instruction, such as reading or vocational training, in the home. They were a nomadic people on the go and on their way to the Promised Land. This basic approach to training children was likely true of the generations that followed them for several hundred years. Formal compulsory elementary education for Jewish children came into existence in the first century B.C. (75 B.C.).[6] This trend developed some 1400 years after the conquest, and completely apart from any biblical mandate given in the Old Testament.

And so, while children were likely educated in the home for one and a half millennia after the giving of Deuteronomy 6:1–9, it is important to understand that the text does not command parents to teach their children to read and write or to train them in a given vocation while in the home. In other words, Deuteronomy 6 does not mandate parents to personally give (teach) their children basic education and training. However, what the text does legislate or demand is that believing parents be the primary "teachers" of their children in the ways of the Lord. That is the inescapable point of verse 7, "*You* [parents and grandparents] *shall teach them* [God's precepts] *diligently to your sons and shall talk of them* [morning, noon, and night]." Jewish parents were called to mentor their children spiritually, and that basic responsibility carries over into the New Testament (Ephesians 6:1–4).

Let me be clear, no one can make a mandate from Deuteronomy 6 (though some erringly do try) that all Christian parents must homeschool their children. Do I personally believe that more Christian parents need to consider homeschooling as an option? I absolutely do. Can we mandate it? Absolutely not! So again, what is this text teaching us in principle? Here is what Scripture is clearly telling us.

My fellow parents, we need to make doubly sure that the covenant activity of God—and by this I simply mean that which we are bound to do as parents before the Lord—the teaching of God's truth, the formation of biblical values, the development of character, the shaping of the mind, must be accomplished first and foremost in the home. Because, you see, according to Scripture, the spiritual moral formation of our children is not the responsibility of the schools, nor is it, as we have previously considered, the principal responsibility of the church. That privilege belongs first and foremost to the parents with the community of believers coming alongside to support the instruction in the home.

You are your child's pastor

Let me tell you something, Mom and Dad, you are your children's primary pastors. Someone might object, "Whoa there, just a minute, partner. What do you mean, I'm my children's pastor? I'm a layman. I've never been to seminary. I've never been trained to work with kids." Well, I hate to be the one to break this to you, but if you're a parent, you've been working with kids for as long as your flock of ankle biters have been around, and whether you acknowledge it or not, you are a pastor to them. You already have the job.

What is a "pastor"? A pastor is another term for "shepherd." What does a shepherd do? We borrow the term from animal husbandry, and a shepherd is a person who works with livestock. His basic responsibility is to take care of his herd, and so the shepherd protects, provides, feeds, nurtures, heals, guides, and trains. Doesn't that sound remarkably like the job description of a parent? It is! You've been shepherding your children from the day they were born.

You swaddled them in the hospital before you came home so that they would feel safe and warm. You fed them when they cried so they wouldn't be hungry. You rocked them through the night when they didn't feel good so that they would be comforted. You picked them up and consoled them when they fell down and scraped their knees. You bought them their first bike, put it together for them, and taught them how to ride it. You took them to their first ballgame and explained the rules. You corrected them when they needed correction and provided guidance for them when they were perplexed. You have spent countless thousands of dollars on clothes, food, shelter, playthings to provide a safe place to grow. You know how they think; you sense when they're sad, and your heart bears their burden; you rejoice when they're happy. You feel proud when they're honored. You would give your life for their welfare. Why? Because you are their pastor, their shepherd, and you love them more than life itself.

No one knows and cares for your children like you, and divine sovereignty has placed them in your care to lead them to God and to equip them for a godward life. God has made you their shepherd, and He has called you to mentor your flock spiritually with the word of life He has entrusted to you. My dear fellow parents, the home is the hub, the center for the moral, spiritual training of our children, and you and I (parents) are the overseers of this process. That truth is inescapable.

These words, which I am commanding you today, shall be on your heart. You shall teach them diligently to your sons and shall talk of them when you sit in your house and when you walk by the way and when you lie down and when you rise up. You shall bind them as a sign on your hand and they shall be as frontals on your forehead. You shall write them on the doorposts of your house and on your gates (Deuteronomy 6:6–9).

For He established a testimony in Jacob and appointed a law in Israel, which He commanded our fathers that they should teach them to their children, that the generation to come might know, even the children yet to be born, that they may arise and tell them to their children, that they should put their confidence in God and not forget the works of God, but keep His commandments (Psalm 78:5–7).

For I have chosen him, so that he may command his children and his household after him to keep the way of the LORD by doing righteousness and justice, so that the Lord may bring upon Abraham what He has spoken about him (Genesis 18:19).

Fathers… bring them [your children] *up in the discipline and instruction of the Lord* (Ephesians 6:4b).

CHAPTER 8

The Investment of Time in Our Children

The consistency of discipleship

Deuteronomy 6:1–9 is the fulcrum of the Bible's teaching on the family. In this text we recognized the importance and centrality of Scripture in the believing home.[1] We discovered that Scripture is God's gracious provision for our obedience and also for our blessing—both personally and for our homes.[2] Furthermore, we discerned that God's word is the road map for knowing and loving Him, the chief pursuit of life and mentoring.[3] This brought us to explore one more pivotal idea in this text, and that is that God's word is the Lord's chief provision to disciple our children in the faith, which includes the content, the context, and the consistency of discipleship.

So far we have considered the "The Content of Discipleship," which is the whole of Scripture, as well as "The Context of Discipleship," which is the home. Now we come to the final focus of our consideration: "The Consistency of Discipleship." This addresses three consistent commitments of the disciple-making parent that arise from Deuteronomy 6:6–9. We will explore these three commitments necessary to effectively shape the minds, the hearts, the values, indeed, the very lives of our children in this chapter and the next. Think of them if you will as three essential principles of parental discipleship.

Three key principles of parental discipleship

Whether we are talking about mentoring a fellow Christian in the truth of Scripture or discipling our own children, the precepts we are about to discuss are necessary for the effective training of all believers. You will recognize that the Lord Jesus Himself employed these three precepts in the training of the twelve. We will briefly look at the example of the Lord and see that these three nonnegotiable truths of discipleship also arise out of Deuteronomy 6 to form the framework for the effective spiritual mentoring of our children.

The first axiom consists of the investment of time we are obliged to pour into our disciples. We must commit ourselves to give our children the priority of our time. No discipleship relationship can thrive without this valuable asset. This is especially true in the parent/child discipleship bond. Secondly, we must also be committed to engage in purposeful living. Every growing disciple learns best from observing a life lived well. Therefore, God calls parents to showcase His truth for their children on the stage of life. Finally, the third principle we will unveil is related to the second, yet it is especially emphasized by the text and key in the transformation of disciples. It is the compelling commitment to passion. Specifically, we're talking about God's desire for us to live out the truth with vigor. An evident love or zeal for the truth is a vital force in stamping God's ways on the hearts of our children.

Principle #1: The consistency of discipleship realized with the investment of time in our children

The Lord's example

Jesus invested the precious asset of time in His men. Time is to a discipleship relationship what fuel is to a fire. You must have the first (fuel/time) to grow the second (fire/discipleship). The simple math is obvious: you and I cannot have a mentoring relationship with anyone—let alone our kids—unless we pour significant amounts of time into them. The Lord Jesus modeled this by investing the vast sum of His earthly ministry into the lives of His disciples. Jesus Christ, God in the flesh, poured the three most important years of his terrestrial existence into twelve men. Simply stated, He lived life with His men. He shared meals with them; He prayed with them. He taught them in the ebb and flow of daily life; He traveled from town to town with them and ministered with these men at His side for the duration of His public ministry. During that time, they were the focal point of His care and training.

This short ministry period in the Lord's life (10 percent of the Lord's earthly sojourn) is so important that it requires the preponderance of the four gospels to unfold the events. By comparison, very little is said in the gospels of Christ's previous 30 years of life. Essentially, He came to earth to accomplish what He fulfilled in His three-year plan. The Lord had three precious years to carry out His ministry, and He chose to pour the lion's share of that time into the lives of these beloved followers. In order to mentor these select disciples effectively, in order to release them into the world fully equipped to carry out His great missionary task, Jesus gave them the heart of His most important time on earth.

The fabric of parental discipleship: Time

What do you need to give your kids so that they may grow into spiritual health, so that they might be equipped for life and service? What must you lavish upon them in order to successfully transfer *"these words,"* God's precepts, to their souls? One inescapable conclusion that arises from Deuteronomy 6:7–9, and especially verse 7, is that we must give our children time. Notice the translators of the Hebrew supply the relative adverb "when" four times in the span of one verse: *"You shall teach them* [God's words] *diligently to your sons and shall talk of them when you sit in your house and when you walk by the way and when you lie down and when you rise up"* (Deuteronomy 6:7, emphasis added).

A necessary assumption in this text is that the training of our children demands the absolute investment of time, to be specific, time spent in the company of our kids. Parental discipleship, the effective training of our children in God's ways, will take the lion's share of our time as adults. Some would argue that this is an obvious reality and that it is hardly worth noting. It may be obvious, but few principles for effective discipleship are as easily neglected as this one— especially with the frenetic pace of our present-day lives. Investing time in one another is a significant challenge for many contemporary families.

Really, time is like currency. There's only so much of it to spend; it will be spent one way or another, and the vendors of life pitching for their share of the wealth are numerous and convincing. Typically, the things that scream the loudest for our attention in life receive the largest chunks of our time (career, personal interests). Conversely, the quieter voices receive the gleanings of time left over on the margins of daily schedules. Often the faintest cries (the ones easiest to ignore because they do not hold the collateral of a paycheck, authority, or worldly gravitas) come from those who need to be heard and heeded the most, our children. The biblical reminder to invest this currency into the lives of our children, our families, is not simply helpful, it is urgently necessary considering the milieu of our culture which so aggressively competes for the precious treasure of our time.

But I object

Someone will object, "But I'm a busy person. I'm short on time. I can't afford to give my kids big chunks of time." I would beg to differ. I would say you can't afford not to give them time. I realize for some this is especially difficult. You may be part of a growing number of Christian single parents. At this point in your life, you find yourself in the challenging position where you are both mom and dad; you are the provider and the nurturer. When you come home from work, you are beat and ready to tune out and turn in. You may feel you have little left to give, yet the inescapable reality is that the currency of time you do have—abbreviated as it may be—you must invest primarily in your children.

This is what God requires of us as parents for the welfare of our kids; and therefore, you and I must take inventory of our stewardship of time and adjust our lives and those of our children so that we may give them the most time we can. It may take the wise counsel of several godly people to guide us. It may take us a prayerful while to figure out how we're going to free up our schedules and how we're going to implement our plan. It will likely take great sacrifice, but we must give our children the heart of our time.

There are many purveyors vying for our time as parents. The list of variables is long and we cannot afford to delve into details, but allow me to give you four basic modern realities that compete for and often rob parents of time with their children.

1. Splintered by activity

One challenge parents face as they endeavor to spend time with their kids is the unflinching taskmaster of an ever lengthening, bewildering list of activities. Often families simply allow themselves to be splintered by busyness. It is so easy for today's family to find itself going at mind-numbing speeds in different directions. An almost limitless array of time-consuming events—none of them necessarily bad in and of themselves—draw parents and children away from one another and tear at the very fabric of discipleship: time. Multiple sports, social events, extracurricular commitments, competing priorities, take us in multiple directions and in the process plunder us of time spent together.

The tyranny of manifold activities is especially tricky, because quite often they fool us into thinking we're spending time together, when in actuality we're spending time "about" one another instead of interacting meaningfully with one another. In other words, I may spend time "about" my kids while taking them to our various commitments (like soccer or ballet), but the time I spend dodging traffic or blindly staring off into the middle distance while my son or daughter zones out on their iPod, or the hours they invest on the field or dance floor while I'm lost in my smart phone is not time meaningfully invested in one another. Busyness can give us the illusion of time shared with our family while actually robbing us of that very thing. The convincing lure of countless activities can be a subtle but real brigand of the time we need to pour into our kids.

Certainly in preindustrial days (which is the vast sum of human history), this was not nearly the problem it is for families today. Before modern transportation and communication, a family's activity cycle looked quite different than it does for us today. By the time the sun inched its way down on the horizon, families pretty much found themselves at home. I love my present-day conveniences as much as anybody, but the fact remains that our great advances in technology have made it quite easy for families to be splintered. Unfortunately, many of us mindlessly slip into a breakneck pattern of round-the-clock bustle or become lost in the time gobbling seduction of our modern devices. In part, the net result is that parents and children exist in separate worlds though they live under the same roof.

2. Relinquishing parental prerogatives

Another present-day reality that robs us of time with our children is the pressure on modern parents to parcel out their children to youth experts—especially during the teen years. In the last century, we have witnessed a growing chorus of voices telling parents they need to hand over the mentoring of their kids to others who are more knowledgeable in the field of training children—teachers, coaches, and assorted mentors. This message has cut across our cultural strata to convince parents from all walks of life, including Christian parents, that this is so.

Even within the contemporary church many parents are taught—and believe—that they must surrender the role of spiritual mentor to the church (see chapter 1). Sadly, this is more a reflection of present-day cultural values than it is a biblical understanding of God's pattern for the family. To the degree that we buy into that message, parents are deprived of their God-given role and the time they need to invest in their children.

3. Narcissistic value system

It's difficult to live in a fallen world without being tainted by it. In fact, it is inevitable for every Christian. We are born "tainted" (in sin, Romans 5:12–21) and even after we are delivered from the penalty of sin through salvation in Jesus, we continue to live in bodies of unredeemed flesh subject to temptation and failure. Our ongoing fight against the world's influence in our lives is a daily struggle that will continue until the Lord gathers us to Himself. Until that day, armed with His word and by the power of God's indwelling Holy Spirit, we must fight the ever-present presence of sin within ourselves and the sinful influences of the world that entice our flesh overtly and often imperceptibly. In spite of our vigilance, however, the world's way of thinking can creep into our minds and infect our personal values. One of the ways we are frequently tempted and influenced by the world is in the area of self-absorption, or narcissism, that is, an obsession with our own needs and wants. Ironically, few things can rob us of needed time with our children like ourselves.

Narcissism is pervasive in our culture. One area where self-absorption flexes its powerful influence is in the realm of time. It appears that people today increasingly value time in relation to themselves. Generally speaking, contemporary culture does not value time spent for the benefit of another. Our biggest value seems to be "personal time," "my time," time "invested in my career," time for "my leisure," "mommy time," "man time." Our culture is obsessed with personal gratification, and its narcissistic call for personal time drones in our ears constantly.

Narcissism is an anti-Christian outlook and the opposite of the attitude exhibited by the Lord Jesus toward us, His beloved. Based on the example of Christ's selflessness, His self-emptying, the Bible beckons us to have an outward-looking perspective. God's Spirit tells us through Paul, "*Do nothing from selfishness or empty conceit, but with humility of mind regard one another as more important than yourselves; do not merely look out for your own personal interests, but also for the interests of others. Have this attitude in yourselves which was also in Christ Jesus*" (Philippians 2:3–5). God's call to selflessness applies to the entirety of a Christian's life and must govern our relationship to our children in all areas, including our stewardship of time.

Even with the clear example of our Lord and the unambiguous teaching of Scripture, Christian parents are still susceptible to this narcissistic view of "personal time." We need to be aware of the subtleties of this ubiquitous message and our susceptibility to it, because when we buy into it, this cultural value puts us at odds with God's standard and what He desires of parents—i.e., that moms and dads sacrificially and selflessly give their children the lion's share of their time.

Look again at God's command to parents to teach their children His precepts and notice once again the obvious references to time. "*You shall teach them diligently to your sons and shall talk of them when you sit in your house and when you walk by the way and when you lie down and when you rise up*" (Deuteronomy 6:7, emphasis added). The simple truth is that the spiritual development, mentoring, shepherding of our sons and daughters takes place in the outworking of a day, in the context of life, and that assumes the investment of our calendar.

4. Luring moms out of the home

Let me address the moms for a moment because their investment of time in their children is so essential to their spiritual development and (not surprisingly) so challenged by our contemporary cultural values. It is vital for mothers—especially if they have young ones at home—to embrace Paul's exhortation in Titus 2:4–5 and stay at home to shepherd their children. In a day and age when two-income households are all but normative, the concept of a stay-at-home mom has become a controversial issue even among Christians. Yet Paul is crystal clear on the responsibility of mothers to invest their time in their homes. Paul writes, "*so that they* [older women who have raised children and kept a godly home] *may encourage the young women to love their husbands, to love their children, to be sensible, pure, workers at home, kind, being subject to their own husbands, so that the word of God will not be dishonored*" (Titus 2:4–5).

The key point of contention arises from the phrase *"workers at home."* The question is often asked, "What does Paul's phrase really mean for us today?" and usually in a desire to avoid offense, the phrase is parsed, and punched, and kneaded, and stretched to mean just about whatever the verbal masseur wants it to mean. However, given the plain sense of language, what does *"workers at home"* mean? Allow me to answer that inquiry with another question. What does "workers at Walmart" mean? It simply means that the people identified by the phrase "workers at Walmart" work at... you guessed it, Walmart. When Paul—under the inspiration of the Holy Spirit—instructs younger women to work at home he means that they should invest their time in the home. Why? The answer is simple and profound, there is business of eternal consequence to accomplish in the Christian home, and the world is watching to see if and how we fulfill that command.

God knows the forging of young minds and souls in His ways takes the dedication of a mother's love applied with perseverance and patience over the course of many years. In the home, young souls come to know the Savior, and as they grow and blossom in discipleship, they then become a testimony to the truth and power of God's word and the gospel itself. As the process of spiritual mentoring plays out, the fruit of our homes (a family ordered by biblical precepts and maturing disciples) adorns God's truth with honor. Those who honestly look into a Christian home will have to conclude that God's design for the family makes a difference and that His ways are not broken. Outsiders looking in move that much closer to the crossroads of the gospel. What will they do with the evidence of a transformed family? Let me tell you, my friends, a godly home is a powerful apologetic for the veracity of God's word and the gospel!

Because of the powerful testimony of a godly home, the enemy has worked overtime to disrupt the order of Christian relationships and to pull the mother out of the home. Apart from the economic pressure brought to bear on one-income families these days, the pressure of social stigma heaped upon stay-at-home moms has been especially intense since the post–World War II years. In the 1940s, the stay at home mom was transformed into Rosie the Riveter, and the expectation for women to join the workforce has only grown and intensified since then. In fact, the role of mothers has morphed so much that the stay-at-home mom is the exception rather than the rule today—even among contemporary evangelical circles. According to the latest data, nearly two-thirds of moms work outside the home, and in 40% of households that have children under 18, the mother is the sole or main wage earner.[4] Often this social reality is mirrored in the evangelical community.

Facilitating this change in a mother's role is the shift in attitudes toward the identity of women. The contemporary mindset tells us, "No modern woman in her right mind would want to 'stay home and bake cookies' when she can have an impact on the real world—the world outside the misogynist cloister of the home." We as a culture have embraced the notion that women find their greatest fulfillment outside the home in their role as provider, co-provider, and/or in their career or profession. In other words, a woman's true sense of identity and fulfillment comes primarily from her role in the workplace. We have therefore minimized, devalued, and even disparaged the importance of a mother's work at home.

You can bet the world (and sometimes the church) will mock believing parents for their decision to keep mom at home with the kids. Present-day society denigrates Christian women for following their husband's leadership and dedicating themselves to the welfare of their kids. Modern culture will even sneer at children raised in such an environment and tag them odd and peculiar. They will call a lifestyle reflective of biblical priorities "puritanical" (a good term mongrelized by the world) and cast aspersions on it, comparing biblical thinking to the Taliban.

Yet God has spoken clearly on the essential and honored role a full-time wife and mother plays in the Christian home. What's more, when we align our families by God's prescription, we will find ourselves in the place of blessing and reflect God's glory to the world. As we have suggested, precious lost people will inevitably see in our homes the lovely interplay of harmony, healing, grace, forgiveness, joy, and spiritual strength that God pours into a Christian family over time, and that those looking on so desperately need. A mother who stays at home to love her husband and invests her life (time) into the souls God has granted to her for care is critical to the stability and health of a Christian family.

A personal word of encouragement

My wife Valorie has been a stay-at-home mom ever since we brought our firstborn home from the hospital twenty-nine years ago. Up to that time she had been working as a speech pathologist in a hospital. Valorie received her master's in speech pathology from one of the top schools in the country for the discipline in the 1980s (Purdue University). She graduated summa cum laude at the top of her class with a perfect 4.0 G.P.A. She found a gratifying job with ease when we returned to Southern California and helped put me through seminary until we became pregnant with our first child, Joshua. She retired from her profession when she came home with our son scarcely two years into her career. I was in my senior year at seminary, and the financial constraints we faced at the time were considerable, but we made up our minds even before marriage to bring Val home when we started having kids. As the Lord would have it, He tested our resolve and also graciously provided for all our needs while I finished my Master's of Divinity (a four-year graduate degree).

Since Val left her job some twenty-nine years ago, my gifted wife has received many job offers. In fact—I'm not exaggerating when I say this—she still receives multiple job offers every year, sometimes several in the same month. Like most ministry families, we have struggled financially over the years and could have used the extra income. To be truthful, Valorie's income would have put us in fat city because she could have earned much more than me.

Would we welcome more cash? Are you kidding? Does a professional whistler have lips? Yes! It would be nice to have newer cars, to help my kids out with school, to take exotic vacations to places I can't pronounce. Val could have jumped back into the professional workforce and helped supply our needs, and most of our wants, but—and here's the key value question—at what cost? That is the question with which we always tempered our desire for a more comfortable life. The answer always came back the same: the cost of affluence for us was always "time," and that's a priceless commodity that first needed to be invested in our home and especially in our children.

Quite honestly, the lure of Val returning to work has never been a temptation for us because the cost of that move would have been unspeakably high. Val's employment would have taken her away from our home and the eternal treasure of our kids. When we did the domestic math early on in our relationship, our initial decision to invest Val's time in our family was and continues to be the right choice. It has resulted in an incalculable windfall, the souls of our kids, a close relationship with our children, a close relationship between the siblings, and a happy home, not a perfect home (not even close. I'm the husband and dad, remember?), but a home where the love and grace of God has coalesced a group of redeemed sinners into an oasis of love and grace.

We still get a kick out of the job offers prospective employers regularly dangle before our ears on our voice mail. We listen to the messages and often look at each other and ask ourselves the rhetorical question, "What would we have gotten from your career in exchange for the time you (Val) actually spent with our kids?" The vaporous prestige of professional recognition? Certificates to hang on an office wall? Stuff? A string of new cars maybe—most of which would be in the junkyard by now—a couple of decaying jet skis leaking oil on our garage floor, a flat-screen TV the size of my family room wall, hundreds of pounds of clothes now hanging on the coat racks of multiple thrift stores or decomposing in a landfill, postcards, stubs, and tickets to line a scrap book? Not to mention the kissing cousin of "more income," "more debt," and all of that for what? For the time Val invested in our kids, for the fruit we are enjoying from their lives, and the eternal dividends that investment will yield! No, no job, no "thing" is worth the time my wife has poured into our children and the forever results and joy we will relish because of it. In a few thousand years when I reflect back on my life here on earth, I will not mourn not having had a bigger TV or a nicer car because Val invested her life into our children and home. I will, however, rejoice eternally in the fellowship of my children who are fellow saints in Christ.

Mothers have a special, God-given mentoring opportunity with their children, but the call to invest one's life in their young ones applies to fathers as well. In fact, the logical priority of this call in Deuteronomy 6:7 belongs to the dads. In short, the biblical exhortation to give our children the substance of our days belongs to both mom and dad. The only question remaining is whether or not parents will choose to give their kids the valuable endowment of time.

Who or what will step in if we don't?

You must realize that to withhold time from your kids, for whatever reason, is to withhold the mentoring they need, which also means you must surrender them to other mentors. The critical question at this point becomes, if you as the parents do not give your children your time, who or what will take your place? Will it be their own peers, the media, the Internet? Will you surrender that duty to other men and women in their lives who may be sincere, but whom you may not know well and who may hold an unbiblical worldview at odds with your own?

When my son Josh was in grade school he had a terrific teacher. She was a lovely person, a good educator, and she truly loved the kids. We, like most parents in our shoes, felt no hesitation about our son spending six-plus hours per day under the tutelage of this gregarious lady and her persuasive teaching skills. My son liked her, and we were happy as clams—assuming clams are indeed happy.

Apart from my son's constant struggle with distraction (like that of his old dad when he was in school—Josh's mind seemed perpetually on a voyage to some distant thought), he was enjoying school. We certainly saw no red flags in terms of his teacher's skills and content. Then one day my son came home and informed us that whales once walked on land and that his astrological sign was Leo. Both these propositions were news to his mother and me. Joshua's teacher believed both these ideas were true (evolution and astrology) and passed them on to the children under her educational care.

Josh's teacher was an extremely nice lady—I'm sure she still is—but she had a radically different worldview than we did, and she was teaching our son theories and conjecture with broad ramifications for his outlook on life. Needless to say, we did a little retrofitting with Josh's learning. The next year we started educating him at home, and I began to teach Joshua his science lessons. We had a blast as we filtered scientific knowledge through the grid of Scripture. Today my son is a scientist (he earned a graduate degree in chemistry from New York University), and he confidently believes and affirms that the God of heaven and earth directs our lives (not the stars and planets) and that "*in the beginning God created the heavens and the earth*" (Genesis 1:1).

My friends, if you are wrestling with the question, "Do I have time to mentor my kids?", you need to do so with the following reality firmly fixed in your mind. You need to understand that someone or something will mentor your kids if you don't. It is that simple. It's not a question of "if" but of "who" or "what." Regardless of what educational model you use (public, private, or homeschool), God intends for you to disciple your children in the light of His truth. That's His design for you and your children, and so we must find the hours in a day to shape the minds and souls of our kids because if we don't, someone or something else will.

My brothers and sisters, we need to evaluate our commitments, our time constraints, our leisure, our debt load, and if need be (dads) our careers, and indeed our very lives, and prayerfully make choices that will allow us to give our children time and the shepherding God commands of us and that they so desperately need.

Quantity vs. Quality

People who have known me for almost any length of time have heard me express a particular familial axiom that I have found to be true. In one way or another I have told many parents (new parents and mature parents), "You will never regret decisions that give you more time with your family (i.e., spouse and children)." Apart from some ridiculous or irresponsible application of this maxim (e.g., quitting one's livelihood to spend more time with the kids or refusal to serve the body of Christ to be with the family), this truism has always helped families make good decisions. In response to this principle, however, some have reasoned, "Well, Marcelo, I appreciate what you're trying to say, but quantity of time itself is not the issue. You're missing the point. When it comes to our kids, the most important idea is quality of time. I want to give my kids 'quality' time—that's what I'm shooting for, 'quality.'"

That kind of thinking, however, creates more questions than it answers. First of all, I'm not sure what "quality time" means. How do you create quality time? Do you tell your kid, "Okay son, this is now officially 'quality time.' You've got my undivided attention. You're on the clock, thirty minutes, go!" Do you create quality time by throwing money at activities? Do you scheme and plan an occasional elaborate and pricey adventure to create that teachable, memorable moment? Can you plan "quality time"?

Quite honestly, sometimes the events I thought were ordinary turned out to be the most momentous. It's hard to schedule serendipitous, teachable moments. What I've discovered as I've poked and prodded this question of "quality vs. quantity" with parents is that "quality time" differs widely in definition from one person to the next and even between spouses. What's more, it is often used as an excuse to justify our failure to give our children the time they need with their parents.

Allow me to give you an exhortation based on the "when" principle found in Deuteronomy 6:7. I would encourage you to shoot for "quantity time." I beg you to give your children "quantity time." I guarantee you quality time will find its way into the mix as you give your children a preponderance of time. Give them big honkin' Costco, bulk-size chunks of time. If you need to do errands, plan to run them with your kids. Dad, take them along with you on your run-about-town after you get home from work. You're tired? It's okay, they're probably tired too. Be tired together, and take the opportunity to put your arm around your son's or daughter's shoulder, tell them you love them, and ask them how you can pray for them or they for you. Think of the "open mic" opportunities you could have while running around town. Let them have the floor. Prompt them with simple questions; listen carefully and long. You have a "honey do" list that needs your attention on Saturday? Take your kids to the home improvement store with you and introduce them to the wondrous world of lawn care, screen repair, building fences. Take them with you to the Department of Motor Vehicles. Take them to the Post Office. Teach them the art of standing in line. Hey, it's a life skill!

I recently read that the average person spends three years of their life waiting in line.[5] For me, it would be much longer than that, because I have an unwitting, almost magical ability to pick the wrong line. No matter what the situation, I will inevitably choose the most time-consuming line anywhere, guaranteed (grocery store lines, gas lines, bank lines, preferred customer lines, express lines, ride lines at Disneyland...)! If you could subtract the years I have spent waiting in line from my life, I would be about twelve. Regardless of how skilled you are at picking the quickest lines, the truth is we spend a lot of time going about our weekly routines, going hither and yon, waiting here, waiting there. Think of the impact you could have on your family if you purposed to redeem as much as possible of that time interacting with your children and grandchildren!

Think of the important discussions, teachable moments you would encounter if you gave your kids more of your ordinary time. Think of the impact such talks and happenings would have on the depth of your relationship with your kids. Obviously, not many errands will involve an epiphany. Thank goodness! Personally, I couldn't handle the stress of life-altering conversations every time I ran to the store with my kids. I'd be afraid to step out of my house.

Valorie: "Thanks, honey, for running to the store for me and getting the soy sauce. Didn't you take Aaron with you? Where's Aaron?"

Me: "Oh, we were looking in the Asian food section and he decided to become a missionary to China. He's left. He says he'll write soon."

The value of the ordinary moment

Yes, special moments and life-changing experiences will come, but equally as important are the bonds we build with our children and grandchildren as we share life with them and purposely, consistently speak to them about God and what He desires for us. Strong family relationships, spiritual mentoring, is built out of the brick and mortar of mutually shared, day-to-day life. The foundation and integrity of a godly home is laid down precept upon precept over years (time) of discerning instruction, much of it in the ebb and flow of ordinary, daily routines.

Sadly, time is one commodity that is easily misspent, and once it is lost we can only acknowledge its passing; we cannot retrieve it and reinvest it in the lives of those we love. On a family trip to Ann Arbor, Michigan, to visit the University of Michigan, we stayed at a local family-friendly hotel. On our first morning there— feeling the wear and tear of the drive from Southern California—we got up lazily and made our way to the dining room for their complimentary breakfast. Having no pressing agenda that day, we ate and visited for well over an hour and enjoyed ourselves in each other's company.

About fifteen minutes into our breakfast, a dad and his preteen son took the table directly across from us. They were in my direct line of vision, and I could not help but notice that these look-alikes separated by some thirty years were not talking with one another. The boy looked to his dad for cues and direction, and while the dad did not seem angry or upset, he appeared completely uninterested in the company of his son. As time pressed on, I was astonished and saddened to observe that the dad did not address his son once while eating breakfast. Not one word or as much as a smile in the span of approximately twenty minutes! Yet the father did manage to take three business calls over that same stretch of time, each one with great personal warmth and enthusiasm.

I wondered then as I do now how that father's neglect made that boy feel. I will never know. I have a sense that what I saw between that dad and son was part of a pattern of behavior, a pattern of wasted ordinary moments, lost opportunities to nurture intimacy between father and son. Men and women, as Christian parents, we need to appreciate the value of time spent with our children and seize the precious moments given to us by God to pour into their souls, to mold their minds, and shape their character in the warp and woof of daily life, even over a complimentary breakfast with forgettable food.

Time flies

They say "time flies." Well as a father of older children, I testify to the truth that the days to shape their souls zoom by much too quickly. This may sound cliche to you, and yet too often Christian parents fail to invest a significant amount of time in their children because there are always other important things to do, and "there's always tomorrow." Frequently, we do not recognize the value of "today" and the ordinary moment, yet that's exactly what our children need from us so that they might grow into the kind of men and women God wants them to be. That kind of life-on-life discipleship takes place in daily-shared existence. It is the flux of the ordinary that creates the shaping force of a life lived together and inevitably also gives rise to special moments that will forever change our relationship with our kids and their future as men and women of God.

Unfortunately, the failure of parents to invest their lives—with the currency of time—into the lives of their children is a growing problem in our day and age. Parents can dutifully provide for the physical needs of their kids, faithfully take the family to church and yet find themselves pulled away from home by the constant activities and distractions of life. Time with the kids gets relegated to a place of tertiary importance, and with the absence of time you have a corresponding lack of discipleship. Often the heartbreaking assumption parents make, and the gamble they take, is that their children will find their way to God by spiritual osmosis. Just have them live under the same roof, provide what they need, and expose them to church and Christian influences, and they will turn out alright. Many Christian parents believe that somehow their children will grow up to embrace the God of the Bible even though He has not been consistently and accurately explained and modeled in the home. That is an illogical assumption, and reality tells us this gamble often carries an eternal and horrible cost, the souls of our children. Our children need to be led to God, and that journey takes the investment of parental time.

Kids are like a garden

In a way, children are like a garden. Allow me to make the assumption that most people reading this book like to work with the soil as I do. If you don't like gardening, just pretend that you do for a moment and work with me. Certainly all of you enjoy eating, so let's talk about a vegetable garden. "But I don't like vegetables!" Sha, no kvetching (Yiddish for 'Quiet down and no complaining.')! Work with me! Like any cultivated plot of soil, our children need to be nurtured, fed, pruned, weeded, watched over, and fussed over like a valued garden.

Imagine thoughtfully choosing the vegetables you want to harvest and painstakingly planning your little plot out on paper. Then one bright, sunny, spring day you mix in your amendments, till your soil, and lay out your earthy bed, envisioning the produce you will enjoy when your garden bears its fruit (and vegetables). You line up your furrows, sow your various seeds, and carefully place your ready seedlings into the expectant soil. You plant a section of tomato plants, followed by a few rows of carrots, perhaps some cucumber and lettuce, several rows of scallions, and round off your hopeful garden with a couple of different types of squash. Your sprinklers already in place, you turn on your water and watch with satisfaction as the dark, thirsty soil soaks up the welcomed moisture. What a promising start! With your temporal lobe culling its files for favorite vegetable recipes, you set your irrigation timer and walk away dreaming of the great harvest that awaits you. But imagine planting your vegetable garden in May, setting your irrigation system, and then just letting your work go untended until late summer.

Now that everything is planted and in its place, you leave your budding vegetable garden to itself and don't come back until August. You and your family leave on a very long trip, fully anticipating a cornucopia of summer produce when you return. You anticipate harvesting all this food with your kids. Maybe you envision purchasing some pilgrim outfits to wear for the entire family, big strange-looking black hats, square-toed, patent leather shoes with massive buckles on them, and knickers for dad and the boys. In your mind's eye, you picture your daughters looking like Betsy Ross, you contemplate getting a bonnet for your dog. (Naw... that's taking it too far.) Granted, the scene would likely appear odd and disturbing to your neighbors and concern some of your closest relatives, but you don't care because you're so excited about your promising garden. And so off you go for three and a half to four months satisfied with your labors, rubbing your hands in anticipatory delight for what you will find upon your return.

But if you did that, if you were to sow and split as I mentioned above, what would you find come harvest time? Would you come back to a flourishing, fruitful victory garden to satisfy your agrarian dreams? No! You would come back to discover a pest breeding ground overrun by weeds, a patch of dirt, overwatered in some areas, totally dry in others. You would find diminished, diseased, insect-stripped plants, gopher holes, perhaps a nest for ground squirrels and other varmints, a Uruk-hai, a dwarf, a troll or two and probably no vegetables or few edible ones.

Now, what would be—pardon the pun—at the root of your farming disaster? Is the problem with your seeds? Would you say, "Oh no! Look at what's happened? I don't understand. The soil was good; I planted the seeds in perfect order. The garden had water, sun. What is up with this? Hey, wait a minute, hmmm? I get it! It's the seeds. Must be bad seeds! Yep, I think I'll plant another garden with different seeds, but first I'm going to write the seed company and give them a piece of my mind. The nerve of that company selling such seeds!" Obviously, that would be a ridiculous assessment of the situation, wouldn't it? The problem would not lie with the seeds but with the neglect of the gardener.

As you know, gardens need lots of attention—not simply undiminished sunlight or arbitrary watering. In fact, some plants need a little water, others need abundant water, and even those needs vary according to the plants' development. Plants need ground cultivation, fertilizer, pest control, pruning. In short, gardens need a lot of nurture if you expect them to yield good results. It takes a lot of work and time to raise a fruitful garden, but if you love gardening and its produce, it is satisfying and worth the effort—trust me.

Children, my friends, are like gardens. Birthing them, or the finalizing of that adoption, is simply the exuberant beginning of a labor-intensive and joyful process, the fruit of which is eternal! As such, our children need us in the form of nurturing time: hours, days, weeks, months, years teaching them, nurturing them, correcting them in the truth of the Lord so that they may grow to be fruitful branches of the strong and true Vine.

CHAPTER 9

Purposeful & Passionate Living

Principle #2: The consistency of discipleship expressed in purposeful living

In order for people, including our children, to become disciples (literally "learners") they must observe the truth lived out. That is how we learn best, by seeing the truth fleshed out in three dimensions.

Living and dying: The example of Jesus

Jesus Christ lived His life with absolute clarity of purpose, and by so doing He saved His disciples from their sin and left them a clear pattern for living. The Lord Jesus came to serve by giving His life as an atoning sacrifice so that He might redeem sinners to God. The Lord stated this purpose in the familiar words of Mark 10:45, *"For even the Son of Man did not come to be served, but to serve, and to give His life a ransom for many."* That statement by the Lord came as a corrective to the twelve who at this point in the Lord's ministry failed to adequately perceive and embrace His exemplary life and mission (Mark 10:42–45). Instead of humbly serving one another as Jesus taught and demonstrated, the disciples were locked in a head-to-head competition for preeminence. Believing the millennial kingdom was about to appear, they were jockeying for position in the new administration (Luke 19:11; Mark 10:35–37, 41). Anticipating the immediate establishment of the messianic kingdom, they were engaged in an ongoing argument to assert "top dog" status.

The Lord's life and words unmistakably pointed them toward humble service, and yet the disciples were slow to understand and mimic the Lord's clear and unfaltering example. Sadly, they continued bickering right into the last days of the Lord's ministry on this earth. How that must have grieved His heart. Three years of constant instruction wedded to the integrity of a perfect example, and still these men were not picking up the purpose of the Lord's first coming.

Were we in a similar situation as mentor to these men, I suppose the temptation for us would be to give up, to say, "Okay, I'm done. These men are absolute dolts. I'm flunking the entire class! I should have gone with the Phi Beta Kappa group from Judea." We would be tempted to throw in the towel, but what did the Lord do on the last night He spent with his bickering men? Did He throw in the towel? No, instead He quite literally picked one up in order to serve His beloved friends and to yet again patiently demonstrate the attitude He longed for His men to own. Once their Seder meal was over, Jesus calmly got up from His seat, took off His outer cloak, picked up a towel, girded His garments, stooped, and began to wash the disciples' feet (John 13:1–17).

The Lord persisted to the last hour in modeling what He taught His men from the very beginning of His ministry. He knew His men needed to see the truth as well as hear it, and that the truth would change their lives (John 1:14; 1 John 1:1–3). The Lord Jesus taught the truth, modeled it, and persisted in so doing until the end so that His men would have an example to follow. This is why the Lord said to Peter, "*What I do you do not realize now, but you will understand hereafter*" (John 13:7). In other words, "Keep watching, Peter, because the light is going to come on when you remember how I lived and what I taught you." Jesus understood His men needed to hear the truth and see the pattern, and in part, that's why He lived as He did.

Jesus lived His sermons. Moments after washing the disciples' feet, He explained to the remaining eleven, "*You call Me Teacher and Lord; and you are right, for so I am. If I then, the Lord and the Teacher, washed your feet, you also ought to wash one another's feet. For I gave you an example that you also should do as I did to you* (John 13:13–15, emphasis added). In less than twenty-four hours, Jesus would take this example of humble service to its highest form. At Calvary, Jesus would display the greatest act of selfless service the disciples and the world would ever see. The next day, the Lord willingly hung on a Roman cross, bearing the wrath of God for the sins of His people. Why? So that He might redeem His people from their iniquities and also show them how to live the way of love.

We have an audience

Jesus lived with purposeful intention, aware that His disciples were watching. He understood that "hearing" and "seeing" would guide the truth to its mark and transform their lives and with ripple effect impact the lives of countless other disciples to come. Jesus made disciples by showing them what the truth looked like, not simply what it sounded like.

We too learn best when we see the truth modeled before our own eyes, and so it is with our children. They will learn about God and His ways best when they see the truth of God's word fleshed out on the stage of life. Now, there is not a one of us who can live out the truth as Jesus did, perfectly—but it is incumbent upon Christian parents to follow their Master's example and humbly, with dependence upon the Holy Spirit, live out the Bible before their children. Indeed, purposeful living is a believing parent's calling.

That reality is one of the key permeating principles of Deuteronomy 6:1–9. The text makes it clear: the instruction of our children in the ways of the Lord cannot be divorced from modeling the truth daily. Parents, we have an ever-watching audience in our kids. Listen once again to the words of verses 6–9,

> These words, which I am commanding you today, shall be on your heart. You shall teach them diligently to your sons and shall talk of them when you sit in your house and when you walk by the way and when you lie down and when you rise up. You shall bind them as a sign on your hand and they shall be as frontals on your forehead. You shall write them on the doorposts of your house and on your gates.

The simple appeal of the text is for parents to take the truth that rests on their hearts (i.e., the truth that saturates and shapes their reason and emotions), and to flesh that truth out in the flow of their daily lives. This is an urging for moms and dads to incarnate biblical principles so that their children may see what the truth looks like in HD.

The Lord Jesus came to this earth to preach, to proclaim God's kingdom to the lost by means of words, but He also explained God by His actual life (Luke 4:43; Mark 1:38; John 1:18). The God whom we could never see, we saw explained in Jesus Christ (John 1:18; 1 Timothy 1:17; 1 Timothy 6:16). And so the Word—the eternal God, the second person of the Trinity—took on flesh to reveal the Almighty to His creatures so that they might know Him through His Son (John 1:14, 18). Likewise, God's words must be fleshed out, lived out, modeled, so that our children might understand them and make them their own.

I realize this is no small or easy task, and mark it, as I have mentioned above, we will fail. In fact, the most consistent biblical command I have had the opportunity to practice before my dear wife and beloved children is repentance. My family has gotten quite used to the sight of dad eating crow. After a while you get used to the taste of confession and asking for forgiveness. It's not bad. It tastes like chicken! As challenging as living a life of integrity is, we must—with an ever deepening dependence upon God's Spirit—demonstrate God's transforming truths to our families. Our kids need to hear and see the truth.

I'm not denying the rightful place of catechistical training. Some wrongly believe that the only thing disciples need in order to learn is a good example, but the fact remains that God has given us His truth in propositional statements to understand first and then apply (live out). Without understanding what God has said in His word, living out the truth is impossible. That is explicitly taught in Deuteronomy 6:7–9. "*You shall teach them* [God's precepts] *diligently to your sons and shall talk of them.*" We need to teach our children information about the person of God and His ways. They need to know about who He is and how He works, e.g., His dealings with His people, His plan of redemption for mankind, the beauty of His glory, the outworking of His magnificent plan for the ages. We need to sit down with them and in a systematic fashion tell our children about God and His gracious deeds. As we said, the Bible consists of objective truth; as such, we need to communicate it in propositional statements—that is most certainly true.

That said, you will notice much of the "teaching" and "telling" referenced in Deuteronomy 6 happens in the warp and woof of everyday life. Truth is transferred to the next generation as it is talked about and modeled by mom and dad and played out in the classroom of life, not just in a lecture hall. Life is the schoolroom where parents equip their children. Notice the all-encompassing venue parents need to employ to teach their children in verse 7. It starts within the four walls of the home, extends to life lived in the outside world, and demands continual conscious engagement on the part of mom and dad.

Give us this day our daily bread

First, parents are commanded to "*diligently*" teach or sharpen their children in God's word. How and where? Moses tells us this must take place in the day-to-day flow of routine duties and conversations within the context of the home. "*You shall teach them diligently to your sons and shall talk of them when you sit in your house*" (Deuteronomy 6:7a). God tells parents to exercise and explain His precepts for life in the life they share with their children at home. In other words, live the truth purposely before the eyes of your kids and seize the many unique opportunities that living together affords you to explain/model biblical truth to them.

Obviously, the text in front of us does not give us specific examples of how to prioritize our commitments in order to better model the truth before our family. It simply commands us to live out biblical precepts before our children and to talk about them in our homes. Where do you begin to do that? Allow me to give a simple, biblical starting point to begin to fulfill the imperative of Deuteronomy 6:7. It is a renewable point of contact that we have virtually every day, and yet it is an opportunity that is almost entirely ignored by many busy families. I'm talking about breaking bread together, sharing a meal as a family around a family table. In Jewish culture—which is the context in which this passage was written and delivered—shared meals were a daily point of contact between parents and children and served as prime opportunities to adorn life with God's precepts.

Have you ever wondered why God made us to experience hunger, the irresistible need to replenish and refuel our bodies multiple times a day? Let's face it, God could have designed our bodies to pick up necessary nutrients in any way He pleased. He could have created us to absorb nourishment through our pores from the air or from a solar panel on our heads. Ridiculous? Yes, but it underscores this question, why did the Lord design us to have appetites and consume food the way we do? I'm sure there are many reasons why the Lord wired us the way He has, not the least of which is that we may experience our need for His provision throughout each and every day, several times per day. Needing to eat is yet another reminder that the Lord is God (self-sustaining) and we are not. We experience the need for food every day, morning, noon, and night, and the Lord opens the bounty of His stores to feed us.

God has designed us to eat so that we may also know His goodness. Think of it, unlike so many of God's other creatures who have a mono-dimensional diet (eucalyptus leaves for Koala bears [marsupials actually], krill for blue whales), we have an amazing panoply of foods God created for us to enjoy. The spectrum of colors, smells, tastes, textures arranged and rearranged by the creativity of man never ceases to amaze us and please us, and spawn endless TV food competitions. Why didn't the Lord simply create one lukewarm-bland-grey-gruel (I guess I've just described oatmeal) that would meet our nutritional needs and call it good? Just go to the Gruel Station, pump it in once a day or once a week and it's done—like we fuel our cars. The Lord created us to enjoy a cornucopia of culinary delights so that we might know His kindness. He created us to want food and to satiate our palate with a rainbow of choices because He is good and the Giver of good things to His creatures. He delights in our ability to taste of His goodness, as it were, and man knows of God's goodness in part through his ability to eat. Experiencing and satisfying hunger makes our souls cry out, "*Praise the Lord! Oh give thanks to the Lord, for He is good... who gives food to all flesh, for His lovingkindness is everlasting*" (Psalm 106:1).

Yet one of the main reasons God has created us with the necessity to eat (in my opinion) is to bring us together, mostly for the purpose of fellowship, but very importantly in that process, to learn. Before man was bewildered by thousands of choices and the mixed blessing of mobility, people had to come together with their people, their families, to share a meal, to partake of life together, to speak, to hear, to learn. It would be an interesting study to see how often the Bible references people eating together. One thing is certain, the Bible talks a lot about breaking bread with those who are close to us or with those we desire to know. For example, think of the many times the Lord Jesus is referenced in the gospels eating with people. The Lord ate with sinners, with the multitudes, with the religious leaders, with friends, with His disciples. He even took time to eat with His circle of friends after the resurrection to reassure them and instruct them (Matthew 9:9–10; 15:32–38; 26:26–29; Mark 14:3; Luke 7:36; 10:38–42; 19:1–10; 24:30, 41–43). What is interesting is the Lord Jesus used meals to bring people together in order to display and teach the truth until the very last hours of His post-resurrection ministry on earth.

Shortly before Luke describes the Lord's ascension into heaven in Acts 1:9–10, we read the following in Acts 1:4: "*Gathering them together, He* [Jesus] *commanded them not to leave Jerusalem, but to wait for what the Father had promised* [the coming of the Holy Spirit and the birth of the church], *'Which,'* *He said, 'you heard of from Me.'*" The Lord brought His men together for one last important instruction, and how did He do it? The vehicle He used for this last essential teaching was likely a meal. The actual Greek term translated "*Gathering them together*" means literally "to eat with."[1] God wired us to eat, in part, to bring us together for fellowship and learning. This was a favorite and effective teaching opportunity that the Lord Jesus used during His three-year ministry on earth.

My friends, many of us need to rediscover the joy of eating together with our families. Sharing a meal can be a prime opportunity to teach our children in the context of daily life. A lot of the wonderful interaction and dialogue referenced in Deuteronomy 6:7 can happen around the family table.

Obviously, modeling the truth and speaking of the truth at home is not limited to mealtimes. The upshot of Deuteronomy 6:7 encourages parents to flesh out God's words in the whole of family life lived under the same roof. Shared meals, absolutely, but also in the practice of household chores, when interacting with one's spouse, when exercising discipline or counseling our children, when resting from labor—normal, daily, home-centric interaction. Biblical truth must of necessity be modeled, consistently lived out by mom and dad, in the flow of life at home. I would go so far as to say that the rule of God's precepts in the lives of parents as they lovingly lead their children within the intimacy of domestic life is likely the single most important ingredient in the salvation and discipleship of children. Where people see truth married to practice, people's lives are deeply impacted.

The opposite is frequently true as well. All too often I have dialogued with broken people who struggle in their walk with God, or who have rejected a personal relationship with Jesus Christ, and found that at the core of their inner conflict or disbelief lies the failure of parents to model at home the Christian image they projected to the church and the outside world. Incongruity between a believing parent's life at home and what they portray to others can be devastating to the spiritual health of our kids. Parents must adorn their lives with the truth of God's word, and that starts within the four walls of intimacy we call our homes.

The highways and byways of life

From the hub of life in the household, parents are also instructed to model biblical integrity in the highways and byways of everyday existence outside the home. "*You shall teach them* [biblical principles] *diligently to your sons and shall talk of them... when you walk by the way*" (emphasis added). This phrase beckons parents to teach their children in the balance of life's activities and relationships and would extend to all interactions that take us out of the home, e.g., errands, leisure, socializing with other families and friends. God tells us that all things, all places, present teaching opportunities. Just as important, this mandate governs our character and dealings with people—believing and unbelieving—and reminds us that the way we treat others (those who live outside our homes) helps teach our children how to respect those outside the faith and love those within the household of faith.

I've known a handful of vocational educators in my life, and without exception, all of them coveted their "time off." Be it Christmas, Easter break, or summer vacation, each one looked forward to hanging up their chalkboard and hanging out away from school. Long breaks from the teaching schedule are a great perk for professional educators, but there are no such breaks for parental educators. Our educational vigilance goes 24/7. Life is a parent's schoolhouse. Note the closing thought in verse 7, "*You shall teach them diligently to your sons and shall talk of them when you sit in your house and when you walk by the way and when you lie down and when you rise up*" (emphasis added). That covers the twenty-four-hour cycle. As far as modeling and teaching goes, parents are never off the clock.

In other words, both within our homes and outside our homes, from daybreak to sunset, the truth that rests in a parent's heart, the truth that enlightens our thinking, that feeds our emotions, that shapes our character and volition, that transforms our inner self, this same truth must continually be on our lips and on display in our lives. It is in this spiritually stimulating context that children learn most effectively about God and become familiar with His paths. Primarily, this is how God designed truth to be assimilated by our young, through their parents in the warp and woof of life.

What God is teaching us implicitly, but very clearly, is that the learning curve goes way up when truth is observed, when it is modeled in the context of life at home. Our sons and daughters learn best when we naturally talk about God's precepts in the flow of conversation and when they see biblical principles come to life in our everyday coming in and going out. To reiterate, truth takes firm root in the souls of our kids when it is couched in ordinary day-to-day life.

This is both a positive and negative axiom, isn't it? Mom and Dad, be aware that our children are watching us and they are learning. Really, we are always teaching our children. Our biblical mandate is to seize the opportunities of life in order to teach and model God's truth positively, but one way or another we will teach by what we say and do. Our young people are observing how we react to life. They are taking mental notes on how we respond to adversity, success, and failure. We're not "off the clock" when we're tired or "off the hook" when we get a flat in the middle of a busy day. Our children are observing how we regard people, how we use our words, how we treat our spouse. They are considering how we spend money and the other resources God entrusts to us. They take note when we encounter the frequent forks in the road of life and we have to decide whether to follow God's way or the world's way. What will we choose? Whatever we do, mark this: as they watch, they learn. This is why the Lord calls us to conscientiously speak and flesh out His precepts before the ever observant, ever learning eyes and ears of our sons and daughters.

Sometimes parents can plan great teachable moments, such as when we purposely engage our kids in an activity where we can talk about and model a particular biblical virtue like hard work (e.g., work projects around the house), or kindness (e.g., preparing and taking a meal to someone who is ill or shut in). We can create wonderful learning opportunities for our children, for example, by taking the fruit of the Spirit outlined in Galatians 5:22–23 and creatively finding ways to demonstrate what those virtues look like in real life. For example, you can display kindness by befriending a new family at church and inviting them to your home for a meal. You can show love by volunteering to do housework or property upkeep for someone who is incapable of physical work, or participate in a short term missions project with your kids to serve the local church and its ministries (digging wells, building structures for the needy, or assisting in medical missions). Such lessons can display for our children the beautiful character of God, His grace toward us, and how He desires we treat others. Without question, these purposeful object lessons can help shape our children for a lifetime.

And yet, while premeditated instruction is a wonderful way to display the Bible, most of the positive teaching and learning our families experience takes place not as the result of our careful schemes and nifty plans, but rather as the outcome of consistently living a godward life, not a perfect life obviously, but a grace-filled life adorned with the practical beauty of God's eternal word. Our journey through this earth is the road that providentially rises up to meet us. Each day has divine teaching opportunities that we must discover and employ to showcase the truth in real-life circumstances, and as we do, learning happens. When our children see and hear the truth in the three dimensions of daily life, that truth can shape their minds and change lives.

On the road again!

Several years ago, this was literally driven home to my mind. I was invited to speak at a weeklong family camp in Colorado, and so early on a cool, June, Southern California morning, my wife Val and I packed up the kids and headed to the Rocky Mountains for a week of family ministry. We had a long ride ahead of us with some eleven hundred miles between our home in Temecula, California, (just northeast of San Diego) and our destination in the beautiful Sangre de Cristo mountain range of south central Colorado.

We planned to travel over a couple of days, leaving early on a Friday morning, hoping to tackle eight hundred miles on the first day and then cruise into camp the following day with plenty of time to spare. (Camp started with dinner and a teaching time on Saturday evening.) As usual on long trips, we determined to face our big driving stretch on the first day of our journey when we were the freshest. Keeping with our tradition on long drives (especially when the kids were young), we preferred to take off really early in the morning, 3:30 a.m., and put as many miles under our wheels as possible before the sun rose and the kids roused.

It's actually a routine we have grown to love. We wake up to strong brewed coffee, the car is packed with the front end pointing down the driveway ready to roll, and of course there's always the anticipation of some long hours spent together as a family reading, laughing, eating, sleeping, and erupting into the goofy antics generated by cabin fever. Typically, the initial early morning dash happens under the cover of predawn darkness and is among my favorite parts of the journey. While the kids sleep, Val and I get some wonderful uninterrupted time to talk, and then when Val gets sleepy, she takes a nap and I put on some music, sip my coffee, munch on some sunflower seeds, think, and pray—with my eyes open. Before we know it, we're three-plus hours down the road, at which time the family begins to stir from their slumber. On this particular trip, things ran like clockwork. The kids slept for the first part of the morning, and by the time they woke up, four hours of dotted highway and several million California tumbleweeds, sagebrush, and Joshua trees had whizzed by. As soon as everyone stretched themselves awake, we were all ready for breakfast and a break, but before we stopped I had a little something in store for the final thirty minutes of our first stretch.

On this particular morning, Val and I visited for a couple of hours before she succumbed to drowsiness. As she napped for a good long while and I drove, my thoughts turned to a series of Old and New Testament Scriptures that focused on God's provision, His great faithfulness, and our privilege of exercising trust in Him even when things look bleak and deliverance seems far off. I can't tell you why these thoughts were working their way through my mind. My topic for the weeklong camp was quite different, but the thoughts were coming forcefully and clearly, and I pursued the Scriptures with which God's Spirit bathed my mind. I recall being refreshed and energized by the flow of these ideas, and when the kids woke up, I decided to lead my bleary-eyed clan in a family Bible time to start the day. I had about thirty minutes before we pulled over for breakfast, Val and the kids were as alert as they would be all day, and they were cooped up in the car with nowhere to go. It was perfect, a preacher with a sermon and a captive audience.

I began to wax eloquent on trusting God, on how He always takes care of His people, and that He's worthy of our trust. I tell you, I was humming along pretty well, and I remember thinking as I heard myself waxing lyrical, "Man, this is good stuff! I mean really good. This is printable!" I couldn't look back at my kids for long because I had to keep my eyes on the road, but I was certain that my children were sitting in their seats in astonished amazement of their father's biblical depth, breadth, and wisdom. Mind you, they didn't say that exactly; in fact, they said nothing at all, but they must have surely been thinking along these lines—I believe I was.

They were no doubt saying to themselves (again, not audibly, but assuredly in their minds), "Oh father, you are so wise! You are like a walking Bible theological dictionary. You are like Berkhof's Systematic Theology with legs—only not so square and so much more interesting. Yes, you are indeed like Apollos of old, mighty in the word and eloquent of tongue. We shall call you our Bible Father, and because you are also so accessible, we shall call you Bible Dad. Yes, that shall be our name for you! We shall call you Bible Dad. You are our very own Bible Dad." I'm pretty sure they were thinking something like that.

When I had finished my little devotional spiel—quite happy with myself and sure I had inspired my children to faith—everyone was ready for a break and some breakfast, so we pulled over to stretch our legs and eat. After breakfast, we quickly got back on the road and proceeded to our first fueling stop (St. George, Utah), but as is usually the case, I could only drive an additional 20 to 30 minutes after breakfast before the deficit of sleep and the food in my stomach conspired to shut me down. I always think, "I can do this! I'm a guy! I could drive across the North Pole on a cup of coffee and thirty minutes sleep. I can do a couple more hours after breakfast, no problem." But before long I'm seeing double horizons and drooling out of the corner of my mouth. At that point, for the safety of my family and to avoid the very real threat of physical injury from my wife, I reluctantly hand over the wheel to Val and try to grab a few winks. That scene repeats itself on our first day of travel as sure as the sun rises and the seasons change. This trip was no different.

Val relieved me of driving; I settled down into a comfortable position and was fast asleep before another mile clicked on the odometer. We continued north on Interstate 15 through the arid Nevada desert en route to St. George, Utah. For those of you not familiar with this stretch of highway, Interstate 15 takes an interesting twist as it leaves Nevada. It traverses a beautiful and rugged canyon called the Virgin River Gorge while at the same time cutting through a tristate area, beginning in Mesquite, Nevada, then passing through the northwest corner of Arizona, and finally arriving in St. George. It's about a 40-mile desolate stretch of road with dramatic scenery. Within the relative short distance between the flat Nevada desert and the plateau that is St. George, you pass a parade of sheer canyon walls, red-to-orange rocky landscapes, the silty and sometimes turbulent waters of the Virgin River, frequent narrow shoulders, and a consistently steep uphill grade on the northbound lanes. In fact, as you travel north on the I-15 you climb about 1,500 feet in elevation from Mesquite to St. George.

Until recently, the Virgin River Gorge had an exit at the beginning of the trek (Mesquite) and one at the end (Utah Port of Entry station), and as you might have guessed, back in the day there was absolutely no phone service between the parentheses of Mesquite and St. George. To top it off, on this particular trip it was unusually hot for that time of year. That part of the southwest was gripped by a heatwave, and by the time we hit the gorge the thermometer was topping one hundred ten degrees. It was sizzling!

During our ascent into the gorge, I was out, blissfully drooling on my pillow, when all of a sudden I heard the distant voice of Val calling me to wake up. She rubbed my arm vigorously and continued with, "Marcelo, wake up! Wake up!!" Confused, I wiped the drool off my chin and blurted out, "Honestly officer, I thought I was going much slower." Not really. Actually, I was simply groping for a handle on reality as I came out of that zombie-like twilight world that exists between napping and wakefulness.

Startled, I asked Val, "What's wrong? What's going on?" With concern in her voice she responded, "The van is losing power. When I try to give it gas, it begins to sputter." So in my mechanical wisdom I told Val, "Uh, hold off the gas and then punch it. Maybe it's choking on a fur ball or something and it's trying to pass it (yes, I actually said that)." Valorie followed my ridiculous instructions and when she thumped the gas pedal the engine flat-out died. We lost power immediately and were losing momentum fast on the upward incline of the northbound right lane. At that same moment, the steering column locked up and we (both Val and I) were barely able to coax the behemoth Ford van conversion onto the tight shoulder, just barely enough to get the vehicle off the road.

So there we were, stuck in Dante's Gorge, broiling in the triple-digit temperatures, not knowing what to do next. I guess that's when a man's autonomic response kicks in. Searching my foggy brain for an answer, I instinctively did what any normal male would do when faced with a car problem. I stepped out of the vehicle to check under the hood. I pulled the hood up, propped it up with the metal rod thingy, and scrutinized the bewildering array of mechanical stuff. It looked like the surface of a galactic Star Destroyer. There were belts, hoses, assorted blocks of metal, wires, and little tiny pieces of engine I could not identify all jammed into a compartment the size of an average cooler. I thought, "Man, Ford mechanics must have really tiny hands."

As you have probably guessed, I don't know anything about cars. I'm shamefully and utterly useless with cars, but it's my duty as a man to check under the hood even if it doesn't solve anything. I think it makes my wife feel better somehow. So there I was like a deer staring into the headlights, looking at a tangled mass of mystery before my eyes, needing to say something helpful or encouraging to my dear wife. Lamely I blurted out,

"Yeah Val, we have a problem here."

"Really? What is it honey?"

"Oh, it's a uh, umh, it's a mechanical problem. We need a mechanic (thought bubble: "...with freaky small hands.")"

Having done that, I slammed the hood closed, my wife slid over to the back seat to comfort the kids, and I plopped myself back into the driver's seat. I gripped the steering wheel with all my might and started to fume. I went from clueless to angry in about ten seconds.

Little sleep and Marcelo don't get along, and I am not pleased to say that as I wrung the steering wheel I began to lose grip on my emotions. In fact, I was getting quite angry. My first impulse when confronted by the problem was not to talk to the Lord about it, to pray with my family and comfort them. My knee-jerk desire when the initial hopelessness of the situation hit me was to *kavech* (whine) and vent. I began to think, "Oh great! Here we are stranded in the middle of nowhere on one of the outer rings of Dante's Inferno with no communication and no air conditioning. It's Africa hot, and I'm due to preach tomorrow in a town 900 miles from here with no apparent way to get to where we're going. That's just peachy! Absolutely lovely!" Then I bellyached to heaven under my breath, "And Lord, I'm doing this for you. I should have been a doctor. I really don't appreciate this very much."

As I allowed the frustration to build up within me, I remember just wanting to slam my fist into the dashboard of that suddenly worthless van. For all I knew our car problem was all the dashboard's fault—not to mention it was slightly padded and convenient to hit. I would show it a thing or two. I wanted so bad to lose my top and wallow in my misery. It was in the midst of contemplating my personal encounter with the dashboard that I suddenly recalled the little family devotional I had delivered earlier that morning when things were bright, hopeful, cool, and operating smoothly. I remembered my little soliloquy on trusting the Lord and then, sure as the sun rose that morning, it dawned on me that the present turn of events were linked to my homily and I wondered knowingly, "Oh, so that's what this is about, eh? Ah, man?! Why couldn't I have picked a different topic for our devotional, like how to deal with a sudden influx of wealth from the benevolence of a long lost uncle? Why did I pick the trusting-God-even-when-delivery-looks-far-off-and-painful thing? What was I thinking?"

Unfortunately, my sudden enlightenment did not immediately help my mood nor prompt me to obey. In fact, for a moment the thought of my topic selection and present circumstances made me all the more steamed and vexed. At this moment, I clearly realized I needed to trust in the Lord. The problem was I did not want to trust! I wanted to be justifiably angry, and so, compounding my emotions was a healthy dose of justified guilt. That dashboard was mocking me now, taunting me to hit it. All this played out in my tired, selfish, conflicted little mind over some thirty seconds or so, and just before I gave in further to my petty impulses I happened to glance back at my precious family in the rearview mirror. My eldest, Josh (10 at the time), was hanging tough, though concern was written all over his glistening face. My son Josiah—who was just a little guy then—had that worried look he got in stressful situations. His anxious brow knit, his little nostrils flared, his baby blues darted back and forth accenting a countenance that said, "It's hot; we're in a desert, and I'm probably going to be eaten by an iguana." His barely-four-year-old emotions were in a vulnerable place.

Then my eyes bounced over to my six-year-old, Rebekah, nestled under her mother's arm. She was crying. Little girls do something to their daddies when they cry. I can't explain it, but dads will just about move heaven and earth to assuage their tears. Seeing Rebekah rattled was a check for my unruly emotions. In that moment I thought, "If I lose my temper, I'll crush my fragile children, upset my dear wife—and I'll probably deploy the airbag." That would definitely not help because then I would be mad at the airbag as well as the dashboard, and I would look unbelievably stupid! So in that brief moment of spiritual lucidity, I asked the Lord for His grace, gathered the little bit of wits I had left (about half an ounce), turned to my wife and kids and weakly offered, "Hey guys, remember that talk Daddy gave this morning about trusting God to take care of us? Hey (ha-ha), well? Who knew? Here we are. Talk about timing! Let's entrust ourselves and our situation to the Lord, okay? Let's pray." I then uttered a magnificent prayer that went something like this, "Lord, help, please. Thank you. Amen." One for the books!

As soon as I finished praying, I got out of the van—probably to assess the tire situation and count them—when a subcompact driven by an elderly gentleman pulled up behind our van asking if we needed some help—probably the easiest question I have ever fielded. "Yes!" I offered astutely. To make a long story only slightly shorter, this kind gentleman took me to the Port of Entry station for the state of Utah; I called the Auto Club and we got the van towed into St.

George. A local mechanic's shop put a temporary Band-Aid on our problem, and late that evening we managed to sputter and limp into Green River, Utah. It was not quite as far as we had hoped to go on our first day (about 170 miles short), but we were able to find a hotel room and settle in for the night. The beginning of our day (3:30 a.m.) and our early family devotional seemed a distant memory left behind in the California desert three states and several hundred miles behind us.

There were no restaurants open in Green River when we pulled into town at 11:00 p.m., but we had milk in the cooler and Cocoa Puffs in our stash, and that was good enough for dinner that night. The kids loved it. We were relieved to be off the road and have a safe place to spend the night. We were extremely joyful. We all felt a sense of gratitude to the Lord for His protection and gracious provision, and our gratitude quickly morphed into a celebration of sorts. In fact, by the time we finished our nutritious cereal, we were kind of giddy and just plain old goofy. The boys were bouncing off the walls and I was relishing and contributing to the madness—maybe it was the sugar.

In the midst of our revelry, I'll never forget this as long as I live, I spotted Rebekah on the other side of the hotel room with this "Aha!" look on her little face. She then excitedly ran to me—her big, beautiful, green eyes wide with wonder—looked up at me and tugging on my shirt exclaimed, "Daddy! Daddy!!" And I said, "What is it, honey? What's going on?" to which she replied, "Daddy, we really can trust God with our troubles, because He does take care of us!" I paused, looked down at her and said, "Didn't I tell ya'? I'm Bible Dad! Hang with me girl; I've got all kinds of gems like that. Bible Dad, that's me!"

Actually, I had a Mike Myers' moment and got *verklempt* (choked up with emotion). All I could do was cup her face in my hands, smile, and nod in agreement. "Out of the mouth of babes." God had adorned our day with His truth—in this case His great faithfulness—for all of us to see, appreciate, and embrace. The point is this, I could have lectured from Temecula, California, to Montrose, Colorado, about God's providential care for His people and our need to trust Him, but my kids could never have learned that truth half as well if they had not seen God's precepts working themselves out in our lives. Not that the truth was modeled in an exceptional way, mind you. In fact, it was quite tenuously and reluctantly portrayed by their father, and yet my children were able to see God's word working in and directing the events of our ordinary lives. That drove the truth home in a manner that serves them to the present day.

You and I as Christian parents must live life with a purpose to know the truth and to live it out. As our children see God's word adorning our lives, truth will have God's intended effect; it will inform and transform our families. We must strive to live purposefully, knowing that our children are watching, and as they watch, they are learning from us how we live. Effective mentoring of our children takes time; it demands that we model the truth, and just as important, efficacious discipleship requires a passion for the truth.

Principle #3: The consistency of discipleship demonstrated by passionate living

People who have the greatest impact on others are those who hold their convictions deeply and live out those precepts with passion. They teach and live the truth with infectious fervor. Think back to the mentors, teachers, pastors, professors, or coaches who shaped the way you think and live. It's a safe bet to say that those men and women believed deeply in what they taught and communicated it with passion in word and deed. In so doing, they impacted your life in significant ways such as the shaping of your values, your character. Perhaps they infused you with a philosophy of parenting or influenced your career choice, interests, or imparted to you a love for a field of study. As we have stated earlier, an evident love, a passion for God's truth is essential in imprinting biblical values on learners and especially the disciples under our roofs. No one demonstrated this general principle for us better than the Lord Jesus Himself.

The power of passion to communicate

Think back to the account of the Lord's visit to the temple in John 2:13–22. As an adult Jewish male, the Lord was required by Law to celebrate the Passover in Jerusalem. Jerusalem and its temple were near and dear to the heart of every righteous Jew. David cried out, *"O Lord, I love the habitation of Your house and the place where Your glory dwells"* (Psalm 26:8). If this was true of David, how much greater was the passion of the Messiah, the Holy One of Israel, for Zion and the seat of God's presence, the temple? The Lord assuredly delighted in observing God's prescribed call to worship in Jerusalem. What's more, this was the Lord's first visit to the Holy City and the temple since entering His formal ministry after John's baptism (Matthew 3:13–17). He assuredly longed to observe the Passover in Jerusalem and to commune with the Father in His house of prayer (Luke 2:49; Matthew 21:13).

Sadly, when He arrived at the temple, He did not encounter the sweet expressions of heartfelt worship. Instead, His holy desires were accosted by the corruption and greed that had overtaken the temple and polluted the pure worship of the God of Israel. He observed that His Father's house, a house of prayer, had been turned into a crass market of merchandizing and racketeering. In one of the best known incidents of the gospels, the Lord took command of the temple courts and began literally to clean house.[2] *"And He made a scourge of cords, and drove them all out of the temple, with the sheep and the oxen; and He poured out the coins of the money changers and overturned their tables; and to those who were selling the doves He said, 'Take these things away...'"* (John 2:15–16a).

Can you imagine the ruckus this must have caused? A whip-wielding, righteously enraged rabbi begins to drive large skittish animals (oxen and sheep, v. 14) out of the temple enclosure by force along with their merchandizers. Outraged men scream their objections while trying to control their agitated, fleeing beasts. Coinage flies, crashing and scattering wildly on the stone courtyard floors. Tables are overturned, pitching their assorted accounting paraphernalia into the bedlam of the rabble, and out of the cloud of this tumult the impassioned preacher's voice cries out for the vindication of God's holiness and the sanctity of His dwelling. As the crowd and uproar begin to settle, the rabbi's fervid words hang in the air for all to hear and ponder. *"Stop making My Father's house a place of business"* (John 2:16b). An uncomfortable, awkward silence settles over the crowd, and the disciples of the teacher look on with quizzical amazement.

Do you think this incident made an impression on the Lord's men, His disciples? Perhaps as it was happening they were a little bewildered; perhaps they were taken aback by it all. But as the dust began to settle in the moments right after this event, or possibly later as they discussed what happened, the narrative tells us the disciples experienced a collective epiphany. John 2:17 informs us that *"His disciples remembered* [remembered what?] *that it was written* [i.e., Scripture, Psalm 69:9], *"ZEAL FOR YOUR HOUSE WILL CONSUME ME."* Do you realize what Jesus was doing here? He was instinctively acting upon a clear, biblical maxim that was ingrained into the fiber of His being—biblical truth that was on His heart, shaping His thinking, attitudes, and directing his actions.

You see, the Lord didn't simply talk or lecture about the holiness of the temple; He was passionate about it. He lived it, and that zeal transferred this biblical reality (zeal for God's house) to His disciples in an indelible way. Do you think the disciples ever looked at the temple complex in the same way after seeing the Lord's passion on display? All of a sudden, a forgotten, obscure, Old Testament verse came alive in three dimensions. The truth was driven home, embossed on their collective hearts never to be forgotten, ever shaping their attitudes and actions in worship. Passion for the truth is a powerful catalyst to impact the lives of those around us.

Parental mentoring driven by passion

The shepherding, the instruction, the teaching of the learners under our care must be driven by an ardent love for God and the things of God in the same way Jesus taught His men. Put another way, if we want the truth to stick, we must display it with true vivacity. People (big or little) as a general rule remember precepts in relation to how vividly or passionately they observe those precepts taught and lived. Therefore you and I as parents must live out biblical truth passionately.

We don't want to model the truth technically or mechanically like some computer or machine going through its programmed cycles. We must live out the truth with zeal, because we believe it, because we love it, because it has become part and parcel of our being. It rests on our hearts, shaping our attitudes, and driving our words and deeds. Kids need to see more than simple rote, correct, heartless obedience. They need to see conviction in action. That's how they come to know, love, and live the truth themselves.

Conversely, if we want to turn off and turn our kids away from God and His ways (quoting Paul, "*I speak as if insane,*" 2 Corinthians 11:23), one of the most effective ways to do that is to be passionless about what God decrees in His word. Just be boring with the Bible and you'll turn off future generations to the things of the Lord. And the best way I know to be boring with the Bible is to not know it nor understand it, yet under its banner demand obedience from our children to a list of "Christian" rules. Simply reduce biblical Christianity to a mindless litany of rules that we can't explain and/or fail to model, and I guarantee we will turn away the next generation from following after Christ and His words of life.

Bursting with zeal (Deuteronomy 6:1–9)

Our calling as parents is quite the opposite of such folly, isn't it? We are to model God's truth with diligence and genuine affection! Our passage is pregnant with zeal!

> *You shall love the LORD your God with all your heart and with all your soul and with all your might. These words, which I am commanding you today, shall be on your heart. You shall teach them diligently to your sons and shall talk of them when you sit in your house and when you walk by the way and when you lie down and when you rise up* (Deuteronomy 6:5–7).

Please take note of just a few of these passionate markers in the text. For example, consider the repetition of the word "*all*" in verse 5: "*all your heart, all your soul, all your might.*" And what are we to be "all-ing" about? Loving God. In the late seventies, a popular bumper sticker invited people to "Try God" as if God were some kind of sampler platter made available to satiate man's fickle curiosities. Verse 5 implores and commands believers to love God with abandon, with all our being, not simply with the tepid interest of the unbelieving.

In verse 6, we are commanded to put God's word on our heart, and as we have seen, this word is a term rich in meaning with reference to the entire inner person, the real you.[3] In other words, this is not a suggestion to dabble in the truth, but a command to be immersed in it and to be transformed from the inside out by it.

Then in verse 7 we read that our communication of God's life directives is to be characterized by fervency, "*You shall teach them* [God's precepts] *diligently to your sons.*" The word "*diligently*" is a very forceful command.[4] In other words, teaching and modeling God's word needs to be intentional, purposeful, and energized by passion.

Everyone is passionate about something!

Over the years, I have spent quite a bit of time meeting with men to talk about life issues, biblical truth, etc. Some of these men have shown only a lukewarm interest in God's word and spiritual conversation. This is true of ladies also, but allow me to pick on the guys for a moment because I spend so much of my time with men who often share my weaknesses. Frankly, some guys I have tried to encourage spiritually have a hard time getting excited about spiritual things. However, whenever I turn the conversation to "man talk" and introduce football, baseball, basketball, golf, fishing, hunting into the flow of our interaction, most of them predictably light up like a match! Their countenances change; their energy level goes way up. Their eyes brighten; they get more animated and become virtual Italians and start talking with their hands. They speak louder; they laugh more and readily show their approval or displeasure with their teams, brands, or prospects for next season. They display a visceral response to the things they are passionate about. They show a mild interest in the things of God but light up when we talk about sports and competition.

Now please understand, I'm not trying to knock sports. I love sports. If my knees were healthier, I would be a weekend warrior. I'm a competitive person. I love to win—sometimes a little too much! If I could afford it and I had more time, I would play golf, but I'm short on both. Those who know me will posit that I'm short on skill as well, but that has never stopped me from playing golf before. Take me out on the links and I'll tear up the course (literally, grass is going to fly!), and I'll come after you with a driver between my teeth and go down swinging, all the while laughing at your shank before and after I'm struck by lightning. Then, I will dutifully mark my gain on my scorched scorecard and drop to the ground unconscious, smoldering, somewhere out of bounds. I'm competitive!

I also love to watch sports on TV, especially football. I'm a hopelessly dyed-in-the-wool Rams fan, always have been, always will be. In a parallel universe, I would allow myself to watch all levels of competitive sports. If I were not a Christian, not married, and unemployed, I would be one of the top five sports junkies you would ever meet. I would slip into a depression after every Super Bowl because the season ended—truth is I struggle with that a little now. If I lived an undisciplined life, I would burn countless hours watching anything that vaguely resembled sports on television. I would watch competitive lawn mowing if they had such a sport—and enjoy it! I understand a passion for sports and competition.

My friends, I'm not trying to knock sports. I'm simply saying many men are passionate about sports, and all of us are passionate about something. You fill in the blank. We are "zealous," if you will, for the things that are important to us, the things we value. Whether it's sports, scrapbooking, politics, quilting, cooking, stamps, investments, ad infinitum, we are all passionate about something, and we display that passion for others to see. The point of Christ's example at the temple and the upshot of our text is that we need to be passionate about God and the things that are important to Him.

Five minutes with your kids

At this juncture some of you will protest, "But Marcelo, I'm not a passionate person. I'm not a 'Rah! Rah!' type of personality. I can't be someone I'm not. I'm laconic; I'm a person of few words and fewer emotions. Why I'm practically Norwegian—maybe even Icelandic. I have to lay my body on a hot rock in the noonday sun just to start my blood flowing. Have you ever seen Mount Rushmore? That's a portrait of my forefathers in a fit of ecstasy! I'm just not an excitable person, nor am I an exciting person. I love pocket protectors. I enjoy shopping for paper clips and assorted cleansers. My idea of a roaring party is busting out a Barry Manilow CD, organic chips, mild low-salt salsa, and a generic diet cola. I make Mitt Romney look like Mick Jagger. I don't show much passion about anything." Oh yes you do!

I would wager that you are passionate about several things and that you express your passion for those interests plenty. We are mistaken if we think passion is mostly demonstrated by the loud, trembling voice of a TV preacher, or exhibited by the energy of a hamster, or the zeal of young love. Passion, in fact, is frequently revealed by the value or the priority we assign to things in our lives. *Mom and Dad, you give me five minutes with your kids, and I will tell you what you are passionate about.*

Here are some of the questions I would ask your children about you, and I think this brief query would be valuable for you to answer for yourself. Take a personal inventory of the values you are displaying to your children. What do you spend time thinking about? What do you like to study and read about? What do you make time for? What do you find easy to talk about? What do you save up for? What do you spend your money on? What are you Googling? We display our passion in many ways, and here's an important truth you and I need to keep in the forefront of our minds: our children pick up on those values and priorities. They know what is truly important to us, and that is making an impression on them.

Dear people, God wants us to value and have a deep affectionate priority for Him and His ways. God give us this passion! And by the way—we keep coming back to this reality—the only way to develop a healthy appetite for God and His desires is to begin to ingest His word and allow His heart to become ours, to settle His word on our heart and allow that dynamic treasure to transform our values, our lives before the ever watchful eyes of our children and grandchildren.

Are we feeding our God-given desires?

As you know, we as Christians are locked in a lifelong struggle between the desires of God's indwelling Holy Spirit and our old passions, our unredeemed flesh (Galatians 5:16–24). The apostle Paul reminds us that this battle rages, *"For the flesh sets its desire against the Spirit, and the Spirit against the flesh; for these are in opposition to one another"* (v. 17). A longing for God's word, a hungering for what is good and holy is a healthy spiritual appetite, and ultimately these spiritual longings need to be fed. This begs the question, "Which appetite are we feeding?" Are we nurturing God's priorities brought to our hearts by His Spirit through His life-changing word, or are we nursing the cravings of our fallen, corrupted flesh? The only way we will own and passionately display Christ in us and His eternal values (for others to see and emulate) is by daily laying God's word upon our hearts and nurturing the longings God's Spirit gives us in the Bible.

Putting Feet to What We Believe

—Practical Suggestions

CHAPTER 10

How to Get Hungry for God's Word

An appetite for God's word

So where do we start this process of becoming a transformed Christian and parent, a man or a woman who genuinely loves God in truth, a parent who diligently teaches the stewardship of his children the treasure of God's precepts in word and deed? First, let me mention that you and I must start where we are, and we must stand firmly on God's all-sufficient grace. Only the powerful and abundant grace of God can enable us for this great endeavor of parenting, and only God's grace can work through our weakness and cover our failures. By His grace we must begin where we are and from there continue on in this same enablement.

A believer's fundamental need

But let me ask that primary question again. How do we become transformed Christian parents who impact their children for Christ and for eternity? Some would say that we must look to the word of God and make it the cornerstone of our life and our parental discipleship. They would argue that we must go to the word and study it, mull it over continually (Psalm 1:1–2), apply it, obey it, and teach it to our families. I agree heartily with this pursuit! Seeking a growing knowledge of God's word is absolutely worthy of our undivided commitment and essential for our spiritual well-being and the spiritual health of our families. However, I would suggest to you that before we can effectively fill our lives and homes with Scripture we must pursue a more basic underlying need in relation to the word of God.

It is a fundamental need that prepares us for the effective pursuit of the word, a passionate relationship with its Author, and a transformed personal and familial life. That foundational need, my friends, is an appetite or a hunger for the word of God. Before we can effectively feast on the truth and experience its life-altering effect, it is necessary for us to have an appetite for the Bible. That appetite or craving makes devouring and applying the Scripture possible; it is therefore essential to all that we have talked about in this book.

As a matter of priority then, if we want to be transformed by the word of God and benefit from its catalytic ministry in our lives and families, we must stimulate an appetite for it. If our spiritual appetite is lagging or absent, we will not partake of the biblical feast God has provided for our spiritual health. For example, in the physical realm, when people are sick they have little or no appetite, and when such conditions exist, people don't eat. This results in diminished nutrition to the body and the manifold health problems that accompany privation and compound illness.

When my wife was diagnosed and treated for breast cancer 10 years ago, the life-saving intervention she received made her extremely sick. Her treatment not only attacked her cancer, it all but rendered her unable to enjoy food for a time. Though many folks are blessed to experience less intense side effects than my dear wife, the chemotherapy she underwent hit her particularly hard and robbed her of her appetite and much of her sense of taste. Eating became a drudgery to be endured. She had to force herself to eat, but even so she really could not keep up with the kind of nutrition her body needed to be well.

She lost weight, became weak and vulnerable to other illnesses. One particular bout of the stomach flu that made its way through our entire family—which the rest of us shook off in forty-eight hours—landed Val in the hospital for several days. Happily, when her body recovered from the toxicity of her treatment, Val's sense of taste and appetite returned along with the pleasure of eating and subsequently her physical strength and autoimmunity. Eating good food became central to my wife's recovery, and key to her ability to eat well was her appetite.

Regardless of age, human beings need good food to stay healthy, but in order to partake of and process healthy nutrition there must be a hunger for it. We would do well to remember that this basic physical reality is akin to our spiritual need and condition. If we want to be spiritually healthy, we must partake of the pure nutrition God gives us in His word, but in order to eat of the bounty of God's table there has to be a hunger for what He provides for our good. God's banquet table of truth stands set and ready, a veritable cornucopia of divine blessings, but it does not benefit us at all unless we partake of it, and we cannot partake of it unless we hunger for it. Not surprisingly, the Holy Spirit—by way of the apostle Peter—commands us to stimulate a desire for the book He has authored. In Peter's first epistle, God's Spirit charges us with this interesting exhortation, "*like newborn babies, long for the pure milk of the word*" (1 Peter 2:2).

A command to get hungry!

Look at the entirety of this brief but packed paragraph of 1 Peter 2:1–3, "*Therefore, putting aside all malice and all deceit and hypocrisy and envy and all slander, like newborn babies, long for the pure milk of the word, so that by it you may grow in respect to salvation, if you have tasted the kindness of the Lord.*" There are two basic commands in these short verses, the secondary one introduces the paragraph with the words "*putting aside*," but the principal command is found in the word "*long*," which means "to intensely crave," "to desire greatly."[1] The central exhortation of this passage, then, is the command to "*long*" for the pure, undiluted word of God, and the image Peter uses to illustrate the eagerness of our longing is that of a little baby and his or her ravenous appetite for its mother's milk.

How hungry does God want us?

The vocabulary Peter uses in his principal exhortation is very specific. The desire Peter describes is that of "*newborn babies.*" The term "*newborn*" is a compound word in the Greek made up of an adverb meaning "just now" or "right now"[2] and a verb which is primarily rendered "born" throughout the New Testament.[3] To this Peter adds the plural noun "*babies,*" which refers to the smallest of little ones, i.e., a baby still in the mother's womb or a child who has been recently born (Luke 1:41; 2:12, 16).[4] You could literally render Peter's words "*newborn babies*" to read "just now born infants."

Do you get the picture of what Peter references here? He's talking about a little infant who has just now, this moment exited its mother's womb and craves the sustenance it urgently needs to survive. I'll never forget the births of my four children. Their advent into my life is so vividly etched in my memory that it seems to me they were born yesterday. In each case, the first few minutes of life outside the womb were as wondrous as they were simple and predictable.

Each one of my kids came into this world by the hands of a doctor who immediately cleared their breathing passages, clipped their umbilical cord, cut it, passed him or her to a nurse who proceeded to clean them up and really tick them off. That's when the yelp came, which was followed by a thunderous complaint and the wild erratic flailing of their limbs. Once out of the womb, my kids began to complain violently with their entire bodies.

Imagine yourself in such a condition, screaming at the top of your lungs, crying inconsolably, kicking at nothing in particular and boxing at the air like a drunken sailor. (That's how I behave after every Rams' loss!) That's how my babies came into this world. It was truly an upsetting experience for them and the nurse could do little to fulfill their existential need. All she could do was work quickly and say something like, "It's okay, honey. There, there!" and frankly, that was completely useless because not one of my children came forth from the womb speaking or understanding a word of English. All they heard underneath the squall of their screaming was, "Bah blah-blah blah-blah. Bah blah!"

From the baby's perspective, the people in the colorful cotton PJs were not helping at all. In fact, the more the nurses cleaned, measured, weighed, and fussed over my children, the madder they got until—in the midst of their first-ever desperate fit of longing—they were brought to their mother's waiting arms and there, instinctively began to nurse. If you've been in a birthing room you can guess what happened next. In a moment they quieted down and in a desperate calm drank like their little lives depended on it. Their lives did!

Given the helpless state into which they were born, it always amazed me that my little ones knew exactly what they needed and instinctively knew what to do. They came into this world with one overwhelming impulse (milk), how to get it (screaming), and how to go about it (nursing). My kids needed no manual, lecture, or instructional YouTube video on how to survive their first day out in the real world. Unless there is an unforeseen problem, babies know exactly what they need and how to get what they need once they arrive into this world.

What's more, infants are not interested in alternative food sources. They want milk because it is what they viscerally desire, and if we try to give them something else like a hot dog, an Oreo, or a Twinkie, guess what? They will not go for it. They will have none of it! "Mommy's tired, let's try chips and salsa today" will not work for them. They want milk; they demand milk multiple times each day, and it is milk that they will get. Why? Because it is the sole food that they instinctively, desperately crave and need.

Those are the images Peter uses. He's talking about a brand-new baby that has just been born with its God-given, overwhelming, resolute appetite for its mother's milk. Peter reminds us that just as a brand-new little one craves the pure nutrition of its mother's breast in order to develop in health, so Christians must similarly "*long for the pure milk of the word*" in order to nurture the spiritual life God has given them. We are commanded, then, to desire the "*pure milk*" or undefiled, genuine, spiritual nourishment that is God's word. Note that when using the term "*pure milk*," Peter is not referring to the "ABCs" of Christianity, but to the unmixed truth of Scripture (1 Corinthians 3:2; Hebrews 5:12). The primary analogy is found in the longing of a baby for its mother's milk.[5] And so, just as a baby is absolutely dependent on its mother's nutrition in order to grow in health, so we are completely dependent on the unpolluted word of God to develop spiritually, to grow up into the kind of mature Christians God would have us to be. God's word is essential for our growth as believers and for our development as Christian parents. This is why we are commanded to hunger for God's word.

Fostering a hunger for God's life-transforming truth

Even so, though Scripture is so essential to our spiritual health—and by extension to the spiritual vitality of our homes—there are times when our desire for the word of God lags and falters, and when it falters we often fall prey to the temptation not to eat, and when we stop eating regularly, we grow weak and vulnerable. Nothing could be more dangerous to our health as Christians. Because of this perilous dilemma, God commands us to hunger for His word, and in order to help us implement this command, the Holy Spirit in 1 Peter 2:1–3 gives us four practical encouragements to help stimulate our craving, our hunger for God's life-transforming truth. With this essential appetite enlivened and satisfied, our souls will find the nourishment we need to revive and grow. In so doing, we will enjoy a renewed intimacy with our Savior and experience the transforming power of God in every area of life, including our home life.

In these three verses then, Peter first beckons us to **recall** the life-changing power of God's word at salvation and to eagerly seek its active and present transforming power in our lives. Secondly, Peter exhorts us to **reject** encumbering sin, to cast off the habits and attitudes that rob us of our appetite for divine truth. Thirdly, we are encouraged to **recognize** our need to grow—a need for which God has abundantly provided—and lastly, we are enjoined to **remember** the gracious favor of the Lord, the blessings of which come to us via His marvelous promises.

Recall the amazing power of God's word

First of all then, Peter encourages us to recall the transforming power of God's word when we embraced Christ through the gospel. This great encouragement comes to our attention with the first word of chapter 2 "*Therefore.*" In the original Greek manuscripts of the New Testament, there is very little punctuation. In fact, all the words are written in capital letters and run together without spaces. In such a system, the chief way to discern new ideas or, as in the case of 1 Peter 2:1, a connection between ideas or paragraphs is with words like "*therefore.*" This conjunction connects the previous paragraph, 1 Peter 1:23–25, with Peter's commands in 1 Peter 2:1–2, the chief command being found in verse 2 and the verb "*long*" ("to deeply desire").[6]

The theme of Peter's previous paragraph is the grand principle of the power of God's word in the salvation of believers (1 Peter 1:23–25, emphasis added). Peter writes,

> *For you have been born again not of seed which is perishable but imperishable, that is, through the living and enduring word of God. For, 'all flesh is like the grass, and all its glory like the flower of grass. The grass withers, and the flower falls off, but the word of the Lord endures forever.' And this is the word which was preached to you.*

Peter states the amazing truth that God's word, the gospel, miraculously and powerfully produces the new birth in Christians. Peter then connects this idea with the term "*therefore*" to his principal command in the next paragraph, "*long for the pure milk of the word.*"

In essence Peter is saying, "God's word was powerful to give us a new birth and vibrant spiritual life. That power still resides in the Bible and it is ever available to us. The same eternal word that saved us is available and powerful to grow us spiritually. Since this is true, we ought to recall the transforming might of God's word at salvation and hunger for its active power in our lives." Pastor John MacArthur, commenting on this passage, puts it well. He states that the conjunction "therefore was a concise reminder to Peter's readers to remember the saving power of God's word in their lives as a basis for ongoing commitment to Scripture as the only power to live the Christian life."[7]

The Lord brought life to our souls through His "*word of life*" (Philippians 2:16). James, the half brother of the Lord Jesus and the faithful pastor of the first church said, "*In the exercise of His will He brought us forth* [i.e., saved us, how?] *by the word of truth*" (James 1:18). God uses the imperishable seed of His truth to germinate life in the heart of unsaved people. That, my friends, is miraculously powerful!

We need to think back to our pre-saved condition and recall our desperate and helpless state. Before God rescued us, Paul tells us we were "*dead in your trespasses and sins*" (Ephesians 2:1). That is to say, we were spiritually cut off from God and the life that is in Him. In that position, we were utterly helpless to change our condition. We had no more power to come alive spiritually than a corpse has the ability to will itself to live. We were locked in a spiritual tomb, the sphere of death, trespasses, and sins. As such, we were spiritually dead men walking.

All we could manage to produce apart from God were the miasmic ideas, attitudes, and deeds of this world and of our sin-stricken hearts (Ephesians 2:2–3; Matthew 15:19). We performed the very evil championed by our former despotic ruler, "*the prince of the power of the air*"—the enemy of our soul—"*the ruler of this world*" (Ephesians 2:2; John 12:31, 16:11). Before God rescued us, we were dominated by death, and sin, and in the grip of sin's strongman, Satan. Is it any wonder that in this condition we were heirs of frightening judgment? Paul tells us that we "*were by nature children of wrath*" (Ephesians 2:3). What we had coming to us was the burning, vengeful fury of a holy and just God against sin and sinners. That was our only and rightful inheritance!

Apart from Christ

The Bible teaches us that all men who die without placing their trust in Jesus as their sin bearer on the cross, die in their *"trespasses and sins,"* the natural state into which every human is born (Psalm 51:5; Romans 5:12). Consequently, apart from Christ, men will bear their own sin for eternity and suffer the eternal indignation of a holy God against that sin. That is no small matter, because the eternal wrath of God is a grave and frightful thing. The Lord's eternal punishment is described in the book of Revelation chapter 14, and it is a terrifying specter to contemplate.

The immediate context of Revelation 14 speaks of the punishment awaiting those who follow the Antichrist in the closing years of our present age, yet the description of God's judgment toward them is no different than the wrath He will express toward all sinners who have rejected His grace. In Revelation 14:10–11, we read these sobering words regarding the cup of God's wrath (judgment) and those who will drink it: *"He* [the sinner] *also will drink of the wine of the wrath of God, which is mixed in full strength in the cup of His anger; and he will be tormented with fire and brimstone in the presence of the holy angels and in the presence of the Lamb. And the smoke of their torment goes up forever and ever."*

The most poignant and precise explanation of divine wrath I have ever read comes from my study Bible and the commentary it makes on this very passage. Regarding Revelation 14:10 it states that unbelievers "will suffer the outpouring of God's collected wrath, done with the full force of His divine anger and unmitigated vengeance. Divine wrath is not an impulsive outburst of anger aimed capriciously at people God does not like. It is the steady, settled, merciless, graceless, and compassionless response of a righteous God against sin" (cf. Psalm 75:8; Isaiah 51:17; Jeremiah 25:15–16).[8]

Because believers experience the boundless mercy and grace of God in Jesus, it is difficult for us to imagine the full expression of God's wrath. Praise God we will never know it experientially because the Lord Jesus suffered the full fury of God's anger against our sin on the cross. He was our substitute and carried on His sinless divine person our sin and received and suffered the full, fierce, and unrestrained vengeance of God against our wickedness (Isaiah 53:4–12). In His mercy, God redirected His just and burning anger for our trespasses away from us and to His beloved Son, who bore our sin on the cross so that God might justly transfer the perfect righteousness of Jesus to us, the vessels of His infinite and matchless love and grace (2 Corinthians 5:21).

This salvation is available to every person who puts his or her faith in Christ as his or her sin bearer. At the moment of belief, God pours His mercy and grace on the believing sinner, rescues them from His wrath and imputes to them the righteousness of His perfect Son. That's all Christians will ever know, God's infinite grace in Jesus. But again, those who reject God's mercy and grace in Christ will bear the full unmitigated hatred of a perfectly holy God against sin in "a steady, settled, merciless, graceless, and compassionless" eternal outpouring. God's wrath is real; it is storing up, and it will be expressed (Psalm 7:11; Acts 17:31). No wonder the writer of Hebrews exclaims, "*It is a terrifying thing to fall into the hands of the living God*" (Hebrews 10:31).

Powerful to save; powerful to transform

My friends, such was our pre-saved condition. You and I "*were dead in your* [our] *trespasses and sins... and were by nature children of wrath, even as the rest*" (Ephesians 2:1–3). We were rushing headlong toward God's wrath and were completely unable to obviate its certain, crushing reality. Yet we were rescued! Who saved us? God did, and He brought about that great rescue from sin, death, and His wrath through His imperishable, life-giving, and eternal word. "*For you have been born again not of seed which is perishable but imperishable, that is, through the living and enduring word of God... and this is the word which was preached to you*" (1 Peter 1:23, 25b, emphasis added).

God uses His powerful word to rescue a sinner "*from the domain of darkness* [the dominant and deadly grip of Satan through unbelief], *and transfers us* [or 'rescues' us, with the key idea being that of deliverance from severe and acute danger][9] *to the kingdom of His beloved Son*," i.e., God transfers us to the realm where Christ rules, the sphere of spiritual light and life that He gives (Colossians 1:13). My dear fellow believer, that is an awesome, unparalleled display of divine might, is it not? How is that power realized? It is brought about through the word of the Lord, the Scriptures. God's word is powerful to save!

What wonderful news that is, but the good news does not stop there, because God's word is still powerful to transform us for the balance of our lives on earth. The writer of Hebrews reminds us that Scripture is dynamically alive and able to continue its work of transformation. He writes, "*For the word of God is living and active and sharper than any two-edged sword, and piercing as far as the division of soul and spirit, of both joints and marrow, and able to judge the thoughts and intentions of the heart*" (Hebrews 4:12). Paul reminded the Thessalonians of the continuing power of the word to transform them when he wrote, "*For this reason we also constantly thank God that when you received the word of God which you heard from us, you accepted it not as the word of men, but for what it really is, the word of God, which also performs its work in you who believe*" (1 Thessalonians 2:13). This is truly Peter's point in our focal text, isn't it? Because God brings His saving power to fruition in the lives of believers through His word, Peter encourages Christians to recall that power and greatly desire its ongoing transforming effect in their lives (1 Peter 1:23–25). Hence, the apostle commands all believers "*like newborn babies, long for the pure milk of the word*" (1 Peter 2:2).

Have you lost your hunger for the word of God? Perhaps this is so because you have lost sight of the Bible's amazing power when you first believed. God made you spiritually alive in a moment when you embraced Jesus through the gospel, the word of life. Recall that power to mind, my friend, and allow that reality and memory to stimulate your appetite for the life-transforming truth of His word in your life right now!

Reject encumbering sin

Secondly, in order to stimulate our appetite for God's word, Peter urges us to lay aside, to strip off and cast away, the sins that dull our hunger for the word of God. The participle "*putting aside*" (1 Peter 2:1) has the same command tone as the main verb ("*long*") and is used with the sense of "to put away from oneself."[10] We ought to view and deal with our nagging sins as we would filthy clothes. No one in his right mind would go about town meeting and greeting people after mucking out a dozen horse stalls on a hot and sticky August afternoon. Our first inclination after finishing such a job is to divest ourselves of our filthy garments and get clean. Just as we cannot tolerate wearing grungy, smelly, soiled clothes, Christians ought to have the same intolerance for the sin that encroaches as we walk through life. Our primary inclination ought to be to put such sins aside.

That's the upshot of Peter's exhortation, "*Therefore, putting aside all malice and all deceit and hypocrisy and envy and all slander, like newborn babies, long for the pure milk of the word.*" The apostle reminds us and commands us to put off the sin that diminishes our hunger for God's truth. We cannot grow spiritually as individuals or as Christian parents if we do not continually strip off the sins that pollute our desire for the Scriptures and therefore keep us from partaking in God's pure source of spiritual nutrition.

Sins that steal away our hunger: Malice

Peter mentions several categories of sin, the first being "*malice*" (1 Peter 2:1). This is an umbrella term. The Greek vocabulary employed for "*malice*" is the word *kakia*, which is an extremely broad designation for evil in the New Testament. It is used to refer to all sorts of vice[11] and can be rendered "badness" or "wickedness"[12] and refers to the "depravity or malignity" of the flesh.[13] Peter starts with this broad term for sin that expresses itself in a particular way in each of us. Regardless of where each one of us stands in relation to the sins Peter mentions in verse 1 (*deceit, hypocrisy, envy, slander*), we all struggle with the wickedness, the depravity of our own unredeemed flesh. Do we not? What's more, our struggle with wickedness expresses itself in a particular sin or group of sins over which we stumble and that we must therefore strive to strip away. Does a specific sin come to mind as you read those words? Every one of us has weaknesses; we must identify them and by the power of God's Spirit continually put them aside in order to reinvigorate our appetite for God's truth.

The baited hook: Deceit

The second sin Peter mentions is "*deceit.*" This familiar term comes from an old Greek word which means "to catch with bait,"[14] i.e., a baited hook! Peter uses familiar terminology that instantly illustrates to his readers the vice he admonishes them to throw off, deceit. Nothing is more deceitful to a fish than a baited hook. The intentions of the fisherman are pretty clear. His design is to disguise his hook with alluring bait so as to bamboozle and ensnare the witless creature into the frying pan. The clueless fish thinks it's going to get breakfast but ends up being breakfast because of the trickery of the angler and his culinary cleverness. While fishing is a worthy pastime (unless you're a hapless fish), deceiving others as a fisherman deceives a fish is wicked, defrauds people, and destroys our spiritual vitality.

Peter refers, then, to the sin of deceitfulness that seeks to harm or defraud others by the means of trickery and falsehood.[15] The relationships believers share with all men (friends, family, employers, employees, other Christians) and institutions (governments, businesses, educational entities) must be ruled by honesty. When deceitfulness infects our relationships, this sin will corrupt our associations; it will corrupt us personally and therefore corrupt our hunger for "*the pure milk of the word.*"

Putting on a show: Hypocrisy

Thirdly, Peter warns against hypocrisy. This is almost a transliteration of the Greek term *hupokrisis*. In secular Greek, this word was used to refer to an actor,[16] i.e., to a stage player who pretended to be someone else. When wickedness and deceit invade our thinking and behavior toward God and people, hypocrisy cannot be far behind. In our self-interest, we will seek to cover up our true selves and put on a show of piety to disguise our shame regardless of how our duplicity wounds the heart of God and hurts those around us.

As when our first parents (Adam and Eve) fell, when we sin, often our first response is to hide from God, to pretend that our sin is not as bad as we think, to rationalize it, to explain it away, so that we may deaden the pain of our guilt. Consequently, we put on a show before the Lord, but the only one swept away by our hypocrisy is ourselves. When we fool ourselves, we carry on the charade to fool others about the true state of our hearts. Peter beckons us to stop pretending, to stop playacting before the Lord and to be real, to be true with Him and allow authenticity to saturate all our relationships. Put another way, he commands us to stop being actors and to acknowledge our sins to the Lord, who will deal with our iniquities by forgiving us and by restoring us to a right relationship with Himself and our fellow man.

The beloved apostle John, echoing the heart of Peter, invites us into that blessed state with these well-known words, "*If we confess our sins, He is faithful and righteous to forgive us our sins and to cleanse us from all unrighteousness*" (1 John 1:9). Interestingly, the word "*confess*" means simply "to speak the same" or to say the same thing, "to agree."[17] God desires that we not hide our transgressions but that we agree with Him about what they are and how dangerous they are. He calls us to put away deceit and stop the hypocrisy, to stop the pretending so that He may clear away the sin and the pretense that obstructs our relationship with Him and with others. He calls us to disown the hypocrisy that takes away our desire for the genuine (the truth) and the restoration it brings to our souls and relationships.

Coveting what we do not have: Envy

Envy describes the ill will felt toward another person because of some real or perceived advantage they may have in the eyes of the beholder.[18] It is despising or hating someone because their situation is not ours.[19] We can allow this sin to be conceived, grow, and fester when we desire the position, the talents, the possessions, the familial situations that others have. It is a sin that can express itself in many situations and begets, coexists with, and feeds on bitterness, which in turn fuels enmity, division, and fights. Envy and its kindred vices are toxic poisons to our spiritual, emotional, and even physical well-being. Envy will never rightly motivate us to improve our condition. Yet, it will contaminate our souls, worsening our spiritual state, for as our principal text reminds us, where the toxin envy exists—along with its noxious family of venom—there can be no vibrant, healthy hunger for the word of God.

Standing tall on the backs of others: Slander

Lastly, Peter exhorts us to put aside *"all slander."* The Greek word *katalalia* is only used one other place in the New Testament, 2 Corinthians 12:20, where the King James Version renders it *"backbitings."* This includes all manner of malicious speech that denigrates people, especially when they're not present. Frequently, it flows from envy (the previous vice mentioned by Peter) with the aim of tearing someone down to make ourselves look better.

Do you struggle with the sins Peter lists above—malice, deceit, hypocrisy, and envy? Many Christians would consider themselves fairly free from such misdeeds. Yet when called to account for the sin of talking behind people's backs, they would have to admit a tendency to stumble in this area more than they care to admit. If that is true of you, then you may not be as free as you think from the other sins Peter mentions. You see, there is a logical flow to the five sins Peter enumerates.

If you struggle with some form of *"malice"* (which is arguably the most general term for sin in the New Testament), whatever your area of weakness is, the default response in our fallen nature is to cover it up, to hide our sin, i.e., "*deceit.*" Where there is deceit you will find "*hypocrisy*" because we want to be perceived as free from the very things with which we struggle; therefore, we need to present an image different than who we really are. That playacting or phoniness on our part often leads to the "*envy*" of the authentic virtues, and talents in others, which can and often does result in their "*slander.*"

I understand that these sins don't always follow in a chain with mathematical precision, nor does an unkind word about someone else reveal a long succession of unconfessed sins. What I am suggesting is that when we speak evil of others, "*slander,*" especially if we easily trip over this obstacle, we need to seriously evaluate what is leading us into this evil, identify the issues and repent of our sin. Often we will find we are falling prey to some if not all the evil Peter mentions in 1 Peter 2:1.

"*Therefore, putting aside all malice and all deceit and hypocrisy and envy and all slander, like newborn babies, long for the pure milk of the word.*" Peter's exhortation is plain to see; there cannot be a strong and growing hunger for God's word where sin is allowed to flourish in the shadows of our life. As Wayne Grudem puts it, "Someone who is practicing 'deceit' or 'envy' or 'slander' will not be able to long for pure spiritual milk."[20] If we indulge ourself with such practices, we will in effect poison our desire for the truth our souls desperately need. We must reject, put aside (confess and repent of) our sin so that we may purify our desire and stimulate our appetite for God's word.

Recognize your need to grow

Thirdly, in order to long for God's truth we must recognize our need to grow and that spiritual growth comes to us by means of the word. We are called out of darkness, saved from the power of sin, so that we might become more and more like our Savior the Lord Jesus and in that transformation experience the joys of an abundant spiritual life (growth). That's the magnificent direction our lives must take; we must grow, and the key source for that growth is Scripture enlightened by the Holy Spirit. When we recognize that absolute axiom, we will more intensely crave what God has generously provided for our spiritual development. Consider the straightforward simplicity of 1 Peter 2:2, "*like newborn babies, long for the pure milk of the word, so that by it you may grow in respect to salvation*" (emphasis added).

Peter tells us plainly that in order to grow we must have "*the pure milk of the word.*" True spiritual growth cannot take place in the life of a Christian apart from the word God has given to us. Jesus Himself said, "*It is written, 'Man shall not live on bread alone, but on every word that proceeds out of the mouth of God'*" (Matthew 4:4). We cannot thrive apart from Scripture. We must recognize, then, that the word is our source for spiritual growth, and in that recognition, we will long for the Bible's spiritual nutrition like a little baby desires its mother's milk.

One thing that is unmistakably true about brand-new babies is they desperately, pressingly, eagerly need to feed, and they desire to eat often! You can't just feed a baby every now and then. Newborns typically need to eat eight to twelve times a day,[21] and it seems that the biggest cluster of those feedings happen when mom is trying to sleep. That, however, is not a concern for the hungry baby! When it comes to eating, babies are absolutely tyrannical. If a baby gets hungry at 2:00 a.m., it doesn't think, "Wow, it's really early. Mom and Dad are probably sleeping. Maybe I shouldn't cry right now even though I'm so ready to eat. I think I'll be a good baby and let my parents sleep in a bit. I'll let them know I'm hungry around 7:00 a.m. or so. I'll wait until I hear Dad making coffee. Yeah, I'll just ignore my appetite, look at my fascinating mobile for a while, and suck on my fists. My parents could use the rest." Those thoughts never cross the mind of an infant! Ever!

Little babies will dictate terms when it comes to satiating their appetite, and they do not give a tinker's toot about what you think is convenient or fair. They will cry out when they're hungry, and they will not stop their crying until their need is met. That hungry baby does not care if you're in the middle of a worship service, a wedding, a funeral, or if your team is at the one-yard line and about to score the winning touchdown in the Super Bowl. When that little guy or girl is hungry, he or she will let you know about it and you (the parent, especially the mom) will do whatever is in your power to meet its need and to stop the wailing.[22] The baby wins every time! Why? Because that's how committed babies are to devouring the nutrition their mothers provide for their growth. Why the radical commitment? Babies long for milk because in that life-sustaining provision a baby receives two basic things: everything it must have to grow and everything it needs to stay healthy as it grows.

In their mother's milk, babies first of all have all the building blocks their little bodies need to grow. Think about how incredible that is for a moment. All that a baby needs to strengthen bone, to make muscle tissue, all that the child needs to develop its vital organs, its vision, to make skin, nails, and grow hair, comes from one God-given superfood, its mother's milk. Babies are literally transformed by the milk they crave. Secondly, in that same nutrition an infant inherits antibodies, important proteins, and immune cells that are essential to its ability to fight off disease. All that the baby needs to survive, thrive, and grow comes from this one pure food source, and so they are instinctively and supremely committed to it.[23]

Peter's analogy corresponds beautifully to our spiritual condition. We must grow, and in order to grow we must ingest God's all-sufficient word. That is the means by which we thrive spiritually. Few things are sadder than a weak, stunted, defeated, spiritually vulnerable Christian. We need to grow so that we may become more and more like our great Savior Jesus, full of spiritual knowledge that renders us strong and full of faith to face life, joyful in what's real and true even in the midst of great hardship, growing in our love for God and increasingly becoming more detached from this passing world, bold and abounding in the service of the Lord rather than timid and unfruitful in our short earthly journey. My friends, we need to grow! We should be yearning, aching, longing to grow so as to please the Lord in all of life, and as we desire to grow we need to recognize that spiritual growth comes only through the untainted word of God. If our desire is to grow, and we recognize that growth comes through God's truth, then we will long for that truth with a similar devotion that a baby longs for its mother's milk.

Remember the gracious favor of the Lord

The last motivation Peter gives us to stimulate our spiritual appetite for "*the pure milk of the word*" is a precious reminder. In this fourth and final exhortation, Peter tells us to take a short trip down memory lane and count our blessings, "*if you have tasted the kindness of the Lord*" (1 Peter 2:3). The apostle encourages us to remember God's blessings by employing a "first class condition," a grammatical tool that expresses certainty.[24] Verse 3 could also read "since you have tasted the kindness of the Lord."

Peter's exhortation to desire the word comes from our own experience. We have all tasted of the *"kindness"* or good-heartedness[25] of the Lord Jesus, haven't we? The context which follows (vv. 4–10) points out to us that the *"Lord"* of whom Peter speaks in verse 3 is Jesus Christ Himself. The Lord Jesus lavishly pours out His goodness, His kindness, His grace and love upon His people. Remember the words of S. Trevor Francis in his wonderful hymn, "O the Deep, Deep Love of Jesus"? (This was my grandfather's favorite hymn.) His love is "vast, unmeasured, boundless, free! Rolling as a mighty ocean in its fullness over me! Underneath me, all around me, is the current of Thy love, leading onward, leading homeward to Thy glorious rest above!"[26]

We (believers) have all savored the boundless goodness of the Lord Jesus, haven't we? Matthew Henry writes, "Our Lord Jesus Christ is very gracious to his people. He is in himself infinitely good; he is very kind, free, and merciful to miserable sinners; he is pitiful and good to the undeserving; he has in him a fullness of grace."[27] And my friends, of that grace we have all freely tasted.

As we regard His manifold grace toward us, the blessing at the top of our inventory for which we owe our Lord an eternal debt of gratitude is our redemption. Remember, He showed us His infinite kindness by reconciling us to the Father while we were helpless, ungodly, sinful, enemies of God (Romans 5:6–11). That is such a supernatural kindness; it bends human logic and common sense. Imagine if you can an eminent, supremely powerful, just, and offended foe, who has his enemy cornered, vulnerable, helpless, and in his sights for destruction but who instead refuses to annihilate him, and then—in a shocking turn—swaps places with his enemy, bears their just punishment, and makes that enemy the intense focus of his love and riches. We have no reference point for such a scenario in the human realm.

Can you imagine SEAL Team Six, after cornering the world's most notorious terrorist, Osama bin Laden, granting him pardon, honoring him with US citizenship, and setting him up in a lavish seaside mansion for life on the taxpayers' tab? What if that expertly trained SEAL, after zeroing his sight in on bin Laden, refused to shoot? What if instead he decidedly took his finger off the trigger, lowered his weapon and stated, "I've been informed that Osama bin Laden has been granted the legal right to be reconciled to our people. He has been guaranteed full rights and freedoms as an American, including the right to live among us in peace, free of fear."

On a human level such a scenario rings utterly ridiculous to us, if not offensive. We can't deal with enemy combatants in that way. Here's the point: Christ's kindness and goodness defies human example, it stretches and breaks our powers of description, and explodes our earthbound paradigms. That's why Paul cries out, *"For one will hardly die for a righteous man; though perhaps for the good man someone would dare even to die. But God demonstrates His own love toward us, in that while we were yet sinners [even enemies, Romans 5:10], Christ died for us"* (Romans 5:7–8). I've often wondered how the hosts of heaven must have watched the unfolding of God's salvation in Christ with holy astonishment. Heaven must have echoed with gasps of amazement and cries of astounded wonder as the hosts of the Lord observed God's love play out in time and space at Calvary and the tomb (1 Peter 1:12b).

Yes, Christ's kindness to us is unfathomable, and yet it is ours and we have tasted, indeed we have drunk deeply of it in redemption. That is blessing number one, the crown of His goodness to us, and from that one great benevolent gift in Christ, God has filled our lives with His manifold kindnesses. Paul echoes this very truth in Romans 8:31–32, *"What then shall we say to these things? If God is for us, who is against us? He who did not spare His own Son, but delivered Him over for us all, how will He not also with Him freely give us all things?"*

Overflowing goodness

The Lord has filled our lives to overflowing with His goodness! We have experienced His kindness in the institution of marriage and the love and fellowship of our spouse (Genesis 2:24; Ephesians 5:25–33). In that relationship, God has given us the *"gift,"* the *"reward"* of children, the joy of our early years and the crown of our old age (Psalm 127:3–5). God has graced our lives with manifold material provisions and blessings (Matthew 6:25–33). He calls us to rest in Him in our distress and fills us with His peace as we do (1 Peter 5:7; Philippians 4:7). We see the kindness of the Lord as He comforts us in our sufferings through His promises and by His presence (Psalm 119:50–52; 2 Corinthians 1:3–4). What's more, He blesses us with joy in His fellowship and fills us with hope by His Spirit (Psalm 16:11; Romans 15:13). Oh my friends, we have tasted of the goodness of the Lord! These are but a few of His kindnesses, and here's Peter's chief point: all of these graces, all of the goodness of Jesus we have *"tasted,"* all of the kindness we have come to savor has come to us by way of God's great and awesome promises.

Peter exhorts us to take a brief inventory of our blessings and remember that God's goodness, the kindness of Christ, has come to us via the promises of God. God's word brings the grace of God to bear on our lives from the moment of salvation to the day we are translated into his presence. If we contemplate that great reality, we will experience an increasing appetite for His word. Peter invites us to continue to savor, to experience, to explore Christ's goodness through the Scripture. Matthew Henry writes, "The graciousness of our Redeemer is best discovered [revealed] by an experimental taste of it. There must be an immediate application of the object to the organ of taste; we cannot taste at a distance, as we may see, and hear, and smell. To taste the graciousness of Christ experimentally supposes our being united to him by faith, and then we may taste his goodness in all his providences, in all our spiritual concerns, in all our fears and temptations, in his word and worship every day... The word of God is the great instrument whereby he discovers and communicates his grace to men. Those who feed upon the sincere milk of the word taste and experience most of his grace."[28]

How's your appetite?

How's your appetite for God's truth at this point in your life? Wherever it may be on the hunger spectrum, it could always be better, right? I encourage you to meditate on Peter's exhortations and allow them to stimulate your longing for God's word. I will make you this promise: the more you fill your life with the word of God, the more you will desire it. As you humbly take God's word into your heart and mind through personal study, through hearing it taught, hearing it preached, listening to it read as you drive or exercise, God's truth will transform you because Scripture does not leave a man as it found him; it changes the man.

The very nature of the Bible makes it a catalyst for change. It is "*God's word.*" Paul reminded Timothy that the Scripture was literally the "out-breath of God" (2 Timothy 3:16).[29] It comes from God; it is an expression of His mind imbued with His very nature and therefore powerful to conform us to His will. It will give those around you the wisdom that leads to salvation; it will instruct you; it will correct you; it will train you in righteousness and render you mature in Christ (2 Timothy 3:15–16). The word of God will feed your soul; it will make you fruitful (Matthew 4:4; 13:23). Best of all, growing in the knowledge of God's word will bring you into greater intimacy with God and Christ.

God's Spirit will use Scripture to do all that and more in your life, and He will certainly bring the transforming grace of God to your relationships—especially to your relationships at home—as you seek to know Him and order your life by His precepts. And yet, as we have said, without a hunger for God's word, this exciting and rewarding process is difficult to begin and sustain. I enjoin you to **recall** the life-changing power of God's word in salvation. That life-changing power is still accessible to you 24/7; therefore, "*long for the pure milk of the word.*" I exhort you my brother or sister in Christ to **reject** encumbering sin, put aside the attitudes and behaviors that pollute your longing for the word of God. To the degree that sin invades our life, we will lose our appetite for God's revelation, and to the degree we fail to partake of the word, we will grow weak and vulnerable. Purify your desires and awaken your appetite.

Also, I encourage you to **recognize** your need to grow. If you long for the benefits of Christian maturity, a greater faith in God, a greater love for God, a greater pleasure in God, wisdom to live your life and shepherd your family, if you desire greater joy, peace, and victory over sin, then you must grow, and in order to grow you and I must live daily by the bread God supplies (Matthew 4:4). Lastly, I entreat you to **remember** the goodness of Christ to you. He has filled your life with so many good things. He has lavished your existence with His grace and He has brought His goodness to bear on your life through His great and precious promises (Acts 20:32; Ephesians 1:7–8).

May our good and gracious God perform a marvelous work of grace in your life and family by His magnificent promises and through the power of His Holy Spirit. Amen!

CHAPTER 11

How to Study the Bible with Your Kids: Some Suggestions

I believe the message of this book makes it clear that the word of God is one of the most important resources the Lord has given us to raise our children in His grace. The Bible is an essential means of grace by which we lead our children to the Lord. It is an invaluable resource of grace to build our kids up in the ways of the Lord and to keep them growing and maturing throughout their lives until the day they inherit heaven itself—God's promises to us fulfilled!

Enveloping our kids with grace through the Bible

The more I encompass my kids with biblical truth, the more I couch their lives in the grace of God. In the stories and teachings of the Bible, I recount for my children His magnificent acts of past favor to our people. In God's self-disclosure (the Bible), I remind them of the manifold riches of the Lord's kindness and provision for today, a grace that meets their every spiritual need along life's way. In His promises, I point them to the Lord's future benevolence as the Spirit pulls back the curtains and shows us our spiritual inheritance and the unfathomable favor He will pour out on His beloved saints forever. And by these promises, my children, your children, and indeed all believers grow in God's grace. It is no wonder the apostle Paul calls Scripture *"the word of His grace"* (Acts 20:32).

This being so, I encourage you as strongly as I possibly can to study God's word with your children. Set a time aside where it's just you (the parent) and your son or daughter (once a week, every other week, or whatever the size of your family and your schedule can accommodate). While a family devotion time is a great idea and worth pursuing (a brief time of Bible reading with the family in the morning before everyone gets on with their day, or in the evening at the dinner table, or right before bed), I challenge you to find a niche in your weekly schedule to meet one-on-one, or one-on-two, or one-on-three, if necessary, with your children over the study of God's word.

Just a note along these lines, I realize some of you have very large families and meeting one-on-one with each of your children is not feasible, yet the smaller the cluster of your Bible study, the more intimate your time can be. Obviously, the optimum discipleship relationship is one-to-one. Such a context allows for more interaction between parent and child, it results in a greater degree of intimacy, and it gives each child the concentrated focus he or she craves and needs from their spiritual mentor, you the parent.

Obviously, I am speaking to both parents in this section, but as a matter of biblical priority I especially address the dads. Deuteronomy 6 targets the parents of households but does so by addressing the heads of homes, the fathers. In God's economy, He has established husbands to lovingly lead their wives and to shepherd their children (Ephesians 5:22–33; 6:4; 1 Timothy 3:4). Men, that is our role in the home, to shepherd our families spiritually, and that pastoral guidance is expressed beautifully when we lead our children through the pastures of the Bible. Indeed, this is one of the premium ways we can invest time in our families.

Having Bible study with our kids: Getting ready

As you contemplate starting a study with your kids, here are a few suggestions to keep in mind.

Prayerfully resolve to teach your children God's word

Many of you taking in these words see the value of pouring God's precepts into your kids. You understand that you will all be transformed incrementally into the image of Jesus Christ through the process of Bible study, and you find yourself longing to instruct them in the words of life. I encourage you to go before the Lord and express your desire to teach your children the Bible. Pray that He would empower you for the task that lies before you. If this is your heart's desire, then you are echoing God's own heartbeat for your family!

That said, not everyone reading this book finds himself/herself buoyed by such resolve. If your desire is lagging, then plead with God to give you or to revive in you this passion for the truth and to instill it in your kids (read and reread the previous chapter: "How to Get Hungry for God's Word"). Make this your fervent and earnest prayer to the Lord. Honestly express to Him where you find yourself, and pour your soul out to Him.

He will not be surprised by what you tell Him. Confess your personal and parental weaknesses and failures to God. Tell Him about your insecurities regarding spiritual leadership, whatever they may be—a lack of confidence to teach the Bible, inconsistency in your own spiritual pilgrimage, a gap in biblical knowledge, whatever weighs on your heart. Come to God in your weakness, and ask Him to fill you with His desires and His strength for leading your family. Coming to the Lord with empty hands is not a sin, that's a marvelous starting point. Just like the many weak and shattered sinners who came to Jesus with nothing but their brokenness and tears seeking for forgiveness and restoration, you and I can come to Him with empty yet open hands that He can take hold of and fill.

In fact, regardless of where your level of confidence and resolve may be, do remember that you cannot lead your kids spiritually apart from His wisdom and strength. We are all desperately needy for our God, and so whether you are settled in your decision or vacillating in your weakness, confess your absolute need to God for His empowering grace in your endeavor. Tell Him all about your plans and hopes, and proceed forward in faith by His enabling for the sake of your children whom you love so much. Ask the Lord to prepare your heart to understand the truth, to apply the truth, and to teach the truth. By all means, pray for God's strength and resolve to teach your children God's word.

Recognize that you are capable of teaching God's word to your kids

Some of you may feel intimidated by the prospect of trying to teach your children the Bible. Let me assure you, if you are a Christian (i.e., if you love the Lord Jesus), then God has equipped you to study and understand the Bible. You have the resident truth teacher, the Holy Spirit, the third person of the Trinity residing in you (John 14:17; 1 Corinthians 3:16). He is the ultimate Author of the Bible, and an important facet of His ministry is to unfold the Bible's meaning to believers (1 Corinthians 2:10–12; 1 John 2:20, 27). Furthermore, if you are a parent, God commands you to "*bring them up* [your children] *in the discipline and instruction of the Lord*" (Ephesians 6:4b). God calls you to "*teach them* [God's truths] *diligently to your sons* [children]" (Deuteronomy 6:7).

You are not only capable of teaching your children God's instruction, it is your duty and God-given privilege to do so. Remember, God's Holy Spirit resides in you; He desires to unveil to you the book He has penned for you and your family's spiritual health, and God Himself has called you to lead your family in the journey of Bible discovery. Embrace those truths and proceed on in His power and confidence.

Set a time!

Talk to your spouse about your plans; jointly look at all your commitments and schedules; find a time that works and lock it in. You may need to adjust your meeting time in the ebb and flow of life, but setting a time helps keep you accountable and will encourage you in your resolve. Then tell your son or daughter about your plans, and explain to them what you will be doing, that this is your time to learn to walk with God together more intimately and that you are so excited to share this journey with them. I encourage you to not simply think about studying the word with your kids, but prayerfully resolve to do it; recognize that this is your duty, your privilege, and then set a time.

Make it special

You know your child's needs better than anyone. As such, you understand what would make a study outing particularly special for them. Our family has always enjoyed visits to neighborhood coffee shops, and through the years our local Starbucks has provided a warm atmosphere for our studies. Who knew Howard Schultz could be such a spiritual catalyst?

That said, "special" doesn't have to mean "expensive." You don't have to go out to breakfast with each of your kids to your favorite diner or coffee shop regularly. If you can afford that and you choose to do that because it suits your needs, great, but something special can be brewed right at home also. There have been times when money was spread pretty thin in our family budget. During those times we improvised. For example, during one of our lean periods when I was meeting with my oldest son, Joshua, my wife made it a habit to bake our favorite coffee cake the night before or early on the morning Josh and I met. I would brew a pot of dark coffee, then Josh and I would steal away to my office and pore over the biblical text together. We spent the better part of a year studying the epistle of first Timothy in such a manner. It was delicious, affordable, and spiritually profitable!

Perhaps "special" for you and your son or daughter would be enjoying an iced tea in the shade of your own backyard, or cradling a hot chocolate by the glow of your fire ring, or packing a lunch or a couple of muffins and sharing a time of study on a picnic bench at your local park, or simply spreading out your Bible and journal on your family room couch. Speaking of journal, give your son or daughter a brand-new journal to record their personal study of the word of God (see Appendix A, Building Blocks of Bible Study: Getting the Right Tools).

You know what can give your time a dash of something "special" that will help create a positive association with the study of the word for your children. One key ingredient that will certainly make your experience warm and memorable will be the rare fact—in our culture—that you have prioritized your schedule to meet with your kids and to give them the treasure of God's word! That, my friends, will leave its transforming mark on you and your children.

Having Bible study with our kids: Getting started

Studying God's word with our children is one of Christian parenting's great rewards. It will mature you in Jesus, and it has the potential to bring your children closer to the Lord—goals worthy of pursuit in and of themselves—but as you both draw nearer to Him, God will also strengthen the bond between you and your kids. Here are a few helpful suggestions to keep in mind as you launch into your biblical pilgrimage. God bless you in your journey.

Keep it simple and personal

I would encourage you to keep your study as simple and as doable as you can, especially at the start. Also, you don't come together to simply crank through a text. Remember that talking about life and the issues of the heart from God's perspective is an important part of your time together. Establish that from the get-go. On your very first visit, spend a good portion of your time just catching up, talking about school, friends, concerns, what God is teaching both of you in life. Take the opportunity to affirm your love for your child and set a comfortable tone. This should be part of your habit whenever you come together around God's word, but I would include an extra measure of fellowship on your first visits.

By the way, part of keeping it simple is to begin with basic tools. Here are two you will need: a trustworthy study Bible based on a good translation and a journal book for both you and your child. For more guidance on translations and study Bibles see the appendix entitled Building Blocks of Bible Study: Getting the Right Tools.

You are not on a schedule, but on the road of discipleship

After you visit for a good long while, cap off your first time together by looking over the principles of inductive Bible study (see Appendix B, Building Blocks of Bible Study: The Basics of Inductive Bible Study). If your interaction pushes some of your study into the following week, that's okay, you're not on a schedule to finish an assignment. You're on the road of discipleship with your children. There have been times with my kids when we have laid our "scheduled" study aside for an "unscheduled" study and brought the light of God's word to bear on issues of special interest to them or that weighed on their hearts. That will definitely happen from time to time, and when it does, there's usually a spiritual and relational payoff in the offing. Remember, spiritual mentoring is always the goal, and sometimes God's Spirit preempts our schedules and plans.

However long it may take (one, two, or three meeting times), familiarize yourselves with the guidelines of inductive Bible study. A good excursion through these steps will be a great way to start your time together. Keep in mind that these concepts will be reinforced as you mine God's word in the seasons ahead.

Pick a book and dig in!

After you've considered the four Building Blocks of Bible Study (see Appendix B, Building Blocks of Bible Study: The Basics of Inductive Bible Study), it's time to pick a book of the Bible to dig into. Most study Bibles will provide the necessary introductory material (authorship, historical setting, etc.) to acquaint you with the context and flow of the book you have chosen. Introductory information typically will take no more than one visit and will set you on the path to spiritual discovery with your beloved disciple. Once you have walked through the background of the book together, at the end of your time I would suggest that you mention the text you will study over the course of your upcoming week, and if you have time, read it through aloud. Encourage your child (children) to read that section of Scripture several times over the following week. Commit yourselves to making four or five observations from the text by your next meeting time. The following week, assign the next paragraph, and so on, until you work your way through the book. For a personal example of how I have approached Bible study with my kids see Appendix C, Building Blocks of Bible Study: What I Do.

Alternative studies

I strongly encourage you to lead your children in inductive Bible studies and by so doing teach them a critical Christian life skill. Scripture reveals the very person of God, and as such, has the power to bring us into an ever deepening intimacy with God. Learning to study the Bible and actually delving into its teachings has to be a top priority for a disciple-making mom and dad. What's more, by equipping our kids with the gift of Bible study, we enable them to pass on this same life-changing discipline to their children. So, let me say again, I strongly believe in the value of inductive Bible study as a means of spiritual growth for every disciple, including our children.

That said, we can also mix things up and try alternative approaches through the course of time. There are many profitable means of studying the depth and breadth of God's great person and the truths He would have us know. With that in mind, here are a few suggestions for alternative studies with your children. After working through a book of the Bible, we will often switch gears for a time and explore God's truth through a different kind of study. Below you will find a few suggestions.

Workbooks: While going through workbooks doesn't fit my children's learning style, it may work for you and your kids. Recently I had coffee with a friend and fellow Christian dad who is taking his fifteen-year-old daughter through such a study. She really enjoys that particular format. They are working through the

Navigator's 2:7 series *Growing Strong in God's Family: A Course in Personal Discipleship to Strengthen Your Walk with God.* This particular workbook also helps develop the disciplines of prayer and Bible memorization, as well as personal Bible study. One of the advantages of this approach is that it gives some families initial rails to run on. That can be a confidence builder and prove extremely profitable for many kids and parents.

Listening to podcasts: My family and I really enjoy excellent preaching and teaching, and of course with the advent of modern technology, we now have a bonanza of great Bible teachers at our literal fingertips. After you finish one of your inductive studies, you might want to study another book or special series with one of your favorite Bible teachers. Typically what my kids and I do is read several times through the passage we will hear preached before dialing up our podcast. I suggest keeping your journal at the ready for any questions and observations that may arise as you read through your text. When we meet, we listen to the message, pausing as needed to comment, clarify, ask questions, or apply God's word.

This has proved to be an effective and enjoyable way to study the Bible together, and it is especially suited for meeting at home. While it isn't mandatory, I believe some serious baked goods should be thoughtfully considered. I have found that brownies, for example, go well with most sermons, as do chocolate chip cookies. Don't try this at church; you'll distract the preacher! If you're health conscious, have some fruit if you must, but I don't think you'll get as much out of your message.

Some of our favorite teachers are John Piper (Desiring God, www.desiringgod. org), John MacArthur (Grace to You, www.gty.org), Tim Keller (Redeemer Presbyterian Church, www.redeemer.com), and R.C. Sproul (Ligonier Ministries, www.ligonier.org). Listening to these gifted men with your kid next to you over some pastry and coffee early in the morning in your pajamas is a pretty sweet deal! I highly recommend it!!

Reading Relevant Christian Books Together: Reading is a good thing! Pick a subject/ book of interest and process it together chapter by chapter or at the speed that suits your needs. In the interest of stimulating some thought, here is a short list of subject matter and titles that might trigger an idea for you and your child.

• **Spiritual Disciplines & the Christian Life**: Jerry Bridges has written some wonderful works through the years (Please search your browser "Jerry Bridges, Books"). Tim Chester is a refreshing voice who weaves theology and godly living into the beautiful tapestry that it truly is. *You Can Change* is a prime example of Pastor Chester's biblically dynamic teaching ministry. This book deals with God's transforming power in the life of believers and comes highly recommended. He's British, so you might want to brush up on your English accent. *Knowing God*, by J.I. Packer; *Desiring God* and *Don't Waste Your Life*, by John Piper (teens and up); *Practical Religion*, by J.C. Ryle (teens and up) are four other engaging possibilities. Ultimately, these should probably be required reading for all Christians, but since I'm not in charge I can only encourage their consumption most earnestly.

• **Christian Biographies**: Christian biographies can be especially exciting and spiritually challenging. Here is a glimpse of the many offerings available...

The Hiding Place, by Corrie ten Boom, is the story of a devout Christian family who—compelled by the love of Christ—risked all to save Jews during the Nazi occupation of Holland in WWII. Their journey of sacrifice and Christian love will challenge you. *Through Gates of Splendor*, by Elisabeth Elliot, is the story of Jim Elliot and his four missionary cohorts who poured out their lives to reach the Auca Indians in South America with the gospel. *Surprised By Joy*, by C.S. Lewis, is Lewis's account of his journey to faith, from atheist to believer. There are several biographies on the amazing story of the father of modern missions, Hudson Taylor. One of our favorites is *Hudson Taylor and Maria: A Match Made in Heaven*. This story of Hudson Taylor and his wife and their challenges in China draws extensively from personal letters and papers.

An excellent series of short biographies is offered in John Piper's "The Swans Are Not Silent" series. There are five books in total (each with multiple biographies) encompassing the life stories, struggles, and triumphs of Christian greats such as John Bunyan, William Cowper, David Brainerd, John Newton, William Wilberforce, William Tyndale, Adoniram Judson, and others. One of the benefits of these volumes is that the biographies are short and beautifully written, making them easy and inspiring reads.

- **Christian Manhood**: *Thoughts for Young Men*, by JC Ryle is a small book packed full of exhortations, entreaties, and instructions on how a young man can face the trials and temptations of this life. *Stand Fast in the Way of Truth* and *Hold Fast in a Broken World* by Douglas Bond are two books that form a series entitled Father & Sons. This is wonderful discipleship material for Christian dads to train their sons to be stalwart Christians at home, in the church, and in the world.

- **Christian Womanhood**: *Beautiful Girlhood*, by Karen Andreola is a great choice for middle school girls and *Passion & Purity*, by Elisabeth Elliot is excellent for the transition of a girl into womanhood.

- **Apologetics**: One very profitable little book that helped introduce my boys to apologetics (trustworthiness of Scripture, the deity of Christ, the veracity of the gospel, etc.) and helped solidify their Christian faith was Josh McDowell's short classic *More Than a Carpenter*. It's right around 100 pages with easily digestible chapters. This little volume helped lay a foundation for future studies with my kids. We read through this book over the course of three months (meeting once per week) with two of my boys when they were on the cusp of their teen years. Another title by Josh McDowell is *The New Evidence that Demands a Verdict*.

- **Redemption**: *The Stranger on the Road to Emmaus*, by John R. Cross, is an engaging study of redemptive history. It compellingly looks at the beautiful theme of redemption from creation to the cross. This volume unfolds the wonderful doctrines of the gospel for believers to understand and apply to their daily lives. It can also be instrumental as a help to lead some of your children to Christ as Savior.

Audio Books: Here's a hybrid of the last two examples of alternative studies: find a favorite Christian book on audio and work through it as you would a podcast. This would be an interesting change-up from time to time. Don't forget the brownies!

Your Weekly Pulpit: Your pastor's personal study and preaching should provide a steady stream of edifying material for your family as well. One possibility for Bible study with your kids is to turn your Sunday sermon notes into your weekly study. This can be a fantastic way to reinforce what God's Spirit is endeavoring to teach you and your church through your pastor's pulpit ministry, so go to worship on Sunday mornings with Bible, pen, and notebook in hand and be ready to jot down thorough notes on Sunday's message. It would also be profitable to read Sunday morning's text on Saturday evening to prepare your heart and mind to receive the word on the Lord's Day. Then, starting on Monday, take two to four days to read Sunday's text, review your sermon notes, and record your own observations in a journal. This would be your preparation for your Thursday or Friday study time to discuss your comments, questions, and applications.

Here's the point

These are but a few suggestions offered as food for thought. The important objective to keep in mind is to begin to purposely disciple your children in the truth. Immerse yourself in God's truth personally, and as you do, pour that life-giving nourishment into the disciples God has entrusted to you at home. Regardless of what outward form that takes—whether you start with one of the ideas I have suggested, or you tweak one of these ideas, or come up with your own approach—get about getting the truth into yourself and into your kids.

Lastly, allow me to address a couple of questions that will come up from the two ends of the parenting spectrum regarding discipling our young people with the truth: those at the beginning of the parenting endeavor and those on the back nine, grandparenting. Let's start with the question that no doubt has already arisen in the minds of parents with really young kids.

"When should I begin to meet with my kids? If my kids are really young should I wait a few years (until they're more mature) before we study the Bible together?"

If your children are really young (three to eight years old), don't wait until they are older to gather around the word with them. Obviously, in their earlier years they will be limited in their abstract thinking skills and possess a very short attention span, but accounting for all of this, you can still come together around the stories of the Bible and the gospel. If your children are very young, you are in a great time of life to lay the groundwork for the gospel and the foundation for future in-depth Bible study. Once your children have the cognition to be read to, they can begin to process the storyline of the Bible. Just as you would with your older children, set a time aside and select a special place to meet. That's where you can begin to introduce them to the great accounts found in God's word. Begin to tell them how all the stories in the Bible point to the Lord Jesus and His gospel. All you need do is read the stories to them (What child doesn't love being read to?) and ask them the simplest of questions. A special journal book at this point can be filled with pictures and crayon scribbles of Bible stories, just like my sermon notes.

I'm reminded of the story of Philip Doddridge, a Puritan pastor, Christian educator, and hymn writer who had a tremendous impact on the spiritual revival of eighteenth-century England. As an author, he wrote one of Christianity's most influential books for the time, *The Rise and Progress of Religion in the Soul* (short title). This work played an important role in the salvation of John Newton (the former slave trader of "Amazing Grace" fame), William Wilberforce (the visionary antislavery parliamentarian), J.C. Ryle, and Charles Haddon Spurgeon (two powerful evangelical preachers of the late nineteenth century).

Philip Doddridge obviously had a prodigious ministry, yet he was an orphan at the tender age of eight. How did this little boy who had such a difficult beginning (Philip was presumed stillborn and nearly died at birth; he was also physically fragile all his life), become such a stalwart for the Lord Jesus and His gospel? The answer is not all that surprising. He was spiritually equipped by the mentoring of his young, godly mother, Monica Doddridge.

Each day as the fog enveloped the English landscape outside their home, Monica would sit young Philip on her knee in front of their warm fireplace and explore God's story together long before Philip learned to read. In typical Puritan style of the day, their hearth was adorned with Dutch tiles depicting the history of the Bible from the fall of man to the return of the Lord Jesus Christ. Every day Monica would lead her son through God's redemptive story as displayed on the tiles. By so doing she exposed Philip to the gospel and its biblical content many times during their short sojourn together. In this fashion, through the telling of the story and gentle dialogue of a mother with her son, Monica Doddridge mentored her son in the great truths of Scripture and prepared the way for the gospel which gripped Philip's heart at a very young age.

While our children are still quite young, we can unfold God's story to them from Genesis to Revelation. As I have said before, don't underestimate the ability of young minds to process biblical truths. If your children are little, engage them with the accounts of the Bible. These are truths the Holy Spirit can use to cultivate the soil of their hearts for the gospel and the study of His word.

"What material can I use with my little people?"

Here are a few suggestions to introduce your young ones to the Bible and its redemptive message.

• *The Jesus Storybook Bible: Every Story Whispers His Name*, by Sally Lloyd-Jones—for the youngest in your family fold (Ages 3 to 8—these age levels are simply suggested guidelines). This is an excellent resource. It recounts the major events in the Old and New Testaments and how they point to the Savior. The stories are concise, the artwork is bright, colorful, somewhat cartoonish in style, and presented to engage little people with God's amazing and unfolding biblical story of redemption.

• *The Lamb*, by John R. Cross—for children 5 to 10 years of age. This is a children's adaptation of *The Stranger on the Road to Emmaus* and is masterfully illustrated. Like *The Jesus Storybook Bible*, *The Lamb* shows how the entire Bible points to the Lord Jesus and His saving work. The key differences are that in *The Lamb* each section ends with questions to discuss with your child and the illustrations are beautifully realistic (including a vivid image of a sacrificed lamb).

• *Leading Little Ones to God*, by Marian M. Schoolland—for children 4–10 years old. This is a wonderful devotional for parent and child. Each brief lesson includes a story, a Scripture verse, and "hymn" which can be read as a poem. This wonderful book answers the big questions of life in a way a child can comprehend: Who is God? How was the earth created? Why are we here? What is the cause of evil and suffering? Why did Jesus come to earth? This book is a favorite of our family.

• *The Child's Story Bible*, by Catherine F. Vos—for older children in the seven-to-twelve age range. This thoughtful paraphrase of more than 200 stories from the Bible has been around since the time of the apostles, I think (Copyright

1935). It was certainly around when I was a boy before the discovery of fire and the wheel. The fact that so many years after its release this book is still widely employed is a testimony to its faithful conformity to the biblical text, and to its ability to connect Bible stories to children. In it, the narratives of the Bible are expertly paraphrased and occasionally illustrated. This beloved volume has absorbed children with the stories of the Bible for three quarters of a century.

So young parents, have at it! Begin reading the stories of Scripture to your kids while they're babies and throughout their early development, especially as they acquire language. When they are able to simply interact with you over the stories of the Bible, meet with them one-on-one even if it's only for five to ten minutes. In many ways this is the easiest time to start and create a joyful expectation in your children. Set the precedent and begin to shepherd them with the truths that will save their souls and prepare them to lead their own homes in that same way—which brings us to the other side of the parenting spectrum, grandparents.

"Should I try to disciple my grandchildren?"

This is likely the desire echoing in the hearts of many grandparents reading this book. If this question has captured your affections, I would encourage you to pursue the spiritual longing of your heart as much as it is possible. Reach out to your grandchildren in a discipleship relationship. I realize there are many complex family dynamics at work in some of your familial relationships, but as far as it depends on you, prayerfully look for opportunities to connect regularly with your grandchildren over the word of God. Your natural affection for one another and your God-ordained role in their lives can be powerful catalysts to bring about God's purposes for them.

My wife and I have two dear friends whose sons have families of their own. Our friends raised three boys in the environment of the church, but by their own admission never actively discipled them in the word; no one ever talked about the concept. They have decided to take a different approach with their grandchildren. They have determined to have a deliberate spiritual role in their Christian development. Starting with their two oldest grandsons and with the blessing of the parents, these grandparents have decided to have Bible study with their grandkids.

I think that is exceptionally grand (pardon the pun)! It is laudable because it is so biblical. Remember God's exhortation to Israel in Deuteronomy 6, especially verses 1 and 2? *"Now this is the commandment, the statutes and the judgments which the Lord your God has commanded me to teach you... so that you and your son and your grandson might fear the Lord your God"* (emphasis added). God calls on the parents and grandparents to shepherd the next generation in God's ways. Yes, ancient Israel was a deeply patriarchal culture where grandparents were highly esteemed, perhaps even revered. Unfortunately this may not always reflect our cultural values, but this command transcends culture and stands for us today. Oh, how I wish more grandparents would understand that God beckons them to actively mentor their grandchildren spiritually, not to take the place of the parents, but to come alongside them in a joint effort to reach the souls of the young and to strengthen their spiritual vitality. I pray that more and more of our children would experience the enveloping and life-changing grace of parents and grandparents shepherding their souls.

And so I encourage you again, my friend, whether you are a new parent, a seasoned parent, or somewhere in the middle of that herd, pour the word of God into your children. Read it to them from their infancy. Tell them the great stories of the Bible. Interweave the Bible's principles into the web of life as you live it. Model truth for your children when they are little and when they are grown. Talk of God's precepts when you're in your home or when you find yourself traversing the highways and byways of life. Let His words be among the first your children hear when they awake, and allow God's truth to alight on their minds as they drift off to sleep.

Shepherd the family flock God has entrusted to your care by leading them steadily to the green pastures of Scripture, and may the God of all grace, through the word of His grace, transform your family into a trophy of His grace. May people see the beauty of our God in your home and be drawn to His transforming glory.

> *This book of the law shall not depart from your mouth, but you shall meditate on it day and night, so that you may be careful to do according to all that is written in it; for then you will make your way prosperous, and then you will have success* (Joshua 1:8).

Here is the spring where waters flow,
    To quench our heat of sin:
Here is the tree where truth doth grow,
    To lead our lives therein:
Here is the judge that stints the strife,
    When men's devices fail:
Here is the bread that feeds the life
    That death cannot assail.
The tidings of salvation dear,
    Comes to our ears from hence:
The fortress of our faith is here,
    And shield of our defense.
Then be not like the swine that hath
    A pearl at his desire,
And takes more pleasure from the trough
    And wallowing in the mire.
Read not this book in any case,
    But with a single eye:
Read not but first desire God's grace,
    To understand thereby.
Pray still in faith with this respect,
    To bear good fruit therein,
That knowledge may bring this effect,
    To mortify your sin.
Then happy you shall be in all your life,
    What so to you befalls:
Yes, double happy you shall be,
    When God by death you calls.

(From the first Bible printed in Scotland—1576)

CHAPTER 12

Starting Where You Are...
by the Grace of God

Discipling our children is the greatest privilege and challenge we as Christian parents will face, and as with any great task, the overwhelming temptation that will confront us at one point or another will be discouragement. All of us fall short of being the fathers and mothers (for that matter the spouses) that we need to be. Not one of us can claim to be the ideal parent, and only the most deluded would even dare ascend to such arrogance. There is only one perfect Parent and that is God the Father. We, on the other hand, emanate from the fallen line of our first parents, Adam and Eve. Like them, and every man and woman that has followed thereafter, we fall far short of God's perfect and glorious standard (Romans 3:23).

We have all failed to be as perfect as our heavenly Father. He continually showers us with flawless love and never wavers in His holy actions or affections toward us. He is always patient, just, merciful, caring, gracious, and kind, without variance. He is immutable, or unchanging, in His perfect dealings with us, and so James explains that in our heavenly Father *"there is no variation or shifting shadow"* (James 1:17).

He is always good. He is always the same! We never have to worry about what kind of mood we will find Him in, wonder if He possesses all the right information, or whether He will be fair with us, or even if He is available, let alone approachable. In fact, Scripture beckons Christians to enter God's holy presence with boldness. The author of Hebrews describes the perfect availability and approachability of our God with this amazing invitation, *"Therefore let us*

235

draw near with confidence to the throne of grace, so that we may receive mercy and find grace to help in time of need" (Hebrews 4:16).

We may approach God's presence with confidence because of the perfect, saving, priestly work of the Lord Jesus (Hebrews 4:14–15). Based on His accomplishment, when we come before God, we find a loving Father who gladly welcomes us and who delights in our worship and fellowship. Paul reminded the Galatians of this very thing when he said, *"Because you are sons* [God adopts believers as His children through the atoning work of Christ, Ephesians 1:5], *God has sent forth the Spirit of His Son into our hearts, crying, 'Abba! Father!'"* (Galatians 4:6). Paul uses the Aramaic descriptor *Abba*, which is best translated "daddy" in our vernacular. This is a term of endearment, tenderness, and intimacy, and describes not simply our approach to God but the manner in which He receives us. He receives us, relates to us, as beloved children, and that my friends is true 100% of the time! Our Father in heaven is perfect and acts perfectly toward His beloved children—always!

Welcome to the club of the fallen and repentant

But alas, we fall far short of such divine glory. You and I waver, we falter, we sin against God and men, yes, even against our beloved spouse and children. We behave selfishly, sometimes deal inequitably; we can wound with our words and grieve with our actions and fail to consistently lead our family flock in the path of God's good way. This is true of us all, and because we fail, we often grow disheartened. It is precisely at this point that we must guard our hearts against the deception of discouragement.

Over time, the greater temptation that arises from discouragement—especially prolonged and deep discouragement—is a sense of lost hope, a desire to give up. We're seduced to withdraw further from the Lord's prescribed course because we have—in our judgment—failed the Lord too much and too often. We're tempted to throw in the towel, as it were. Failing and feeling hypocritical, we grow weary of trying and retreat even more from God and His precepts. That, my friends, is not the answer to our failures. The urge to distance ourselves from the Lord and His word is a lie of the enemy. Inaction or shrinking back from what we know is true is never the solution to our problems, and this is certainly so when it comes to our parental shortcomings. Instead of prolonging and deepening our failure through greater apathy and disobedience, we must repent of our sin and seek the Lord with renewed fervor.

If you have failed to be the spouse or parent you need to be, I encourage you to join me in the club of Penitent Parents. The room's a little crowded but it's cozy! The chief entitlement is the joy of repentance and the gracious blessings that ensue when we genuinely turn to God. Yet your question at this point is likely, "What is biblical repentance? What does true repentance look like?" Allow me to answer that with five simple points.

1—Repentance begins with confession

If you have failed to be the parent you ought to be, I invite you to repent, and repentance begins by confessing our sin to God (1 John 1:9). "Confession" or "to confess" our sin is a concept that has been distorted by time and usage. However, the true sense of "confession" comes from the oft-used New Testament word *homologeo* which literally means "to say the same thing."[1] Consequently, to confess our evil means that we acknowledge our sin to the Lord, recognizing the horrible offense it is to Him, a holy God. Ultimately, all sin is against God.

After David's sin (adultery and murder) was exposed, he wrote this in his penitent psalm, "*Against You, You only, I have sinned and done what is evil in Your sight, so that You are justified when You speak and blameless when you judge*" (Psalm 51:4). It is God whom we have most offended, and it is to Him that we must openly lay out our offenses. When we confess our sin, we do not rationalize our behavior, we do not dumb it down, we do not shift blame to others, we confess it for what it is and—as much as it hurts—we own it. We cry out to God from our broken condition and acknowledge our failures and transgressions to the Lord.

In 2 Samuel chapter 12, the prophet Nathan was sent by God to King David for the express purpose of confronting the king with his horrible sin (murder, adultery, and abuse of power, to name a few of his offenses). Through the vehicle of a parable designed by God to engage the king and reveal the utter wickedness of what he had done, David's sin was completely exposed (2 Samuel 12:1–7). Even so, it would have been very easy at that point for a man of power and persuasion such as David was to try to shift the blame, to make excuses, to minimize what he had done and to try to negotiate away his culpability.

He could have said, "Yes, Nathan, okay I slept with Bathsheba, but my wives and concubines don't understand me. It's stressful being king, and quite honestly it can be extremely lonely at the top. I feel lonely! But do you know what? Bathsheba understands me. I like her Nathan. She makes me happy, and wouldn't God want me to be happy? Yes, I know I had Uriah taken care of, but as you know he wasn't one of ours anyway. He was a Hittite. I had my suspicions about that man. He seemed a little too eager to please, if you ask me. What if he was a spy? What if he turned on us in battle? And being a gentile, what's he doing with one of our women anyway? No, I felt justified and compelled to act for the greater good of our people, Nathan."

Once David's transgressions were out in the open, what was David's response to the Lord's revelation of his sin? The simple and direct answer is found in 2 Samuel 12:13. David confessed, "*I have sinned against the LORD.*" There were no excuses offered, no shifting of blame, no softening of the sins committed, no "Yeah, but..." David admitted that He had not simply sinned against man but had ultimately sinned against the Lord. He had grieved the heart of the holy God who loved him. He confessed his sin. He owned his sin.

2—Repentance involves turning from sin

Having recognized our sin for what it is, true repentance continues when we turn away from our wrongdoing. It makes no sense to humbly recognize the heinousness of our offense, to be remorseful over our wickedness, and then simply wallow in it without turning from it. That would not be a true confession of our iniquity. That would be simply identifying the filth that makes us uncomfortable but that we enjoy. God does not share this tolerance of sin. Consequently, when we perceive our sin for the evil that it is, we must abandon it. Regardless of what those sins may be—selfishness, moral failure, failure to lead our family spiritually, a spiritually cold and unresponsive heart, pride, putting the world's treasures above Christ, placing ourselves, our desires, and agenda above the parental stewardship we have received from the Lord, clinging to bitterness, an unforgiving heart, tolerating evil influences in our home, or failing to confront sin in our children—we need to renounce our sin. Sin must be abandoned. David, for example, was completely contrite over his great sins (read Psalms 32 and 51). The king had to deal with the consequences of his evil actions for the rest of his life in one way or another, but we have no record or hint that David repeated his former offenses again.

3—Repentance from sin means turning to God

When we repent of our sin, we do not turn aimlessly in another direction without a destination or purpose. When a Christian turns from sin, he or she runs to God! This is certainly implicit in David's straightforward confession of 2 Samuel 12:13, "*I have sinned against the LORD.*" That is, "I must turn away from sin and to the one I have offended, the Lord." In Psalm 32:5 David wrote, "*I acknowledged my sin to You, and my iniquity I did not hide; I said, 'I will confess my transgressions to the LORD'*" (emphasis added). David's heart turned away from his transgression to the Lord.

The exhortations to God's people to turn to the Lord, to seek the Lord, are abundant in Scripture. We are encouraged to "*Seek the LORD and His strength; Seek His face continually*" (Psalm 105:4)—how much more when we abandon our evil practices. This is why after David confessed his sin he wrote, "*Therefore, let everyone who is godly pray to You in a time when You may be found*" (Psalm 32:6). He is near and may be found when we repent (Isaiah 55:6–7), and like the prodigal's father, our heavenly Father awaits our turning to Him and runs to meet us with open arms and an affectionate embrace. Describing the Father's posture toward repentant sinners, Jesus said, "*So he got up* [the prodigal son] *and came to his father. But while he was still a long way off, his father saw him and felt compassion for him and ran and embraced him and kissed him*" (Luke 15:20). That is a picture of God's compassion and affection toward a penitent sinner. We turn from sin to a loving God.

4—Repentance means humbly reaching out in reconciliation to the ones we have wronged

Sadly, David's malfeasance devastated an entire family. As king, the easiest thing to do would have been to push the devastation aside, to remove Bathsheba and her child far from David's presence, throw a ton of money at the problem, and with his wealth and power buy the disregard and silence of many. Instead, what did the king do? David took Bathsheba as his wife. He did not put her away secretly to try to minimize the political and familial damage her presence would bring to the house of David. What's more, David also pleaded with the Lord that the child of their illicit union might live even though the child's life would serve as a living illustration of David's folly for David's enemies. David abandoned his sins and did as much as was in his power to reconcile a morally disastrous situation, as the evidence of his post–2 Samuel 12 life clearly shows.

Just as we must acknowledge our sin to the Lord and turn from it and seek Him, so we must seek the forgiveness of the ones we have wronged and hurt. While we cannot undo the past or control the ability of others to forgive us, it is up to us to humbly seek reconciliation and persevere in this pursuit.

5—The goal of repentance is restoration

When we repent of our sin, when we recognize our sin for what it is, acknowledge it to the Lord, forsake it, and run to our Redeemer in faith, something quite marvelous happens. God in His mercy is moved by compassion to forgive our many transgressions regardless of what they may be and to restore us to a right relationship with Him.

This is beautifully expressed in the words of Isaiah 55:6–7. To the person who genuinely turns from their sin to the Lord, the promise is this, "*Seek the LORD while He may be found; call upon Him while He is near. Let the wicked forsake his way and the unrighteous man his thoughts; and let him return to the LORD, and He* [God] *will have compassion on him, and to our God, for He will abundantly pardon*" (emphasis added). The Hebrew term for "*compassion*" in Isaiah 55:7 is an extremely tender expression. For example, the prophet Isaiah uses it in chapter 49, verse 15 to describe the tender love a mother has for her nursing infant. In all the realm of creation, there is arguably no sweeter expression of human compassion and affection than that which is expressed by a nursing mother toward her little one.

Here's the point of God's use of this language. When a sinner turns with a whole heart to the Lord, God is moved in His innermost and extends His tender love toward that penitent person in the same way a nursing mother extends her caring arms to her needy child. There is no hesitation there, no holding back of affection, only complete acceptance. What's more, God's embrace of a sinner results in total, comprehensive forgiveness! There is more than meets the eye in this beautiful Hebrew word for "*pardon*." This is one of the few words in the Old Testament that is used exclusively of God. It is never used in any way, shape, or form to refer to men forgiving other men. Why? Because only God can forgive so comprehensively, so utterly! It is as though God is telling the penitent sinner, "Look, I forgive you, but I want you to abandon any notion of forgiveness based on man's ability to forgive. Men are reluctant to forgive, they hold grudges, they forgive imperfectly. I forgive perfectly, exhaustively, abundantly to all who call out to Me in repentance."

That is indescribably joyous to me! To think that when I turn from sin our holy God forgives my guilt and embraces me with His love and acceptance, without reservation or hesitation, quite honestly collapses me to my knees in grateful worship. This divine pardon, my friends, is the promise of God in the Scripture to all who genuinely repent. To repeat the words of the apostle John, "*If we confess our sins, He is faithful and righteous to forgive us our sins and to cleanse us from all unrighteousness*" (1 John 1:9). When we repent of our sin, God's faithful and unwavering response is to forgive, to cleanse, to restore. What a gracious God we serve!

We must also understand that God's pardon toward us is exhaustive. As we just mentioned, God doesn't forgive as men do, i.e., reluctantly, grudgingly, imperfectly, partially. God doesn't merely sweep our sins under some celestial rug or wipe away the greater part of our iniquity, leaving behind a dull but unmistakable impression of moral failure on our record. God doesn't hold back some of His forgiveness because of our propensity to grieve Him with the same or worse behavior. No indeed, God expunges our guilt completely so as to leave no trace of it. The Lord wipes out our transgressions and does not remember our sins (Isaiah 43:25)! To put it another way, God literally removes our sin so far from us that it is as though we had never committed it. That's the kind of forgiveness God offers and practices, and that's why in Psalm 103:8–14 David celebrates,

> The LORD is compassionate and gracious, slow to anger and abounding in lovingkindness. He will not always strive with us, nor will He keep His anger forever. He has not dealt with us according to our sins, nor rewarded us according to our iniquities. For as high as the heavens are above the earth, so great is His lovingkindness toward those who fear Him. As far as the east is from the west, so far has He removed our transgressions from us. Just as a father has compassion on his children, so the LORD has compassion on those who fear Him. For He Himself knows our frame; He is mindful that we are but dust.

That is how comprehensive God's pardon is. He removes our sins from us *"as far as the east is from the west"*—an infinite distance! God restores penitent sinners completely!

Beginning where you are

Because the Lord in His beneficent compassion is so sweeping with His forgiveness, when we repent we are given the exhilarating gift of a new start; our past failure is not held against us. We can joyfully begin to obey at the point of repentance. We are given the freedom and privilege to start anew, God's way!

It must be said that this wonderful reality of God's compassion and forgiveness is true for any repentant sinner whether or not he is or ever will be a parent, but it is certainly applicable to all of us who are parents and especially to those who have seen their own families succumb to the ravages of their personal failures. Wherever you are in the parenting journey (first baby to grandchildren), when you fail and repent, God's provision for you through Jesus Christ is a fresh, new start.

You and your spouse may be eagerly anticipating the arrival of your first child, you may actually have little ones, or perhaps your children are knocking at the door of adolescence. Some have children that are in the midst of their teen years, still others of you have sons and daughters who have left home and are on their own. Some of you no doubt have embarked on that great and wondrous journey of grandparenthood, and your heart's desire is to be an aroma of Christ in the lives of your children and a godly shepherd to the little sheep God has graciously added to your family fold, your grandchildren.

Regardless of where life has you, two things can be said with certainty. One, we have all failed to be the leaders we need to be for the next generation—even those of us who are preparing to be parents for the first time. Secondly, in Christ you stand forgiven, and through that exhaustive forgiveness, you have a new start. If your heart is right before the Lord, today you can begin anew to shepherd your family according to God's precepts.

Someone may well object, "Okay, I have a new beginning, but this is not the optimal place for a new start! This parenting thing would be so much easier if my kids were little. My children are older (or out of the home) and we're so set in our ways. I wish we could start all over again." That may be, but you are where you are, and since neither you nor I can wrench one yesterday from history, we must begin by God's grace where we find ourselves. The important thing is to begin to biblically shepherd your family... today, starting where you are!

Embracing God's grace

Still, I know some of you will wonder, "Can God really give me a new start?" Perhaps you have failed so as to devastate your family, and you are asking, "But Marcelo, you don't know how far I've fallen, how far down the road I am in this parenting enterprise. I've failed so terribly. Could God forgive me, revive me, after what I have done? Can He really give me a new start and empower me to make a difference in the life of my family?" The answer to that question, my friend, is a clear and resounding "Yes!" God's grace reaches to the deepest, darkest pit, retrieves and restores all repentant sinners.

The grace of God toward all His people is joyously remembered in the hymn "Grace Greater Than Our Sin."

> Marvelous grace of our loving Lord,
> Grace that exceeds our sin and our guilt!
> Yonder on Calvary's Mount outpoured—
> There where the blood of the Lamb was spilt.
> Grace, grace, God's grace,
> Grace that will pardon and cleanse within;
> Grace, grace, God's grace,
> Grace that is greater than all my sin![2]

Many a redeemed lyricist has described the knowledge and experience of God's bountiful grace that pardons all our iniquities. More importantly, God's gracious pardon is wondrously described in His own testimony, the Scriptures, and ultimately that is where we need to go to understand how deep God's grace is for those who believe. Once we truly come to grips with an understanding of biblical grace and the forgiveness we find through it, then our soul is liberated to embrace it and to experience the fresh start that it affords you and me.

Essentially, divine grace is the sweet, unmerited favor of God primarily expressed in the forgiveness of our sin at salvation. From that key touchstone, grace extends to every area of our existence. Grace permeates our salvation, our ministries, daily lives (including family life), and future existence. Consider the following grocery list of the working of grace in the areas I've just mentioned. God's grace is at the heart of the gospel (Acts 20:24); it has appeared for the salvation of all men (Titus 2:11); it empowers belief (Acts 18:27); it saves (Ephesians 2:8); it justifies (Romans 3:24).

God calls men to ministry through His beneficent grace (Galatians 1:15); grace empowers servants for kingdom work (Acts 14:26); it is the essence of spiritual gifts (Romans 12:6); and it is the very substance of our labor for Christ (Ephesians 3:2). Grace describes the Spirit of God who dwells in us (Hebrews 10:29); it is readily given to the humble (James 4:6); it gives strength to the weak (2 Timothy 2:1); it produces spiritual growth (2 Peter 3:18); and it is utterly sufficient to meet every challenge any believer faces (2 Corinthians 12:9). Additionally, "grace" characterizes the throne on which our God reigns (Hebrews 4:16), and lastly, though we experience its benefits in abundance now, we have yet to experience its fullness. That will come at the revelation of our Lord Jesus Christ (1 Peter 1:13).

Grace touches every area of our experience, and just as important, we must remember the presence of God's favor in our lives is not only exhaustive, but inexhaustible. When I came to faith in Christ, when God poured out His grace upon me and forgave me of all my iniquity, there wasn't a temporary scarcity of grace leaving precious little available for you. The "grace meter" did not dip perilously low. There wasn't a grace "brown-out" in heaven.

When I wrestle with my sins now and my thirsty, listless soul guzzles from the reviving tributaries of grace (God's word, prayer, the fellowship and love of God and His people, the comforting and reviving ministry of His Holy Spirit), heaven does not need to tap into grace reserves because of my great need—although those who know me and love me may be tempted to differ! The fact of the matter is, God's grace comes from the boundless depths of His divine wealth, His very character. There is never a shortage of God's grace because there is never any deficiency in God, and so, it is given to us in ceaseless cascades, without hesitation, interruption, or occlusion.

In Ephesians 1:7–8, we learn that God's grace for our pardon flows from the depths of His infinite riches which He pours upon us in opulent fashion. Paul writes, "*In Him we have redemption through His blood, the forgiveness of our trespasses, according to the riches of His grace which He lavished on us*" (emphasis added). God's wealth of grace is incalculable and He gives us grace in proportion to His abundance.

Paul tells us this divine favor is the "*grace in which we stand*" (Romans 5:2), that we receive in "*abundance*" (Romans 5:17), indeed that is "*lavished*" upon us (Ephesians 1:8), which is surpassing in us (2 Corinthians 9:14; Ephesians 2:7), under whose canopy we live (Romans 6:14–15), and which continually abounds to us (2 Corinthians 9:8). Paul is essentially saying—in these and other passages—that believers live in an atmosphere of divine grace circumscribed above, below, on every side, and all around in unfailing, inexhaustible bountifulness. God has given you an inexhaustible fount of grace from which to drown your great need, and the Spirit of God invites you to glut yourself to the full, my friend. Drink and let your grace-filled, grateful heart rise in worship of the God of all grace.

C. H. Spurgeon, the "prince of preachers" and my favorite deceased pastor and mentor, understood grace and his desperate need of it better than most. My grateful heart leaps in agreement when he says, "Do you sometimes feel so thirsty for grace that you could drink the Jordan dry? More than a river could hold is given you, so drink abundantly, for Christ has prepared a bottomless sea of grace to fill you with all the fullness of God. Do not be frugal. Do not doubt your Savior. Do not limit the Holy One of Israel. Be great in your experience of His all-sufficiency. Be great in your praises of His bounty, and in heaven you will pour great treasures of gratitude at His feet."[3]

Are you in great need of the sweet waters of grace today? Then drink. Don't be tentative, drink! Let your soul be satisfied with God's abundance. Remember this, God's grace is never outmatched or outstripped by our sins, and when we repent of our sundry failures, by His grace, He faithfully removes our guilt and gives us a fresh new start.

Can God restore what sin has devoured?

Let's bring this principle of God's grace to bear on the matter at hand, God's grace as it relates to our failures as parents. The point is fairly obvious, God's grace is far greater than our sins, and it can restore and revive us personally, as well as our families. My desire is to encourage you to repent of your failures as a parent, to turn to the Lord, to accept His full forgiveness and all-sufficient grace, and to begin anew (regardless of where you are) to grow in your love for God through His word, and by His bountiful strength, to order your family by His precepts.

Can God's grace undo the past? In an eternal sense, I believe you can say that. Because of the cross of Christ, one day in heaven we will be free of the manifold devastation sin brings to our lives. All the dire consequences of our sin will be completely done away with, including the greatest consequence and our greatest enemy, death (1 Corinthians 15:54–57). That is not true of us this side of heaven. The promise of complete deliverance is certain beyond doubt, and the present reality of exhaustive pardon from our sin is equally real, but until the wonderful dawning of the great and eternal day of God, believers still live in an unredeemed world and in bodies of unredeemed flesh. That means we will struggle with sin, and we will live with some of the temporal consequences of our failures, the scars of our sins. We're redeemed, healed from the ultimate penalty and consequences of sin, but like the patriarch Jacob we walk with a limp (Genesis 32:25, 31–32). King David found pardon from his great iniquity (Psalms 32 and 51), but throughout the balance of his journey here on earth, he lived with many of the temporal consequences of his terrible choices. He could not undo his adulterous act with Bathsheba; he could not bring Uriah back from the dead, nor could he prevent the devastation that ensued from his destructive behavior (2 Samuel 12:10–12).

Yes, all of the consequences of our sin will be relieved in eternity (Revelation 21:4). Until that day we will have to bear under many of the failures we have perpetrated. If, for example, you have neglected to spend time with your children over the years—for whatever reasons—there is no way of retrieving the time that has passed. In that sense, you cannot undo the past. You are left with the varying consequences of such behavior. However, if you recognize your failure, repent of it, accept God's gracious pardon, and begin by God's mercy to seek out and biblically lead your family, God can do marvelous works of grace in your home. You cannot bring back time, but God can redeem the time you have left.

We can—by His enabling—work through the repercussions of our past and sinful choices. What's more, as we do that, God will restore and renew us and will bring about great miracles of grace in our lives and families. I've seen it. God can rebuild what transgression has destroyed. He can create something wonderful out of the ashes of our failure.

Yes, God can restore what sin has devoured. Moreover, just as the Lord will one day make the waste places and deserts of Israel bloom and blossom like the garden of the Lord (Isaiah 51:3), so God can take devastation in our lives and use it to create something new and spiritually vital. To affirm this encouraging reality we need look no further—as we have been doing—than the life of King David. After David's great sins, his life and the lives of many around him looked like a fresh impact crater—nothing but devastation all around. Yet from that relational, spiritual, emotional rubble, God created a garden of grace that flourishes to this day.

First of all, David's relationship to God was immediately restored when he admitted his guilt to the Lord. In David's famous psalm recounting his confession (Psalm 32), the king launches his song of praise with, *"How blessed is he whose transgression is forgiven, whose sin is covered! How blessed is the man to whom the LORD does not impute iniquity, and in whose spirit there is no deceit!"* David celebrated the Lord's forgiveness of his great guilt because He had been restored to the Lord. Later in this psalm, David exalts, *"You [the Lord] are my hiding place; You preserve me from trouble; You surround me with songs of deliverance. Selah... Be glad in the LORD and rejoice, you righteous ones; And shout for joy, all you who are upright in heart."* The Lord had pardoned David, and the king took pleasure and refuge in God. He rejoiced in a clean heart before the Lord. The bond of fellowship between God and David that had been interrupted by the king's sin was restored, and praise could once again flow from David's heart and lips. David's relationship to the Lord was fully revived to the intimacy of former times and likely to depths he had not known before experiencing the matchless forgiveness of the Lord.

What is truly remarkable is that God made King David the standard of godliness for all the kings of Israel. When the Lord charged Solomon (the first king to succeed David) to shepherd His people, He raised the Davidic standard with these words: *"As for you, if you will walk before Me as your father David walked, in integrity of heart and uprightness, doing according to all that I have commanded you and will keep My statutes and My ordinances, then I will establish the throne of your kingdom over Israel forever, just as I promised to your father David"* (1 Kings 9:4–5). From Solomon onward, the kings of Israel were all held to the standard exemplified by King David (1 Kings 15:3; 2 Kings 22:2, 2 Chronicles 29:2; 34:2).

More amazing still is the testimony of God regarding the sum of David's life. When the Lord considered the life of His servant in sum total, His gracious assessment was simply this, *"David the son of Jesse, a man after My heart."* In God's eyes, that was the life of David in a nutshell, and He tells us so in both the Old and New Testaments (1 Samuel 13:14; Acts 13:22). According to the commemoration of the Lord, David's passions and values, the outworking of his rule, the direction of his life, were in harmony, in sync with God's heart. God absolved David of his great sin and exclusively remembered the fruit of righteousness that sprang from his life. Wow! What an amazing epitaph.

Surely someone out there must be musing, "Wait a minute! God testified to Solomon, *'if you will walk before Me as your father David walked, in integrity of heart and uprightness... then I will establish the throne of your kingdom over Israel forever,'* and to all generations God declared, *'I have found David the son of Jesse, a man after my heart, who will do all My will'* (1 Kings 9: 4–5). Really? Are we talking about the same guy? The one who took another man's wife and had her husband murdered to cover his adultery? Could there possibly be another David in the Bible God is referring to?"

No! You see, my friends, the life of David is a monument to the restoring power of God's grace. Out of the catastrophe of David's sin, God multiplied grace. God forgave; God healed; God restored; and yes, God created something worthy of remembrance and emulation. Furthermore, the outpouring of God's blessing on the life of David didn't stop there. After David's abject moral failure, it would have been enough for the Lord to restore David's relationship to Himself, to establish his righteous legacy, and to testify of David's heart as He did. Yet God had even grander plans for the legacy of His servant. The crowning glory of David's life is found in the advent of Jesus Christ. You see, through the line of David (through Bathsheba), God brought forth the greater Son of David, Jesus, and through Him, God supplied salvation to mankind (Matthew 1:1). Myriads upon myriads of people—including you and me—have experienced and will experience cleansing from sin, reconciliation to God and man, restoration of life and family, renewed purpose in this life, and the eternal delight of heaven because of the blessings that spring from the fount of David. Yes, my friends, God can make something beautiful out of the ashes of our lives.

I know that many, if not most of you who read this book, will at one point or another question the largeness of the grace I have described in the previous paragraphs. As I mentioned earlier, you will do so because you will fall and fail and the enemy—through your emotions—will tell you that your sins have outgained God's grace. You've gone beyond the margins of grace. As a pastor, I have heard people express that very sentiment to me. When those internal voices rise up to condemn you, I want you to recognize them for what they are. They are lies from the enemy of your soul.

After we recognize the source (hell) and substance (lies) of these emotions, we need to reacquaint ourselves with and embrace biblical grace. You would do well to reread, study, and apply the truths of grace we have discussed in this chapter, and remind yourself that no one can exceed God's grace with their transgressions. In this age of grace, God always waits with open arms to receive and restore the truly penitent and in so doing affords them a fresh, clean start.

Wherever you may find yourself in your familial journey today, I invite you by the amazing grace that God affords, to call out to God and take your first step in shepherding your family afresh. Does this mean you need to repent of sin, reach out to recommit yourself to the Lord and His word, or evaluate your priorities and time commitments? Perhaps for you, your "first step" is to persevere in what you are doing.

The "first step" will vary from person to person. In humility, ask God for the wisdom to know what to do, and then walk on in obedient faith by the grace that God supplies. Remember who goes with you to enable and sustain you, the Lord your God! Just as He promised Israel of old, He promises His people today, "Do not fear, for I am with you; Do not anxiously look about you, for I am your God. I will strengthen you, surely I will help you, surely I will uphold you with my righteous right hand" (Isaiah 41:10).

Appendices

Building Blocks of Bible Study: Getting the Right Tools

Essential Tools

A Good Bible Translation: It is important that you get your hands on a good translation of the Bible. Our ministry recommends the following four translations: the New American Standard Bible (NASB), the English Standard Version (ESV), the New King James Bible (NKJB), and the New International Version (NIV)— the most-read translation of the Bible in the US, if not the world. While the NIV is not a word-for-word translation of the Bible, it is a reliable and readable rendering of the original languages of the Scripture.

Study Bible: This can be your all-in-one starting study tool. We highly recommend the ESV Study Bible and the John MacArthur Study Bible (comes in the NASB, NKJB, and the NIV). An interesting option for teens is The Apologetics Study Bible, edited by Ted Cabal. According to its press release, it is designed to "help today's Christian better understand, defend and proclaim their beliefs in this age of increasing moral and spiritual relativism."

A good study Bible will give you all the relevant background material you will need to properly understand a book's context (date, authorship, interpretive challenges, cultural, geographical, historical setting), as well as helpful verse by verse commentary to aide and verify your understanding of the text. Along with the cross-reference and concordance features, you and your children will have all you need to start your Bible study in one volume.

Journal Book: As I mentioned before, a 9½" X 7" journal has worked great for us. You will find a variety of journals at your local office supply store. FYI, Barnes & Noble has a beautiful selection of fancy-shmancy journals.

As your desire to understand more of the Bible grows, you might want to add the following helps to your list of study tools.

Digging Deeper Tools

Exhaustive Concordance: A Bible concordance contains an alphabetical index of words and references to where those words occur in the Bible. A few examples are the *NASB Exhaustive Concordance*, the *KJV Strong's Exhaustive Concordance*, and the *ESV Comprehensive Concordance*.

Bible Dictionary: This important tool will help you discover the places, people, and theological terms of the Bible. I highly recommend the *Holman Illustrated Bible Dictionary*, Trent C. Butler, Editor. It works with the following main versions: NKJV, NIV, RSV, NRSV, REB, NAS, and TEV. It is a great resource aide.

Commentary of Choice: When you want to delve more deeply into the Bible books you study, a good Bible commentary will prove indispensable. When searching for reliable commentaries, it's always beneficial to consult a seasoned believer you trust such as your pastor or other mature spiritual leader to aid you in the process. A great resource to help you wade through the volumes of commentaries and assist in choosing a reliable and appropriate study aide is Dr. James Roscup's *Commentaries for Biblical Expositors*. This one volume organizes, rates, and fairly evaluates (from an evangelical perspective) pretty much every commentary that has been written on the Old and New Testaments. Dr. Roscup is a first-rate scholar and dear man of God.

"How to Study Your Bible": This resource is found in the help section of the study Bible I personally use, *The MacArthur Study Bible*, published by Thomas Nelson. It is one of the most succinct and helpful resources I have found to learn the steps of independent Bible study. There are many good resources out there, and I encourage you to find one you enjoy and feel comfortable with, but the MacArthur guide is a great and helpful place to start.

Free Online Bible Study Tools:

- www.studylight.org/dic/ved/

- www.blueletterbible.org/

- www.biblestudytools.com

Inductive Bible Study Helps Online:

- http://www.desiringgod.org/labs/all

- www.christianity.com/bible/bible-study-tips/the-inductive-method-of-bible-study-the-basics-11530093.html

APPENDIX B

Building Blocks of Bible Study: The Basics of Inductive Bible Study

---

The steps of basic inductive Bible study

Before you begin to study the word of God with your kids, it would be beneficial to familiarize yourself and your children (as much as it is possible given their ages) with the basic principles of inductive Bible study. Inductive Bible study is simply the process of allowing the Bible to speak for itself while examining a passage in its context and applying it to real life. Remember, we must look to the Bible with a humble, prayerful dependence upon the Holy Spirit, who is the Author of all Scripture and our resident truth Teacher (John 16:13; 2 Peter 1:21–22). We must endeavor by His grace to see clearly what it is He intended in any given passage we study. Leaning on Him, we can make careful observations and gather evidence from the text so as to make sound conclusions, order our lives by these precepts, and subsequently teach them to our children.

Regardless of what resources you use to familiarize yourself with inductive Bible study methods, allow me to give four foundational Bible study principles I have taught my kids to get you on your way. I will list them out, briefly explain them, and encourage you to investigate the resources in the preceding appendix. These guidelines have provided the road map for my personal investigation and my family's biblical journey of discovery over the years. Lastly, I will give an example of the kind of study I have enjoyed with my kids since they were little people. First, however, let's have a gander at the four basic precepts we need to keep in mind when mining the riches of God's word.

Step 1—The value of reading and rereading your text

What does the Bible say? We have to read the words of the Bible in order for this to be evident. By "reading" a passage I mean reading it thoughtfully and repeatedly. I encourage my kids to read the passage we study five or six times before we actually discuss it together. Because we want to read a passage repeatedly, we keep the length of the text under consideration reasonably short, and since we meet weekly, this gives us an attainable goal. Reading and rereading a passage allows us to pick up the thrust of the text and familiarizes us with its content. As we repeatedly read a section of Scripture, it is amazing how the text begins to unfold before our very eyes. The thrust of the paragraph or chapter becomes clearer and clearer, words begin to stand out, tenses start to tie ideas together, more and more questions surface, and answers become more evident. Having our kids read a passage of Scripture carefully several times enables them, not to mention us, to understand God's word, and helps establish an essential habit of lifelong Bible study.

Step 2—"What does the Bible mean by what it says?"

Reading what the Bible says leads us to interpretation, or determining what Scripture means by what it says. This is the step where we employ the interpretive lamps of language, culture, geography, history, and especially the testimony of related Scriptures to shed light on our particular passage. This is critical because if we don't understand, or worse, if we misinterpret what the Bible means, we will short-circuit the Bible's usefulness in our lives at that given point. For the Bible to be useful to us, we have to interpret it accurately. In fact, we only possess the Bible to the degree that we properly interpret it. The power of the word is not in the paper pulp or the beauty of its gilded binding and leather covering. Your physical copy of the Bible is not a magical talisman that mystically, magically changes you somehow. The transforming power of the word is in its meaning which we must endeavor to comprehend by allowing the Bible to speak for itself through the meaning of the words, the relationship between words (grammar), within the historical and cultural context in which they are couched, and by comparing the Bible with the Bible (cross-references, parallel passages).

What's more, remember there is only one meaning to scriptural texts. Regardless of how disputed the meaning of a passage may be, or how straightforward it is, there is one true interpretation of Scripture. Happily, the meaning of most Scripture is evidently clear: this is what theologians call the perspicuity of Scripture. It should always be our desire and objective to get to that meaning, to discover the meaning God intended for each text, because this is what leads to life transformation.

Step 3—Assessing our interpretation

In Step One we ask the question, "What does the Bible say?" This logically leads us to interpretation and the question "What does the Bible mean by what it says?" This third step, "assessing our interpretation," allows us to check our understanding of a passage with the interpretation of other faithful servants of the word and trusted pastors. You will find that the tested insight of godly people who have pored over Scripture and whose discernment has stood the scrutiny of many proves extremely valuable. Often God will use their spiritually energized powers of observation to correct our thinking and to further enhance the depth of our biblical comprehension. This is where a good and thorough study Bible is especially useful.

Step 4—Appropriating the truth

This brings us, of course, to the "So what?" part of our Bible study. Once we have arrived at what a passage means, we must ask ourselves the all-important questions, "How does this truth make a difference in my life? Where does this verity impact what I believe, how I feel, and/or what I do?" Repeatedly reading, rightly interpreting, carefully assessing the truth is like mining precious ore; appropriating the truth is where and how we spend that wealth. We have a sure source of priceless truth (the Bible); once we mine it, we are spiritually enriched as we apply that treasure to our lives. And while there is one interpretation of biblical texts, the applications are many, suiting the great and varied needs of believers in every culture and at every stage of life.

Each of our children will vary in their ability to work through this Bible study method according to their age and spiritual maturity. Yet, we must endeavor to instill these precepts and nurture these skills in them. As we do we will equip them for their lifelong journey of discipleship with the Lord.

Nurturing a heart like Ezra's

As believers we would do well to nurture a heart like that of God's faithful servant Ezra who committed himself to study the word of God, to live it out, and to pass it on to his people. *"For Ezra had set his heart to study the law of the LORD and to practice it, and to teach His statutes and ordinances in Israel"* (Ezra 7:10).

Building Blocks of Bible Study: What I Do, A Personal Example

―――

When getting together with my kids for Bible study, I have used an approach that blends together the four inductive Bible study steps I mentioned in Appendix B. It is a simple approach and has provided countless hours of fruitful study with my children. If you prefer to amend my approach or follow another that suits you and your kids' needs better, that's great. The key thing is to process the Bible through sound interpretative lenses with your children. I have found that the following steps take my kids and me approximately twenty minutes when we sit down to review our passage on our own in preparation for our joint study.

Step 1: Reading

Step one for us is reading through our text repeatedly. That means we pretty much read through our portion of Scripture four to five times per week. As we work through our section of Scripture independently from one another, the first couple of times we attempt to absorb the text without a whole lot of personal commentary, although from start to finish we keep our journals with us to write down any thoughts or questions that may arise out of our initial reading. By the third read we engage our journals actively, preparing for our joint discussion at the end of our week of study.

Step 2: In Your Own Words

While our minds are interacting with God's words from the beginning, we kick it up a notch with Step 2. This is where we restate each verse in our own words (Typically we do this by the second or third reading.). We're careful not to insert ideas that are not in the text, and we try to express the central concept within each verse as accurately as we possibly can without getting bogged down in details. The purpose of this is to force our minds to focus in on the plain sense of each verse and of course the extended paragraph we're looking at. Thinking about what each verse actually says and means gives rise to a multitude of observations, questions, and ultimately applications for our lives.

Step 3: Observation

This is the point where we actually write down the majority of our observations, questions, comments, correlations to other ideas within the paragraph, or other Scriptures. Putting this step at number three may sound like a chronological step, but it usually happens simultaneously with Step 2. It naturally arises out of the second step as we wrestle with what the text says and means. After we have restated what the verse says in our own terms, the nuances of words and relationships between ideas begin to surface. This is also where a lot of great questions come to the forefront and are written in our journals.

Step 4: Confirmation

This final step usually comes about in the last couple of days of our personal study when we consider what other wise teachers have said about our passage. At this point, we consult our commentary study tools, which may be as simple as a solid study Bible (primarily what I use with my kids), or one or two commentaries besides. Why save the verse by verse commentaries until the very end? The reason is that I want myself and my children to wrestle with the text on our own and therefore allow the Holy Spirit to lead us in the discovery of life-challenging concepts. I find that coming to our own, accurate, biblical conclusions cements the truth more deeply in our minds and lives. Going to our commentaries or study Bible should be a later step to confirm and refine the truths we have discovered and will attempt to live out.

Step 5: Application

This brings us to our need to apply the truths the Holy Spirit has helped us mine from the passage. It is eminently important that we prayerfully think through how the truth we've gathered affects our lives—I would also encourage you to think about how the text you have studied applies to both you and your children. Share with your kids how God's word has challenged and changed you, and help your young disciples understand how biblical principles make a difference in their lives. Obviously, this will take prayerful, thoughtful contemplation on your part, but the dividends are eternal.

Step 6: Discussion & Fellowship

On our designated meeting day we come together and go verse by verse over our passage. One of us will start by reading the first verse aloud from the actual text, followed immediately by the reader's version of the verse in his/her own words. Then the other person shares their rendition (own words) of the same verse. We find doing this often helps our understanding of Scripture because it forces us to look at the same content through the eyes of another. This step also helps cement the first couple principles of inductive Bible study—Step 1: Reading ("What does the Bible say?") and Step 2: Interpretation ("What does the Bible mean by what it says?"). If we have misread or misinterpreted God's word, this simple process helps us filter and correct such issues.

Once we have heard the verse read and restated in our own words, we take turns bringing up our own observations, comments, notes of interest, and questions. This forms the fodder for our discussion, which takes its own shape and journey every time we meet. Sometimes we'll spend the bulk of our time talking about one or two verses, or we'll smoothly work our way through the Bible paragraph that has become familiar to us that previous week. At other times, our text will take us to a corollary passage that will consume much of our focus. Often questions will come up that demand our immediate attention. Occasionally there are questions that require our exploration apart from our study and necessitate a "hold that thought—we'll come back to this later." Whatever turn our studies take, what I can say unequivocally is that they have proven to be a blessing and an encouragement to my children and me. We have all grown together through the word and bonded to one another in genuine Christian fellowship. With that simple approach we have worked our way through several books of the Bible.

"What does the format of your study look like?"

The physical layout of our Bible study is simple and can be easily done with most journal books. The larger ones give us a bit more room to write out our thoughts and seem to work best. We use a 9½" X 7" journal. If you can imagine an open journal book, we use the right hand side of the journal to write our restated text. We designate the verse, then write it out in our own words.

On the opposite page (left side) we jot down our observations (interpretation), questions, contemplative thoughts, applications, study notes of interest, and the meaning of important words. If you like to organize your thoughts, you can also designate each remark you make on the left side of the journal with an identifying caption, such as an encircled "O" for observation, an encircled question mark for a question, and an encircled "A" for application.

We prefer to keep things simple and just lay out our remarks as they arise in our personal study without any designation—except to label the verse in question. Often we leave our applications for the end of our discussion. Leaving most of our take-aways (applications) for the end of our time allows us to have a fuller understanding of the passage and therefore more skill to apply it.

Endnotes

WHY SHOULD I READ THIS BOOK

1 Robinson, Robert. "Come Thou Fount of Every Blessing." 1757. *Hymns for the Family of God*. Franklin, TN: Brentwood-Benson Music Publishing, 1976. 318. Print

2 "The sum of biblical doctrine" i.e., the New Testament and by extension the sum of the Old Testament Scriptures which reveal Christ—Jesus Christ is the point of both the Old and New Testaments, Luke 24:25–27; 44–46; John 1:45; Acts 10:43; 1 Peter 1:10–11, etc.

CHAPTER 1

1 Tolopilo, Marcelo A. *A Clarion Call to Protect Your Home*. Temecula, CA: Chart & Compass Press, 2008. *Duties of Parents*. 115.

2 Fiddler on the Roof. Directed by Norman Jewison. England: Pinewood Studios, 1971. Film. 181 min.

CHAPTER 3

1 Prothero, Steven. *Religious Literacy: What Every American Needs to Know - and Doesn't*. New York: HarperCollins Publishers, 2008. 7.

2 In a Gallup survey: *Teenagers' Knowledge of the Bible* based on a nationally representative sample of 1,002 teenagers between the ages of 13 and 18 interviewed between May 20 and June 27, 2004, results revealed that 8% of the American teens surveyed thought that Moses was one of the 12 apostles. The Gallup Organization, "Teenagers' Knowledge of the Bible," The Bible Literacy Report: What do American teens need to know and what do they know? (New York City: Bible Literacy Project, 2005). Another telling poll revealed that only 51% of American adults can name between one to three of the four Gospels. Pew Research Center, Religion and Public Life. *Who Knows What About Religion*. September 28, 2010. http://www.pewforum.org/2010/09/28/u-s-religious-knowledge-survey-who-knows-what-about-religion.

3 *The New-England Primer*. Boston: 1777. Aledo, TX: Wallbuilders Inc.

4 Ibid.

5 Ibid.

6 Ibid.

7 Ibid.

8 Smith, Christian. *Soul Searching: The Religious and Spiritual Lives of American Teenagers*. New York: Oxford University Press Inc., 2005. 165.

9 Tolopilo, Marcelo A. *A Clarion Call to Protect Your Home*. Temecula, CA: Chart & Compass Press, 2008.

10 The Spurgeon Archive, http://www.spurgeon.org/mainpage.htm.

11 Prothero, Steven. *Religious Literacy: What Every American Needs to Know - and Doesn't*. New York: HarperCollins Publishers, 2008. 40.

12 Prothero. 45–46.

13 Southern Baptist Council on Family Life Report to Annual Meeting of the Southern Baptist Convention (2002). http://www.sbcannualmeeting.net/sbc02/newsroom/newspage.asp?ID=261; Barna Group. *Six Reasons Young People Leave the Church.* https://www.barna.org/teens-next-gen-articles/528-six-reasons-young-christians-leave-church; Wallace, J. Cold-Case Christianity. *Are Young People Really Leaving Christianity?* February 18, 2015. http://coldcasechristianity.com/2015/are-young-people-really-leaving-christianity.

CHAPTER 4

1 The Shema is Israel's central statement of faith recited twice daily by observant Jews. It originally included Deut. 6:4–9, but later was expanded to include Deut. 11:13–21 and Numbers 15:37–41.

2 Francis Brown, R.R. Driver, and C.A. Briggs, *A Hebrew and English Lexicon of the Old Testament.* Oxford: Clarendon Press, Reprint 1951.

3 R. Laird Harris, Gleason L. Archer, Jr., and Bruce K. Waltke, *Theological Wordbook of the Old Testament.* Chicago, IL: Moody Press. 1980.

4 Francis Brown, R.R. Driver, and C.A. Briggs, *A Hebrew and English Lexicon of the Old Testament.* Oxford: Clarendon Press, Reprint 1951.

CHAPTER 5

1 I wrote this illustration and used it in a family conference in February 2008 long before Pixar released *Inside Out.* The "repeating jingle in the brain" theme struck a responsive chord with audiences across the world. Apparently, more people suffer from this annoying malady than I first realized when I penned my illustration.

2 Louw, J.P. & Nida, E.A. *Greek-English Lexicon of the New Testament Based on Semantic Domains.* New York: UBS. 1988. Accordance Bible Software. Altamonte Springs, FL. 2006.

3 Thayer's definition of hinder: thwart, impede, to cut off, strongly impede, detain, prevent. Thayer, Joseph Henry. *Greek-English Lexicon of the New Testament.* Accordance Bible Software. Altamonte Springs, FL. 2006.

4 *UBS Greek Lexicon.* Accordance Bible Software. Altamonte Springs, FL. 2006.

5 Strong, James. *Strong's Expanded Exhaustive Concordance of the Bible.* Nashville: Thomas Nelson, 2009.

6 Smith, Christian. *Soul Searching: The Religious and Spiritual Lives of American Teenagers.* New York: Oxford University Press Inc., 2005. 261.

7 Farris, Michael P. *Nannies in Blue Berets: Understanding the U.N. Convention on the Rights of the Child.* January 2009. HSLDA. http://www.hslda.org/docs/news/20091120.asp

8 The Huffington Post. *Obama Administration Seeks To Join U.N. Rights Of The Child.* 7/24/09, Updated 05/25/11. Heilprin, John. http://huffingtonpost.com/2009/06/23/obama-administration-seek_n_219511.html; FoxNews.com. *Boxer Seeks to Ratify U.N. Treaty That May Erode US Rights.* 2/25/2009. Abrams, Joseph. www.foxnews.com/politics/2009/02/25/boxer-seeks-ratify-treaty-erode-rights.

9 ParentalRights.org. *Twenty Things You Need to Know About the United Nations Convention on the Rights of the Child.* http://www.parentalrights.org/index.asp?SEC=%7B550447B1-E2C1-4B55-87F1-610A9E601E45%7D&Type=B_BASIC#_fn17.

10 Tolopilo, Marcelo A. *A Clarion Call.* Temecula, CA: Chart & Compass Press, 2008. 46.

11 Louw, J.P. & Nida, E.A. *Greek-English Lexicon of the New Testament Based on Semantic Domains*. New York: UBS. 1988. Accordance Bible Software. Altamonte Springs, FL. 2006.

12 Thayer, Joseph Henry. *Greek-English Lexicon of the New Testament*. Accordance Bible Software. Altamonte Springs, FL. 2006.

13 Strong, James. *Strong's Expanded Exhaustive Concordance of the Bible*. Nashville, TN: Thomas Nelson, 2009.

14 The Septuagint is the Greek translation of the Old Testament

15 Thayer, Joseph Henry. *Greek-English Lexicon of the New Testament*. Accordance Bible Software. Altamonte Springs, FL. 2006.

16 Liddell, Henry G. and Scott, Robert. *Liddell and Scott's Greek-English Lexicon*. Oxford, UK: Oxford University Press. 1940. Accordance Bible Software. Altamonte Springs, FL. 2006.

17 You must remember, Jesus' siblings at this point were not believers.

18 Francis Brown, R.R. Driver, and C.A. Briggs, *A Hebrew and English Lexicon of the Old Testament*. Oxford: Clarendon Press, Reprint 1951.

19 Spurgeon, C. H., *The Power of Prayer in a Believer's Life*. Compiled and edited by Robert Hall. Lynwood, WA: Emerald Books YWAM Publishing. 1993. 48.

CHAPTER 6

1 Henry, Matthew. *Matthew Henry's Commentary on the Whole Bible*. Accordance Bible Software. Altamonte Springs, FL. 2006.

2 Strong, James. *Strong's Hebrew Dictionary of the Bible*. Accordance Bible Software. Altamonte Springs, FL. 2006.

3 "Incommunicable" attributes are those God does not communicate or share with His creation, e.g., His eternality. The characteristics of His person He communicates or shares with man are called "communicable," e.g., compassion.

4 from the Latin words "a"—"from" and "se"—"self" meaning "from himself"

5 Packer, J.I. *Knowing God*. Downers Grove, IL: InterVarsity Press. 1973.

6 Job lost his ten beloved children, his health, and his vast fortune in a series of cataclysmic waves of suffering.

7 National Retail Federation NRF. *Cupid to Shower Americans with Jewelry, Candy This Valentine's Day*. Allen, Kathy. January 26, 2015. https://nrf.com/media/press-releases/cupid-shower-americans-jewelry-candy-this-valentines-day.

8 Ryrie, Charles Caldwell. *The Ryrie Study Bible*. Chicago, IL. 1978.

9 R. Laird Harris, Gleason L. Archer, Jr., and Bruce K. Waltke, *Theological Wordbook of the Old Testament*. Chicago, IL: Moody Press. 1980.

10 Because the Scriptures have one divine Author, the Spirit of God chooses in the text of Colossians 3:16 to call the entire Bible "The word of Christ."

11 Strong, James. *Strong's Greek Dictionary of the Bible*. Accordance Bible Software. Altamonte Springs, FL. 2006.

12 *UBS Greek Lexicon*. Accordance Bible Software. Altamonte Springs, FL. 2006.

13 Louw, J.P. & Nida, E.A. *Greek-English Lexicon of the New Testament Based on Semantic Domains*. New York: UBS. 1988. Accordance Bible Software. Altamonte Springs, FL. 2006.

CHAPTER 7

1 R. Laird Harris, Gleason L. Archer, Jr., and Bruce K. Waltke, *Theological Wordbook of the Old Testament*. Chicago, IL: Moody Press. 1980.

2 Spurgeon, Charles H. *Treasury of David, Volume 2*. Peabody, MA: Hendrickson Publisher. Psalm 78:4.

3 Chapter 3: "The Threat of Biblical Illiteracy to the Welfare of the Christian Home".

4 "disciple" means "learner." Liddell, Henry G. and Scott, Robert. *Liddell and Scott's Greek-English Lexicon*. Oxford, UK: Oxford University Press. 1940. Accordance Bible Software. Altamonte Springs, FL. 2006.

5 Our Mezuzah contains these Scriptures: Psalm 1:1–3; 119:105; Deut. 6:4–9; Col. 2:9–12.

6 Yeshiva.org.il The Torah World Gateway. http://www.yeshiva.co/ask/?id=4804. Come and Hear. *Babylonian Talmud: Tractate Baba Bathra*. http://www.come-and-hear.com/bababathra/bababathra_21.html.

CHAPTER 8

1 See chapter 4: "The Indispensability of the Bible to Your Family's Health".

2 See chapter 5: "God's Word, the Road to Obedience and the Way of Blessing".

3 See chapter 6: "God's Word, the Road Map to Knowing & Loving God".

4 Pew Research Center, Religion and Public LIfe. *Breadwinner Moms*. May 29, 2013. http://www.pewsocialtrends.org/2013/05/29/breadwinner-mom.

5 Answers. *How Long Does the Average American Spend in Their LIfetime Waiting in Lines?* http://www.answers.com/Q/How_long_does_the_average_American_spend_in_their_lifetime_waiting_in_lines

CHAPTER 9

1 Louw, J.P. & Nida, E.A. *Greek-English Lexicon of the New Testament Based on Semantic Domains*. New York: UBS. 1988. Accordance Bible Software. Altamonte Springs, FL. 2006.

2 This was the Lord's first cleansing of the temple at the beginning of His ministry. At the end of His ministry, during the last week of His life, the Lord Jesus cleansed the temple yet again (see Matthew 21:12–13; Mark 11:15–19; Luke 19:45–46).

3 See Chapter 6: "God Word, the Road Map to Knowing & Loving God".

4 R. Laird Harris, Gleason L. Archer, Jr., and Bruce K. Waltke, *Theological Wordbook of the Old Testament*. Chicago, IL: Moody Press. 1980. Strong, James. *Strong's Hebrew Dictionary of the Bible*. Accordance Bible Software. Altamonte Springs, FL. 2006.

CHAPTER 10

1 Strong, James. *Strong's Greek Dictionary of the Bible*. Accordance Bible Software. Altamonte Springs, FL. 2006.

2 *New American Standard Exhaustive Concordance of the Bible*. Accordance Bible Software. Altamonte Springs, FL. 2006.

3 Ibid.

4 Ibid.

5 Grudem, Wayne. *Tyndale New Testament Commentaries, 1 Peter*. Grand Rapids, MI: William B. Eerdmans Publishing Company 1989. 94–95.

6 Louw, J.P. & Nida, E.A. *Greek-English Lexicon of the New Testament Based on Semantic Domains*. New York: UBS. 1988. Accordance Bible Software. Altamonte Springs, FL. 2006.

7 MacArthur, John M. *The MacArthur New Testament Commentary, 1 Peter*. Chicago:IL Moody Press. 2004. 96.

8 MacArthur, John M. *The MacArthur Study Bible*. Nashville, TN: Word Publishing. 1997. Revelation 14:10.

9 Actual text reads "transferred." Louw, J.P. & Nida, E.A. *Greek-English Lexicon of the New Testament Based on Semantic Domains*. New York: UBS. 1988. Accordance Bible Software. Altamonte Springs, FL. 2006.

10 To "throw off, be done with, take off" (clothes) (Ro. 13:12; Col. 3:5ff.; Eph. 4:22). Liddell, Henry G. and Scott, Robert. *Liddell and Scott's Greek-English Lexicon*. Oxford, UK: Oxford University Press. 1940. UBS Greek Lexicon. Accordance Bible Software. Altamonte Springs, FL. 2006.

11 Henry, Matthew. *Matthew Henry's Complete Commentary on the Whole Bible*. Accordance Bible Software. Altamonte Springs, FL. 2006.

12 Liddell, Henry G. and Scott, Robert. *Liddell and Scott's Greek-English Lexicon*. Oxford, UK: Oxford University Press. 1940. Accordance Bible Software. Altamonte Springs, FL. 2006.

13 Strong, James. *Strong's Greek Dictionary of the Bible*. Accordance Bible Software. Altamonte Springs, FL. 2006.

14 Robertson, A. T. *Grammar of the Greek New Testament*. Accordance Bible Software. Altamonte Springs, FL. 2006.

15 Grudem, Wayne. *Tyndale New Testament Commentaries, 1 Peter*. Grand Rapids, MI: William B. Eerdmans Publishing Company 1989. 93.

16 *Theological Dictionary of the New Testament*. Accordance Bible Software. Altamonte Springs, FL. 2006.

17 *New American Standard Exhaustive Concordance of the Bible*. Accordance Bible Software. Altamonte Springs, FL. 2006.

18 Louw, J.P. & Nida, E.A. *Greek-English Lexicon of the New Testament Based on Semantic Domains*. New York: UBS. 1988. Accordance Bible Software. Altamonte Springs, FL. 2006.

19 Barnes, Albert. *Barnes' Notes on the New Testament*. Accordance Bible Software. Altamonte Springs, FL. 2006.

20 Grudem, Wayne. *Tyndale New Testament Commentaries, 1 Peter*. Grand Rapids, MI: William B. Eerdmans Publishing Company 1989. 94.

21 Kid's Health. *Breast Feeding FAQs: How Much and How Often* http://kidshealth.org/parent/pregnancy_ newborn/breastfee/breastfeed_often.html.

22 livescience. *Brains of Breast–Feeding Moms Move Responsive to Baby's Cries*. http://www.livescience. com/14335-breast-feeding-mother-brain.html.

23 WebMD. *Breastfeeding Overview*. http://www.webmd.com/parenting/baby/nursing-basics.

24 Robertson, A. T. *Grammar of the Greek New Testament*. Accordance Bible Software. Altamonte Springs, FL. 2006.

25 *Theological Dictionary of the New Testament*. Accordance Bible Software. Altamonte Springs, FL. 2006.

26 Francis, Samuel T. "O the Deep, Deep Love of Jesus." 1875. *Hymns for the Family of God*. Franklin, TN: Brentwood-Benson Music Publishing, 1976. 24.

27 Henry, Matthew. *Matthew Henry's Complete Commentary on the Whole Bible*. Accordance Bible Software. Altamonte Springs, FL. 2006.

28 Henry, Matthew. *Matthew Henry's Complete Commentary on the Whole Bible*. Accordance Bible Software. Altamonte Springs, FL. 2006.

29 "All Scripture is *inspired*." Greek "*theopneustos*" literally "God-breathed."

CHAPTER 12

1 *Theological Dictionary of the New Testament*. Accordance Bible Software. Altamonte Springs, FL. 2006.

2 Johnson, Julia H. "Grace Greater Than Our Sin." 1911. *Hymns for the Family of God*. Franklin, TN: Brentwood-Benson Music Publishing, 1976. 105.

3 Spurgeon, C. H. Clarke, Roy H. editor. *Beside Still Waters, Words of Comfort for the Soul*. Nashville, TN: Thomas Nelson Publishers. 12.

Walking In The Promises
The Bible teaching ministry of
Marcelo Tolopilo

—

Invite Marcelo to speak to your

Church | Families | Men's Group | Conference Center

Go to www.witp.org

—

Now available for moms:

"The Transforming Power of Reading to Our Children"

and

"A Countercultural View of the Teen Years"

Seminars by Valorie Tolopilo

To order additional copies of this book:
chartandcompasspress.com

www.ingramcontent.com/pod-product-compliance
Lightning Source LLC
Chambersburg PA
CBHW021826090426
42811CB00032B/2046/J

* 9 7 8 0 9 8 2 1 0 3 2 1 0 *